UNDER INVESTIGATION

Has Critical Scholarship Exposed A Corrupted Bible?

Kathryn V. Camp, D.Min.

WESTBOW
PRESS®
A DIVISION OF THOMAS NELSON
& ZONDERVAN

WestBow Press books may be ordered through booksellers or by contacting:

WestBow Press
A Division of Thomas Nelson & Zondervan
1663 Liberty Drive
Bloomington, IN 47403
www.westbowpress.com
1 (866) 928-1240

Because of the dynamic nature of the Internet, any web addresses or links contained in this book may have changed since publication and may no longer be valid. The views expressed in this work are solely those of the author and do not necessarily reflect the views of the publisher, and the publisher hereby disclaims any responsibility for them.

Any people depicted in stock imagery provided by Getty Images are models, and such images are being used for illustrative purposes only.
Certain stock imagery © Getty Images.

Scripture quotations are from the ESV® Bible (The Holy Bible, English Standard Version®), copyright © 2001 by Crossway, a publishing ministry of Good News Publishers. Used by permission. All rights reserved.

Scripture taken from the NEW AMERICAN STANDARD BIBLE®, Copyright © 1960, 1962, 1963, 1968, 1971, 1972, 1973, 1975, 1977, 1995 by The Lockman Foundation. Used by permission.

Scripture taken from the King James Version of the Bible.

ISBN: 978-1-9736-5140-6 (sc)
ISBN: 978-1-9736-5139-0 (e)

Library of Congress Control Number: 2019900539

Print information available on the last page.

WestBow Press rev. date: 5/22/2019

To my mother, who took me to church every Sunday so that I could learn about Jesus, and who has never stopped encouraging me to do the right thing. I love you, Mom.

CONTENTS

PREFACE

I will never forget it. I was taking an exercise walk down a country road with one of my in-laws (whom I respect, which is why I am not mentioning names) during a family reunion in the heat of the summer day, and for some reason the Bible entered into our conversation. Suddenly my in-law stopped, looked at me, and asked, "You don't really believe that the Bible is true, do you?" I looked at this individual and responded, "Yes, I actually do." Little did I realize that this was the beginning of a fifteen-year journey that would end up in a doctorate of ministry in the field of apologetics and an unrelenting passion to raise up the next generation of warriors for Christ (both young and old). It became evident to me that my in-laws were not unique in their perception of the Bible and the church, even though they profess to be Christians. I began to realize that here in the West we are caught up in an incongruent and contradictory mind-set that reduces the God of the universe to a "personal" god who thinks just like we do.

How can you claim to be a Christian and not believe the Bible? That did not even begin to make sense to me at that time, and now that I know so much more than I did on that humid August afternoon, it makes even less sense to me. In my journey, I found it interesting to uncover numerous inconsistencies in the way many professing Christians could look me straight in the eye and tell me "I don't agree with you" when we would discuss the cultural issues of our day and how biblical principles should trump the moral values being practiced in society. I do, however, now understand where that inaccurate thought process comes from, and that is why my ministry is focused on educating others.

It's time for Christians to lose the stigma of being uneducated people. God has called every one of us to know Him above all else (Deut. 6:4–9; Matt. 6:33). In order to know Him, however, it is necessary to read and believe His Word. Given the fact that everyone alive today is the product of the Enlightenment period in history, it should go without saying that sheer belief is not enough. It will take research to find evidence to back up that the Bible is actually a historically valid document. God never once called His people to a blind faith, and to live that way is to live in an inexcusable ignorance. Never before in history has there been so much evidence for a Creator. With every new scientific and technological breakthrough, Christians gain a stronger foothold in professing absolute Truth. The evidence that we have at our disposal today leads to a better understanding of who God is than there has ever been before in human history.

My goal is not only to help people understand what makes the Bible such a profound book, but also to teach them how they can confidently share its historical integrity with skeptics. Knowledge is power, and the more we learn, the more we are able to engage in conversations with eternal perspectives, even in the face of great adversity.

INTRODUCTION

Digging Deeper: The Reliability of the New Testament

This workbook focuses on the historical and theological reliability of the New Testament. What makes this study unique is the blend of historical critical analysis coupled with the theological coherence of the New Testament. A critical view of the New Testament is necessary in order to understand the various ways that you will be able to defend the historical reliability of the New Testament to those individuals who have a difficult time accepting the Bible as an authoritative source. This is tantamount to an understanding of the Creator and Sustainer of life. The core of Christianity is based solely on the Bible and an honest observation of the creation, not on opinion or the philosophical ponderings of humanity.

The best way to use this workbook is to give yourself a minimum of one to two weeks to complete each chapter. Each chapter is divided into two segments. The first part of the chapter is the historical validation that makes the New Testament a historically viable document ("the lesson"). In this first section you will learn how scholars who study history dissect the claims made of historical events. You will be introduced to some of the basic tools used to confirm past events and the legitimacy of people mentioned from history.

The second half of each chapter ("Application with Scripture") will require the reading of scripture and your interaction with the text. Make sure to read the scripture assigned to the chapter before you begin this section so that the people and events mentioned are fresh in your mind. A large part of verifying the reliability of the Bible is placing the people and events in a specific time in history. The purpose of each lesson is to help you see the validity of the New Testament as a historical document and then to recognize how the theological side of scripture works within the context in which the Bible was written. The people and events in scripture can be placed in history, but that does not make the Bible a history book, it is God's disclosure of Himself to humanity.

Throughout the lessons you will see words that are in italics. These are key terms and are reviewed at the end of the historical analysis (which is the first part of the lesson) and then also at the end of the theological section of each chapter. Chapters 2–10 will end with study questions to help you review what you have just learned, also providing a few questions for you to reflect on with your study group. Make sure to give yourself enough time each week to focus on both the critical analysis portion and the theological section of each chapter. Ideally you should take two weeks per chapter, if your group is able to remain cohesive for this extended period of time.

The end goal is to become a more confident Christian not only in your faith walk with Christ but also in the knowledge that God has left His fingerprints all over history and that we can speak about scripture and its historical reliability with assurance and authority.

We live in a time of great uncertainty of many things, both worldly and spiritual. As Christians we cannot sit back and be content with the moral decay all around us. I have sat in on countless prayer groups and Bible studies over the last dozen years, and I am amazed at how easy it is for these wonderful people to tell me that it is not their place to bring others to a better understanding of Christ. It is also greatly disheartening to have a Bible study or small-group leader tell me about a blog that I should read because of my firm stance on the authority and integrity of the Bible, only to find that the "Christian" blogger blatantly compromises the Word of God to suit the cultural morals of the day. It is their way of telling me that the Bible is an evolving piece of literature (which it is not). What is even more difficult is to see the grief on the faces of parents who have their teenage children declare that they do not believe in God and then end up leading aberrant lifestyles.

All of this is happening in our time because of the lack of trust in the Bible and its historical reliability. On the surface it seems that the worldly culture in which we live is winning the war, but I strongly encourage you not to give in or give up. Perhaps you have experienced a few of the same situations that I have, either in the past or recently. How do you get past those individuals who simply do not give serious credence to the foundation of Truth that is established in the Bible? There are many reasons why individuals want nothing to do with any faith-based religion, and we cannot control that. What we can change is the way we engage the world around us with intellectual, faith-based conversations that focus on the historical reliability of the New Testament.

There are numerous people in Westernized cultures who do not truly *know* God, yet are deceived into believing that they do. This study will help you engage not only skeptics in the culture with conversations about the validity of the scriptures but also those who believe that everyone is going to have salvation (universalism). This workbook is structured to help you have thoughtful and coherent discussions about God that will not only bring you closer to the Lord, but will also open the eyes of those who remain blind to the God of the Bible. Christians can no longer afford to tell others that they just need to believe and have faith. People want reasons to believe, and the Creator and Sustainer of life has left us with numerous valid and documented reasons to trust in His Word that will lead us to Him.

This study can be done on your own, but it will be much more beneficial to work on this as a small group. If you do not understand the material the first time around, take the time to read the chapter again, as there may be concepts that are entirely new to you (and that is all right). The Bible is steeped in history, but it is also the way we have been given to come to know God better. As you learn the historical reliability of the New Testament, it is my hope that you will also begin to appreciate the way God has made sure that His revelation of Himself is intertwined with the history of humanity. He has done this so that everyone, from a child to the most intellectual individual ever to be born, should be able to find Him as he calls us to Himself.

CHAPTER 1

The Call to Know God

The Shema

There is a call to every human alive that, if ignored or suppressed, will end in an unfulfilled life as well as certain death in eternity. If answered, this call will capture the heart and mind of the individual and lead not only to eternal life but also to a peace that surpasses all human understanding (Phil. 4:6–7). This is the call to *know* God above all else. Deep down, every person has a longing for this missing piece of his or her life. This part of us can only be filled by an intimate knowledge of the Creator of the universe (Eccles. 3:11). If we ignore this call, we will remain seeking, yet never finding, the peace that we so desperately need and desire.

> **The Shema**
> Hear, O Israel: The LORD our God, the LORD is one. You shall love the LORD your God with all your heart and with all your soul and with all your might. And these words that I command you today shall be on your heart. You shall teach them diligently to your children, and shall talk of them when you sit in your house, and when you walk by the way, and when you lie down, and when you rise. You shall bind them as a sign on your hand, and they shall be as frontlets between your eyes. You shall write them on the doorposts of your house and on your gates. (Deut. 6:4–9 ESV)

The Bible is clear about the first and greatest command for our lives: "love the Lord *your* God" with every bit of your existence (Deut. 6:4–5). Unfortunately, we live in a highly self-centered culture, and even this simple command is many times distorted into a personalized application. The true meaning of this command has become lost in the translation when defining the God of the Bible versus the pluralistic ideals of a personal god that we find in our current culture. Therefore, it is important to break this down for a clear understanding of the true intent behind this call on our lives. Our Jewish brothers and sisters were commanded to continually remind themselves and their families that God comes first, as the *Shema* instructs them to place this prayer on their doorposts as well as at the forefront of their minds. As true disciples of Christ, it is important to keep in mind that we are called to be in this world but not of it. This means that our minds should be at one with Christ no matter what the rest of our world is doing.

It is imperative to always be aware of the culture and society in which our Lord has placed us. Far too many professing Christians choose to turn a blind eye and hope that the discrepancies in our world will simply go away. Christians need to be informed enough to know how to reach others right where they are. No one goes into battle without making a survey of the enemy first (1 Chron. 12:32), and facing our culture is no different. Like it or not, we are all faced with spiritual warfare every day (Eph. 6:10–12). There is a reason for the multitude of religious faith groups in our culture. The list and variety seems to be endless. This list even includes the religion of atheism.

Anytime you have a group of individuals who defend their position on matters of eternal perspective, you have a religion. The more fervent the push for their stance, the more religious the movement becomes. Even those who claim not to be religious or who claim not to care about matters of eternal significance are seeking more than they can find in this world. Much to their despair, however, if they refuse to acknowledge the Creator of the universe, they are forced to limit their sense of meaning and purpose to what the material realm can afford them. Their desires can only be fulfilled temporarily. History is filled with examples of how materialism and humanistic pursuits will inevitably leave people feeling empty and dissatisfied.

This is why we live in a society (especially in Westernized civilizations) in which humankind is cognizant of a need for something beyond the fleeting gratification of the material but remains frustrated at the inability to find it. We have a culture with people who insist they are not religious but say they are spiritual. When the individual has saturated himself or herself with all the material wealth or recognition that the world has to offer, there comes a point when he or she is compelled to comprehend that it is going to take something that transcends his or her own existence to bring the gratification and significance he or she seeks. When individuals begin to pursue fulfillment through a spiritual type of quest for any other god aside from the God of the Bible, however, their journeys will bring them to fashion gods after their own likenesses.

This sort of quest will end up becoming a form of self-idolatry. In an honest effort to find meaning and "happiness" in this life, individuals will naturally begin to accept the writings of the various religions of the world. When a culture claims that there are no clear absolutes, the people who rely on their own personal intuitive god will inevitably amend these scriptures to suit their personal desires. Hence, they fashion a god in their own likeness. Many people eventually turn to the Holy Bible and read God's first and greatest commandment. They interpret "love the Lord *your* God" with all your heart, with all your soul, and with all your might (Deut. 6:5) as a call to love the "designer god" they have fashioned to suit their own desires. This entire process takes place with the best of intentions but without proper direction.

This type of love for a personal, self-designed god misses the intent of the love that we are all called to have for the God of the Bible. The Word of God is clear that we are to seek to know God through His creation and His Word. There is no other holy and inspired book that was given to us so that through it we actually come to know the Creator (Deut. 4; Rom. 1:18–20). All living souls are called to know this God by using their human capacity for knowledge and understanding. We are expected to earnestly seek to know this ultimate Being (God) who will eventually judge our obedience to His Word (Matt. 6:33, 7:7).

Why is it important to know God?

_____

A Call to Knowledge

Humans have been given the ability to retain information from which we are able to transfer any given data into knowledge. The study of how we can gather and assimilate knowledge is better known as *epistemology*. This is an amazing phenomenon that many great minds have studied and written about over the centuries. We have been bestowed with this ability if for no other reason than to know the Creator. This capability that we have been given to know God through His creation and His Word is a gift that will enable us to live out our lives at one with Him. This is the missing component to the lives of many who continue to seek but never find, because they refuse to place their trust in the scriptures. Never before have we been more aware in our Westernized culture of the fact that there are multiple religions and religious people who seek oneness with God yet refuse to acknowledge absolute truth.

What they actually end up finding will be determined by the "god" they seek. For instance, the Hindu religion and many of the Eastern-based faiths seek oneness with the universe through their numerous gods. They have no description of this *telos*, or end result, other than an abstract concept of dissolving into the great cosmic world out there somewhere once they have lived a "perfect life." These individuals place their destiny in these religions even though there is no way to gauge what deems this "perfect life." Others believe in a sort of reincarnation cycle based on the conviction that if they have lived as "good enough" people, they will eventually be rewarded by becoming a part of some mysterious *force* out in space somewhere.

Many more individuals hold to a faith that is based on a patchwork of religions from all over the world. Whether intentionally or unintentionally, these people have managed to create their own personalized faith based on what they wish to believe. This is known as *syncretism*. This sort of religious faith blending is evident in the New Age religions that became prevalent in the West in the twentieth century and are now deeply embedded in our Westernized culture and philosophical ideologies. These *designer faith systems* tend to change with the societal and cultural trends of the times. It is no wonder why so many people are confused when faced with what to believe, when there is no base for absolute truth that will stand the test of time.

> See to it that no one takes you captive by philosophy and empty deceit, according to human tradition, according to the elemental spirits of the world, and not according to Christ.
>
> Col. 2:8 (ESV)

The Necessity for the Purity of Absolute Truth

The Christian faith in its purest form is based solely on the Bible and what one is able to observe in creation, not on the traditions of humankind. Over the centuries, many people have hijacked the Christian faith and blended it with other faith traditions, further confusing people who seek the peace and oneness for which our souls naturally long. Just as disturbing is the fact that many leaders in the Christian tradition tend to amend the authenticity of the Gospel message and add the customs of humankind to its original intent. In other words, they make it culture-friendly, which inevitably changes the meaning of the *metanarrative* (the meaning of the whole work). Ultimately, we are all to blame for allowing this to happen.

The Word of God repeatedly warns how people lose sight of God's directives by deviating from the absolute truth (see Joshua, Judges, Jeremiah, Amos, and others). That is why all of humanity is called to know God personally, not merely vicariously.

Scripture is clear: humans have always desired to be equal with God and to be gods (Gen. 3). The truth is that we are unable to truly acknowledge this tendency in ourselves until we correctly come to know God. Most civilizations have naturally recognized that there is something beyond the physical realm that controls the course of creation; it was never meant to be a mysterious secret. Although there is a *neoatheism* (new atheism) movement on the rise in the twenty-first century, the vast majority of the world's population continues to recognize that there is a God, or that there are gods who somehow influence the world. This fact is just one of the many proofs that what scripture records for us is true in that God has put eternity on our hearts (Eccles. 3) and we will not find peace until we come to rest in Him alone.

> You are great, O Lord, and greatly to be praised: great is your power and to your wisdom there is no limit. And man, who is a part of your creation, wishes to praise you, man who bears about within himself his mortality, who bears about within himself testimony to his sin and testimony that you resist the proud. Yet man, this part of your creation, wishes to praise you. You arouse him to take joy in praising you, for you have made us for yourself, and our heart is restless until it rests in you. (*The Confessions of Saint Augustine*, chapter 1)

But the call to know the God of the universe goes well beyond the cursory assent that the average individual gives by claiming to believe in God. Scripture tells us that even the demons believe in the one true God, and they shudder to think of Him (James 2:19). God expects more than assent to His existence; He expects the knowledge that comes from seeking Him out not only through creation but also mainly through His Holy Word. It is through the consistency of His Word that we are privileged enough to come to know His true attributes, and through our knowledge of His undeniable grandeur we grow not only to trust in Him but also to love Him. Through this knowledge, we also come to revere and fear God for the omniscient Being He truly is.

Scripture is replete with warnings as to what the consequences are if individuals fail to come to know God. God speaks through the prophet Hosea and stresses that the people are perishing for their lack of knowledge of Him (Hosea 4). The book of Judges describes the outcome of entire cultures and their mind-set when they fail to recognize the Creator and His moral guidelines. Jesus chastises the religious leaders of His day because they have overlooked the intent of the Word of God and have added to its meaning, making it out to be a book of man-made rules and regulations (Matt. 2:1–36). He also very pointedly tells the leaders and those listening that *His* sheep will hear His voice (John 10) and that it is only they who will inherit the kingdom of God.

Those who are considered His sheep, however, are those who obey the unamended Word of God. Finally, for those who fail to seek the face of God in earnest, Jesus gives a stern warning when He makes it clear that in the last day there will be many who think they are followers of Christ but have failed to come to know the God of the Bible without distorting His Word in any way. He tells His audience that many will come to Him and expect to be participants in God's kingdom, but He will send them away into darkness for their failure to obey the will of God found in the Word of God (Matt. 7:21–23). Some claim that the writings of other faiths include vestiges of resemblance to the Judeo-Christian Bible. History reveals that every civilization seems to hold to a code of ethics as described in its writings. I would pose that this is not a random coincidence but that it is due to the fact that all of humanity was created in the image of the Creator, and therefore it is natural that the whole human race would draw from the laws and desires that God placed on our hearts and minds. There are, nonetheless, still other religious groups that have used the Bible as a basis for their own writings (like the Qur'an and the Mormon Bible). The mere fact that we have all been fashioned by the same God attests to the reality that we all seek His ultimate truth as noted in scripture (Eccles. 3:11).

What are three of the natural laws that God placed on our heart?
1. _____
2. _____
3. _____

Name two religions that appear on the surface to be similar to the Christian faith:
1. _____
2. _____

The Shortcomings of Other Faiths

Although all of humanity seeks God in some way, shape, or form, it is only the Judeo-Christian God that can be known and understood. Scripture reveals that the Creator began to reveal Himself to the Hebrews (Deut. 4:33) with the intent that eventually all of the world's people would come to know Him through this chosen nomadic tribe (1 Pet. 2). Other faith religions have no sound basis for the character or nature of their deities other than the human tendencies that they witness in their fellow man.[1] Written history records humanity as constantly working to appease unseen gods or goddesses. Their petitions for attention have come in a variety of forms, from human sacrifice to temple prostitution. Yet those performing these acts have no basis for knowing whether or not their acts are satisfying to their mysterious and unseen deities whom they attempt to please.

The gods and goddesses of antiquity, for the most part, portray the characteristics of precocious, vindictive, petulant, hedonistic, inconsistent, and sex-driven individuals. The Holy One of Israel, on the other hand, desires that all might come to know Him (Matt. 6:33; 2 Pet. 3:9) and realize the saving faith through Him that leads to eternal life. Many faith-based religions that have developed post-Crucifixion include vestiges of the Judeo-Christian God. For example, the Qur'an depicts Allah with many of the same characteristics of God that are found in the Holy Bible.[2] However, the Qur'an describes Allah through his willful actions, not as an illustration of his very nature, as one finds of the God of the Bible.

For example, Allah is defined as having a form of "greatness, strength, and majesty."[3] These and other attributes, such as lovingness, forgivingness, and wisdom, are all characteristics that

---

[1] For a better understanding of various deities and their characteristics, see Winfried Corduan, *Neighboring Faiths: A Christian Introduction to World Religions*, 2nd ed. (Downers Grove, IL: InterVarsity Press, 2012).

[2] Anees Zaka and Diane Coleman, *The Truth About Islam: The Noble Qur'an's Teachings in Light of the Holy Bible* (Phillipsburg, NJ: P&R Publishing, 2004), 100–101.

[3] Norman L. Geisler and Abdul Saleeb, *Answering Islam: The Crescent in Light of the Cross*, 2nd ed. (Grand Rapids, MI: Baker Books, 2002), 28.

flow from Allah's will but that do not necessarily represent of his very nature.[4] In other words, the god of Islam may have the characteristics of holiness, righteousness, and kindness when he wills to, but he is not bound by these traits as a result of his very nature, as is the God of the Bible.[5] According to the Qur'an, Allah is a *mutable*, or changing, god who is at liberty to change his mind and make exceptions to his own rules, at his own discretion. Unfortunately, for those who live and rely on this faith, there is no assurance of where they stand as far as living rightly. Nor is there any way to depend on Allah since he is inconsistent in his will and his expectations of his followers.

In contrast to the picture we are given of Allah from the Qur'an and the other Islamic sacred texts, the God of the Holy Bible is quite knowable. In fact, He desires to be known, as is evident by His first and greatest commandment (Deut. 6:5). The God of the Bible did not stop at His exhortation for His people to come to some form of abstract love for Him. On the contrary, God made sure that His prophets recorded information about the universe and the creation that would inevitably reveal His very nature. His *immutable*, or unchanging, attributes make known His deity and providential control over all of creation. Then, in the perfect timing of the Creator, He sent His Word in the flesh so that all the people of the world would come to know Him more fully (John 1:1–18).

As you read the Bible in an effort to better know the God you are called to worship, you will find that He is the fountainhead of all things. When the Lord exhibits such characteristics as love and wisdom to people, it is not because He wills to display love or wisdom but because He *is* love and He *is* wisdom. Unlike the deities of other faiths or *cults*, the God of the Bible does not leave His character up to interpretation. On the contrary, the Word of God reveals a consistent and stable character that stems directly from His very nature. God does not change who He is (Mal. 3:6), just as our chromosomes have determined who we are as humans (Jer. 13:23). In stark contrast to Allah, whose character and attributes stem from his own will (which can change on a whim),[6] the Judeo-Christian God exhibits a will that stems directly from His selfsame nature.

> Can the Ethiopian change his skin, Or the leopard his spots? Just as much can you do good, Who are practiced in doing evil! (Jer, 13:23 TNK)

How does God expect us to come to know him?

The Call to Tell Others

The Struggle to Obey

The Old Testament is a beautiful picture of humanity's struggle with the Creator. God's desire for all of humankind to come to know Him is repeatedly hindered by His chosen people as they insist on doing things their own way. Their stubbornness and refusal to live consistently within

---

[4] Ibid.

[5] Richard Shumack, *The Wisdom of Islam and the Foolishness of Christianity* (Sydney, Australia: Island View Publishing, 2014), 47–68.

[6] James F. Gauss, *Islam and Christianity: A Revealing Contrast* (Alachua, FL: Bridge-Logos, 2009), 204–5.

God's guidelines not only continually causes strife but also is a perfect reflection of the nature of humanity. It is imperative that we never forget why God chose the small band of people from the desert lands of Mesopotamia who came to be known as the Hebrews. God's intent has always been that the whole world would come to know Him through those to whom He chooses to reveal Himself (Exod. 19:6; 1 Pet. 2:9). That fact has never changed.

A Light on a Hill

God's people are to be ready to tell others about Him and the dire need we all have for His unsearchable love (1 Pet. 3:15). Jesus taught His disciples, and those listening, that all who belong to God are to be as lights on a hill that shine brightly so that others notice their purity in character, which will point to the Creator (Matt. 5:14–16; Luke 8:16, 11:33–35; John 3:20–21). Those who profess to be followers of the Christ should be living in such stark contrast to the ways of the world around them that they stand out as upright and distinct citizens in the culture at large. Their actions and behaviors should exhibit the *communicable characteristics* of God, or those characteristics that we are able to emulate, as they represent His kingdom. As ambassadors for the kingdom, we should naturally live with an eternal perspective, knowing that in the end there will be a judgment according to the way we have lived our lives.

> But in your hearts honor Christ the Lord as holy, always being prepared to make a defense to anyone who asks you for a reason for the hope that is in you; yet do it with gentleness and respect. (1 Peter 3:15 ESV)

Living with an Eternal Perspective

Living with an eternal perspective is to live a life that fully understands the consequences for failing to repent and seek true forgiveness from the Creator (Ezek. 18:32; Matt. 4:17; Luke 13:3). This alone should prompt every believer to be convicted to speak to their neighbors, relatives, colleagues, and nonbelieving friends about the things of God. Granted, some of these conversations will be far more difficult than others, but if we honestly love our neighbors the way we are called to, we must find ways to interject faith-based conversations into our time with others (Rom. 10:1–17). Unlike other belief systems, the Bible makes it very clear what is required of every living soul to acquire salvation and eternal life in the presence of the one true holy God. Although the world we live in tells us differently, there will be a separation at death.

Living in Obedience

A split between the wheat and the chaff (Matt. 3:12) is an *eschatological* reality. In other words, there will be a separation between those who have truly feared (revered) God during their earthly lives, so much so that they seek to know and obey Him (Luke 6:46–49, 13:22–28), and those who have not. In other words, regardless of what many Universalist churches, and those like them, tout, not everyone is going to go to heaven. God requires obedience to His Word (Deut. 28; John 14, 15, 17), nothing more and nothing less. Part of that obedience requires that we love our neighbors (Lev. 19:17–18). This is to be a love that truly cares about others in the sense that we are willing to guide them into all Truth. The world in which we live clearly operates on a set of fluctuating moral norms and ethical standards that lie in complete contrast to what is required of us in scripture. There is no question that this stark opposition of standards will be confusing to those who do not know the God of the Bible, and this is precisely why it is imperative that we obey, trust God (Isa. 55:8–11), and share the **G**ospel of His grace with those within our spheres of influence.

> You shall not hate your kinsfolk in your heart. Reprove your kinsman but incur no guilt because of him. You shall not take vengeance or bear a grudge against your countrymen. Love your fellow as yourself: I am the Lord. (Lev. 19:17–18 TNK)

The Consequences

Many have fallen into the temptation to soften the message of the Gospel by leaving out some of the hard truths that it contains—truths that include the fact that we are all fallen and have a natural bent toward sin (Gen. 6:5; Rom. 7:15–24). In other words, humans are not innately born "good." Or perhaps we tend to leave out the fact that certain behaviors are sinful even though our culture would deem otherwise. The danger of these blatant omissions is that they will eventually cause an individual to be drawn to a god fashioned in his or her own likeness and not to the God of the Bible. The logical outcome of any deliberate omission or commission of any portion of God's Word is that it will confuse the individual as he or she begins to see the contradictions in what the Bible states and what the world is telling him or her.

A contradiction is a flaw in reasoning, and a flaw cannot be trusted as ultimate Truth. Therefore, an inconsistency in the understanding of the God described in the Bible cannot be trusted. If this were the case, it would only be natural for a person to try to make amends for salvation purposes by filling in the missing or inconsistent gaps with his own ideas of what the Bible says to *him*. At this point the person has fashioned a god after her own likeness, where there is only a false sense of salvation. Not surprisingly, this is not a modern phenomenon. On the contrary, humanity has always tried to amend the Word of God in some fashion.

It takes only up to the third chapter in scripture to discover how humankind is ready to refute the Word of God and interpret it to suit their desire (Gen. 3). While the Creator began to form His people as a fledgling nation, He made it clear to the Hebrews that they were not to add to or take away from any part of His directives if they expected to seek His care and protection (Deut. 4:1–2). If we consider ourselves God's people, then we must understand that we have been grafted into this chosen race of the Hebrews (Israel) and that this is a warning meant for us as well. If we fail to shed light on the entire Gospel of God, we will mislead others, which will very likely cause them to be drawn *away* from the Lord and not *to* Him. Jesus gives a very stern warning to anyone who misleads seekers (either young or old) by amending the Word in any way, shape, or form (Matt. 18:6–7, ESV), as follows:

> But whoever causes one of these little ones who believe in me to sin, it would be better for him to have a great millstone fastened around his neck and to be drowned in the depth of the sea. "Woe to the world for temptations to sin! For it is necessary that temptations come, but woe to the one by whom the temptation comes!"

Why is it important to approach the Word of God as objectively as possible as opposed to subjectively?

_____

_____

Obstacles to Faith

Meeting People Where They Are

Although human nature has not changed since God created the first people, we live in unprecedented times where individuals go to great lengths to ignore what is true and factual in order to avoid giving credence to an ultimate Being. In the present day, it is a fact of life that people will believe what they choose to believe to accommodate their lifestyles. When it comes to faith-based issues, however, we can usually categorize an individual's reasons for rejecting God into one of three broad categories. These various reasons become obstacles to living the life that God has intended for them. The most common barriers to faith are usually intellectual, emotional, or *volitional* (simply because they do not want to believe) in nature.

Human history has revealed that the main obstacle for those who are philosophically or academically minded has usually been an *intellectual* barrier. There is no question that humans have sought out the ultimate meaning of life as we know it since the dawn of time. History is replete with documentation on belief in unseen gods and goddesses who cause things to "mysteriously" happen. These were undoubtedly the machinations of the human mind seeking the Creator without any clear direction. This is not to say that there were no deep thinkers who began to seek answers in a more methodical fashion. One such individual, Thales of Miletus, is considered to be the first philosopher who began to use the scientific method in his quest to discover why things are the way that they are (otherwise known as ultimate Truth). He was a sixth-century BC philosopher who began his quest for ultimate reality through the method of observation.

His scientific methods were the same ones we continue to use today. He studied life, motion, and being (an examination of the *metaphysical*, a reality that is unseen), thus earning him the title the Father of Western Philosophy. Up until his observation style for seeking life's ultimate truth, suppositions of ultimate reality were based on human imagination, or some form of God's revelation to humanity, such as through the Hebrew people. Today's Westernized societies are not impressed with superstitious beliefs and require factual evidence for basing their confidence in any claims to Ultimate Reality (God). Those are the individuals who, for the most part, have intellectual barriers. There are those, however, who can be given all of the facts known to humankind that will lead to the reality of a Creator and yet who remain unable to place their trust in God.

There are some who, unfortunately, have had such negative experiences in life that they find it exceedingly difficult to believe at all in a good and loving Creator who cares for the world. The emotional hurt they harbor inside has become their greatest obstacle for coming to a saving faith in Christ. Many people fall into this category. The fact is, we do live in a very violent world, but if one has never been taught about the nature of God versus the nature of humanity, then one simply cannot comprehend why evil abounds seemingly unhindered. This is where it is necessary to care enough about people to discover the main reason for their emotional barriers and contend with this obstacle through scriptural reasoning. It is only through the Word that one can learn about the true character of God, and as God is revealed, so too is sinful humanity.

The third category is the volitional obstacle. I have been told by young interns who work with college-age students that this is the most common obstacle for this age group. There are, however, a few high-profile atheists who are fully aware that the recent scientific findings of the last three decades all point to *intelligent design*, yet they refuse to acknowledge an Ultimate Creator. Their reason is that they do not wish to believe in any sort of Designer or Creator who will tell them how to live out their lives. This reason for the objection to acknowledge an Ultimate Reality is probably the most difficult with which to contend as a disciple of Christ who takes the Great Commission seriously. This obstacle will require a concerted effort at long-term relationship building (as do the others) and much prayer.

How important is the Bible when sharing God with others?

_____

_____

The State of Our Culture in the West

A survey taken as far back as 1993 revealed that less than 2 percent of Episcopalian priests actually believed in the inerrancy of scripture.[7] Other denominations did not fare much better, and these sentiments are much worse today than they were more than twenty years ago. Disturbingly, many of these ministry leaders in the same study confessed anonymously not to believe either in the incarnation or the resurrection. As a result, true Christians may have a difficult time finding a Bible-believing church since the majority of the professing churches in the United States have been lulled into a state of complacency.

This mass exodus from the truth of God's Word has been a long time coming in North America. Those who study cultural and philosophical trends are all too aware that this progressive march to disbelief has much of its roots in the seventeenth century. This was a time in history that became known as The Age of Reason. It was a time in which people began to demand empirical evidence for everything that would be considered as reality. If a person could not test an idea or hypothesis using the scientific method (which uses the five senses), then it either did not exist or could not be proven as true and valid. Since the events in scripture happened in antiquity, skeptics began to doubt the veracity of the Bible and everything written in it.

Eventually, scholars began to question the motives of those who wrote history and claimed that historical writings must be taken in the context of their cultural atmosphere (which is true). The idea was that what was considered truth for people of the past was no longer necessarily truth for future generations (which is not true). There was a focus on the here and the now, but not on the metaphysical or the transcendent. As a result, the Bible became a subjective document from the past, and any miracles in it came under great suspicion since they are by nature unexplainable. Truth became relative, and the Western world slipped into secularization.

Our secularized culture has intentionally cast a sense of distrust onto the adequacy of the Bible. This sentiment arose in the seventeenth and eighteenth centuries and was promulgated to

_____

[7] Ravi Zacharias, *Biblical Authority and Our Cultural Crisis* (Norcross, GA: RZIM, 1993), CD-ROM.

the masses mostly through academic institutions. In an effort to remain relevant in an increasingly skeptical culture, the church began to "soften" the sharp edges of the Gospel of Truth.[8] It is no wonder that when the church loses its authority by accommodating the mind-set of the culture at large, which in many instances it has, it is not long before congregation attendance drops significantly. The Barna Research Group has revealed that there is an upward trend in atheism and agnosticism that appears to correlate with the increase of those individuals who are categorized as the "unchurched."[9]

According to a study released in 2007, only about 18 percent of the population frequently attends church on a weekly basis.[10] Researcher, R. J. Krejcir, Ph.D., from the Francis A. Schaeffer Institute of Church Leadership Development, based his study on those who attended church service at least twice a month.[11] His research and final conclusions were taken from data gathered over an eight-year period (1998–2006).[12] Concurrently with the release of his findings, Europe reported a 2–4 percent rate in frequent church attendance.[13] It appears that the United States' church attendance is slowly declining to the level of Europe.

What is the harm of approaching God's Word as a subjective document?

_____

_____

_____

The Mission Field

Although this data may be alarming to some readers, this has come as no surprise to our sovereign God. Scripture gives us many examples of entire cultures that either do not know the God of Israel or have chosen to ignore Him when given the opportunity. The apostle Paul is well noted for proclaiming the clear warning signs and consequences for a people without God in his letter to the Romans. His life was devoted to delivering the message of God to Jews and Gentiles. His missionary journeys took him to areas where people had rarely, if ever, been exposed to the God of Israel.

The Gentile people were steeped in all sorts of lewd behavior that was clearly unacceptable to the God of the Bible, which made Paul's mission that much more imperative. He knew that such behaviors were not only unhealthy for the individuals and the society but were also behaviors that went against the natural conscience, marring any vestiges of the *Imago Dei*. Paul's mission was always to bring the good news of God to the people.

---

[8] D. A. Carson, *The Gagging of God: Christianity Confronts Pluralism* (Grand Rapids, MI: Zondervan, 1996), 77–86.

[9] Barna Group, "2015 State of Atheism in America," 2015, research based on the project Churchless, edited by George Barna and David Kinnaman, accessed March 30, 2015, https://www.barna.org/barna-update/culture/713-2015-state-of-atheism-in-america#.VRmtHGd0xLM.

[10] R. J. Krejcir, "Statistics and Reasons for Church Decline," ChurchLeadership.org, Francis A. Schaeffer Institute of Church Leadership Development, 2007, accessed June 5, 2015, http://www.churchleadership.org/apps/articles/default.asp?articleid=42346&columnid=4545.

[11] Ibid.

[12] Ibid.

[13] Ibid.

> For the wrath of God is revealed from heaven against all ungodliness and unrighteousness of men, who by their unrighteousness suppress the truth. For what can be known about God is plain to them, because God has shown it to them. For his invisible attributes, namely, his eternal power and divine nature, have been clearly perceived, ever since the creation of the world, in the things that have been made. So they are without excuse. For although they knew God, they did not honor him as God or give thanks to him, but they became futile in their thinking, and their foolish hearts were darkened. Claiming to be wise, they became fools, and exchanged the glory of the immortal God for images resembling mortal man and birds and animals and creeping things. (Rom. 1:18–23 ESV)

Paul and the disciples were clear on what their mission was to the world. The purpose was always to enlighten the world with the knowledge of the God of Israel through Christ. Over time, however, many Christ followers forgot the true intent for missionary work, and much of the missionary work effort became synonymous with humanitarian aid. For example; what do you think of when someone talks about missions? Many people begin to imagine long journeys to faraway lands. Still others think about reaching out to the impoverished in their own cities and towns. These are all legitimate missional efforts and goals. However, did you know that there are Christians in China who recognize the darkened state of the West and specifically train to come to the United States to reintroduce us to Christ? As brothers and sisters in Christ, they are greatly concerned about the anti-Christian dogma and the pervasive number of *apostate* churches, those who have left the purity of the Gospel message, that are flourishing and consequently leading vast sectors of the population to certain separation from God. If you have not thought about it already, you should know now that the whole world is a mission field, even your own neighborhood. The mission field is very broad, and we need to be attuned to the world around us because there is not one living soul on whom God does not have His eyes (2 Pet. 3:9).

It has always been important to understand the culture in which we live in order to communicate with those in our spheres of influence. Sometimes as Christians, we would prefer to simply stay out of the secular world and surround ourselves with other Christian friends. Granted, the Christian community is not only a gift to us from God but is also imperative for our spiritual growth. The encouragement that we receive from our Christian friendships notwithstanding, we are all still commanded to reach the world around us for Christ. That means we must prepare ourselves with knowledge. First we need to know God through the diligent study of the scriptures. Second, we must observe and do our best to understand the culture in which we live.

In a culture hostile to the Word of God and hence the God of the Bible, how do we meet people where they are, the way that Jesus did? God has given us countless examples of how He has always met people where they are. To begin with, He spoke in terms that people could understand. He used imagery that the people could comprehend, and finally He sent His Son, Jesus of Nazareth, so that we would better understand how we need to view His Word. The activities of the apostle Paul are also wonderful examples of how we can reach the world for Christ. Paul clearly knew the mind-set behind the *Gentile*, or non-Jewish, populations and used his understanding of their philosophies to introduce the one true God to a *pagan*, or one who does not know the God of Israel, and to a pluralistic society much like our own today (Acts 17).

It is imperative to know with whom we are dealing in order to have meaningful faith conversations. The way to familiarize oneself with the culture is to observe the ethical expectations and moral norms of the society and then measure them against the Word of God. It will not take long to recognize what is important to a culture when one studies the activities of the people in any given social sphere. Anyone who has watched the social trends in the West can safely surmise that there is a definite rejection of the things of God. In fact, we are currently living in a unique time in the history of humanity where there is an almost militant hostility toward the Christian faith, even in the West.

What is the danger of not believing that the Bible is indeed the Word of God?

_____

_____

Focus on the New Testament

History reveals that it was at the dawn of the Enlightenment in the seventeenth century when serious criticisms were raised about the validity of the Bible. Academia touted that in order to know any undeniable truth, one must be able to scientifically test the veracity of the claims being made (Descartes, Kant, and others put forth this view). The purpose of this study is to help you as a Christian understand how the Bible can, and does, indeed stand up to scientific testing and reasoning. Our job as Christians is always to be ready with an answer to questions about our faith and understanding of the one true God (1 Pet. 3:15). Never forget that our answers must be delivered with gentleness and respect, yet never compromise the Word.

If you have been a Bible student for long, you are clearly familiar with the reality that the Old Testament foreshadows what is to come in the New Testament. Without the Old Testament, the New Testament does not make any sense. Conversely, the New Testament is what sheds light on the Old Testament. We live with a clearer understanding of God's revelation to humanity because of His work through the Christ. Jesus continuously quoted the Hebrew scriptures (Old Testament) and made it clear that everything He said was not from Him but from God the Father (John 14:10, 24).

All the writers of the New Testament drew from the Hebrew scriptures and, with the aid of God's Holy Spirit (John 14:25), were able to better understand God's desire for His people. Unfortunately, because of humanity's sinful nature, there has always been the tendency to distort the Word of God to glorify oneself instead of using it to understand God's will for humanity. Granted, this is usually not the intent of the individuals who improvise the Word, but when one veers from the Bible in any way, that is what inevitably happens. There are examples of this behavior in the New Testament as Jesus reprimands the religious leaders of the day for distorting the Word and using it to their own benefit (Matt. 12). What was worse, their misrepresentations misled others (Matt. 18:6–9, Mark 7).

This very same thing is happening all over the West today. Many who are entrusted with teaching the Word of God are willing to compromise the integrity of the Word in an effort to appease the society at large. God's Word was never taken lightly by Jesus of Nazareth, nor should it be taken lightly by those who call themselves Christians (Christ followers) today. The Christ is noted as frequently validating the Hebrew scriptures (the *law*, the *Prophets*, and the Psalms [Luke 24:44]), and we can take full confidence in His validation. As a disciple of Christ in the twenty-first century West, it is necessary to equip oneself with knowledge of the validity of the writings in the New Testament. We need to be prepared to engage the culture with facts that can bring the people thereof to a saving faith.

Historicity

The remainder of this workbook will begin to address the concerns and perhaps the misconceptions of the skeptic who either has an intellectual barrier or finds that the Bible is no different from any other religious material. This study is designed to teach you how the Bible was pulled together and its historical value. My hope is that by the time you have completed all of the material, you not only will be able to share this information with others but also will come to appreciate how God has preserved His written Word for humanity throughout history. In no small part due to critical and liberal academia, coupled with modern-day historical fiction narratives like Dan Brown's *The Da Vinci Code*, there are numerous misconceptions about the veracity of the Bible. The ultimate purpose of this study is that you come to know and appreciate the God represented in the Bible by learning the truth that sets Christianity apart from all other faiths or religions.

The next nine chapters will each be divided into two sections. The first section will be the *technical lesson*, which discusses how the Bible has been tested for accuracy and for the verification of its historicity. The second half of the chapter will be the *application section*. This section is where you will learn how to discern how accurate the biblical narrative actually is when compared to the historical context of the time when it was written. When both the historical facts and the biblical narrative are taken into consideration, the outcome should be a deeper understanding of scripture and an appreciation for God's hand in its preservation.

Review

Obstacles to Faith

List the three major obstacles to a person's faith:

1. _____
2. _____
3. _____

Key Terms

apostate: An individual or group who leaves the faith.

communicable characteristics: Those characteristics that humans are able to share as the image-bearers of God, such as love, forgiveness, compassion, and discernment.

cult: Any religious group that differs significantly in one or more respects as a belief or practice from those religious groups that are regarded as the normative expressions of religion in our total culture.[14]

---

[14] Walter Martin, *The Kingdom of the Cults*, ed. Ravi Zacharias (1965; repr., Bloomington, MN: Bethany House, 2003), 17.

epistemology: The study of how we gather knowledge in order to know reality.

eschatological: The idea of end times in discussing future events that will affect all of humanity.

Gentile: A non-Jew

Gospel: The good news of God's plan of redemption for humankind.

Imago Dei: Latin for "the image of God."

immutable: Something that does not change and represents stability.

intelligent design: The belief that because there is intelligence found in the design of creation, there must be an Intelligent Designer.

metanarrative: The narrative in between. The events in the Bible must be taken into consideration within their own theological and historical context. They must be seen as a whole, not as isolated events and narratives (stories).

metaphysical: The reality of the existence of that which we cannot physically see with our eyes. The spiritual realm and human feelings are part of the metaphysical realm.

mutable: Something that does, or has the capacity to, change frequently and that can be unstable.

neoatheism: There is a movement of new atheism on the rise in the West, which can be traced to the lack of belief in the historical reliability of the New Testament.

pagan: An individual who does not believe in the God of Israel.

Shema: The Hebrew word for "to hear" and "to listen." It is a call to pay attention.

syncretism: This is the practice and worldview that blends the beliefs and practices of two or more faith-based traditions.

telos: Seeking the end results of life or purpose.

the last day: The Bible speaks frequently about the *last day* as the Day of Judgment when God decides to end the world as we know it today.

volitional: A decision made "just because." More often than not, there is no sound reasoning, only the desire to exercise one's free will.

Literature Cited or Recommended

Barna Group. "2015 State of Atheism in America." Barna Group, 2015. Research based on the project Churchless edited by George Barna and David Kinnaman. Accessed March 30, 2015. https://www.barna.org/barna-update/culture/713-2015-state-of-atheism-in-america#.VRmtHGd0xLM.

Carson, D. A. *The Gagging of God: Christianity Confronts Pluralism*. Grand Rapids, MI: Zondervan, 1996.

Corduan, Winfried. *Neighboring Faiths: A Christian Introduction to World Religions*. 2nd ed. Downers Grove, IL: InterVarsity Press, 2012.

Geisler, Norman L., and Abdul Saleeb. *Answering Islam: The Crescent in Light of the Cross*. 2nd ed. Grand Rapids, MI: Baker Books, 2002.

Gauss, James F. *Islam and Christianity: A Revealing Contrast*. Alachua, FL: Bridge-Logos, 2009.

Hauerwas, Stanley, and William H. Willimon. *Resident Aliens: Live in the Christian Colony—A Provocative Christian Assessment of Culture and Ministry for People Who Know That Something Is Wrong*. Nashville: Abingdon Press, 1989.

Hawkins, Greg L., and Cally Parkinson. *MOVE: What 1,000 Churches Reveal about Spiritual Growth*. Grand Rapids, MI: Zondervan, 2011.

Krejcir, R. J. "Statistics and Reasons for Church Decline." Church Leadership.org, Francis A. Schaeffer Institute of Church Leadership Development, 2007. Accessed June 5, 2015. http://www.churchleadership.org/apps/articles/default.asp?articleid=42346&columnid=4545.

Martin, Walter. *The Kingdom of the Cults*. Edited by Ravi Zacharias. 1965. Reprint, Bloomington, MN: Bethany House, 2003.

Shumack, Richard. *The Wisdom of Islam and the Foolishness of Christianity*. Sydney, Australia: Island View Publishing, 2014.

Zacharias, Ravi. *Biblical Authority and Our Cultural Crisis*. Norcross, GA: RZIM, 1993. CD-ROM.

Zaka, Anees, and Diane Coleman. *The Truth about Islam: The Noble Qur'an's Teachings in Light of the Holy Bible*. Phillipsburg, NJ: P&R Publishing, 2004.

CHAPTER 2

Higher Criticism: Internal Criteria and Integrity of the Witnesses

Assessing Internal Criteria

Every historical claim must have witnesses to attest to the fact that the incidents in question did actually occur. The historical claims in the Bible are no different than any of the other events from history. Part of any investigative process is to research the events of the past to validate the credibility of the historical assertions being made. In a court of law, which seeks to confirm truth claims of any past occurrence, it is customary to assume the plaintiff of that inquiry innocent until proven guilty, and the jury is asked to take all of the evidence into consideration. The same criteria are usually applied to any documentation of a given historical event. The technical term used for this process is the *nature of evidential inquiry*. What this means is that when an investigator is conducting his or her research for answers to questions, it is important and helpful to be aware of how he or she is approaching the evidence. If, for instance, the researcher is approaching the past events from a "guilty before proven innocent point" of reference, his or her conclusions will most likely be flawed. This is because he or she is forcing an already presupposed outcome on to the evidence. If, on the other hand, the investigator allows for the evidence to speak for itself and approaches the testimony or writings from an "innocent until proven guilty" standpoint, the final assessment will more than likely provide for a more accurate conclusion.

Unfortunately, the philosophies that became prevalent during the Age of Reason (the seventeenth century) encouraged a great deal of skepticism, and as a result the integrity of the Bible was brought under a tremendous amount of scrutiny. Over the next three hundred years, the Judeo-Christian Bible was severely criticized and examined for proof of its integrity from the "guilty before proven innocent" vantage point. Although the facts in favor of the veracity of the claims found in scripture have been mounting up over the last seventy-five to one hundred years, many in Westernized civilizations remain reluctant to take the evidence into consideration. Their unwillingness to examine the facts has created a wide chasm between those who profess to be Christians and those who live as though Christianity is merely another lifestyle choice. It is important for the committed Christian to keep in mind that the evidence for the reliability of the scriptures is sound and that Christians can speak with confidence about the validity of the Bible without compromise. This lesson will begin our research on how the Bible has been tested for accuracy and reliability.

We will begin our investigation using a method of critique known as *higher criticism*. Higher criticism is similar to focusing on the big picture. It is much like any inquiry in that there are certain criteria that must be examined to make any truth claims about a past event. When studying the historical incidents found in the New Testament, scholars approach the manuscripts with both an *internal* and an *external* set of criteria. Our focus for the next three chapters will be on the *internal criteria* for validating the New Testament and its claims. Internal criteria include the following five assessments:

1. the nature of evidential inquiry
2. the integrity of the witnesses
3. the date of the originals
4. the accuracy of the witnesses
5. the accuracy of the documents.

The current lesson will include a look at the nature of evidential inquiry and the integrity of the witnesses.

What is the *nature of evidential inquiry*, and how is it applied? The nature of evidential inquiry is the method of approaching the truth claims made for any historical event, including those found in scripture. The first premise to understand is that one must apply the law of "innocent until proven guilty" when building a case for the integrity of the New Testament. If, as is the case with the vast majority of liberal critical scholarship, one approaches the scripture manuscripts with the presumption that the claims and historical incidents are false, then the entire method will be self-refuting. In his book *Scaling the Secular City*, J. P. Moreland notes, "If such a presumption is universalized (one always assumes someone is lying) lying becomes pointless for the simple reason that lying is impossible without a general presumption of truth telling." In other words, because the incidents of the Bible are historical in nature, how is one to prove that the claims about God's Christ are true if we refuse to begin our investigation by taking the events in question at face value? When we allow the evidence to speak for itself and accept it as truth, then we are able to test the integrity of the propositions made.

Note: If your skeptical friend only believes in nature to explain miracles, it may be necessary to focus on historical facts for the time being.

Embedded in the nature of evidential inquiry is the nature of *historical* evidential inquiry. The nature of historical inquiry focuses the investigative process on three principles. The first principle is the exclusion of any *unfounded* presuppositions. Liberal critical scholarship tends to approach the truth claims of scripture from a negative viewpoint, which includes the presupposition that any supernatural (miraculous) activity is mythical at best. A realistic and thorough investigation, however, must not begin with any unfounded presuppositions and should proceed with perhaps a critical eye for detail but not a skewed negative point of view.

The second principle of historical evidential inquiry is the exclusion of any hearsay. The investigator must seek out primary sources of information. Hearsay is not admissible in a viable examination of the facts. Primary sources are firsthand eyewitnesses. This is necessary to keep in mind as you take note of who is recording the historical events. Third, any claim made in scripture must be able to stand up under cross-examination. A case is made much more sustainable when there is outside evidence of what those who are opposed to either the events in question or the historicity of the people involved do and say. It is one thing to have the witness of someone who is on your side testify on your behalf, and it is quite another deal to learn of what your adversaries say about you, if anything at all.

Overarching Criteria

In addition to the principles involved in the nature of evidential inquiry, historical scholars also have overarching criteria for discerning the authenticity of an historical event. First, they look for *multiple attestations* (or forms) to the events in question. What this means is that historians examine the numerous sources that are available that mention the events being scrutinized and then make comparisons. Second, in the case of the New Testament, they seek *evidences of a Palestinian environment*, or language used in the documentation of the events. This is where the investigator checks to see if the written material matches up with what we know about the culture, as well as the oral and written language of the day.

Third, they test for a criterion known as *double dissimilarity*. The criterion of double dissimilarity is a test that ascertains whether or not the Gospel writings portray a Jesus who is dissimilar enough to the Jewish cultural expectations of the long-awaited Messiah, and a Christ who is different enough from what is found in the perspective of Jesus in early Christianity. In other words, was Jesus exactly what the Jews expected from their Messiah, and did Jesus always do what the people wanted him to do? Many historical scholars note that the authentic Jesus stood out from what was expected by the Jewish religious leaders just as He did from the other people of the day. He was also known for his difficult demands on His followers, as many chose to walk away in the early days of Christianity.[15] Fourth and lastly, historical scholars check for *coherence*. This is an argument that takes into consideration the writing, or manuscript in question, and its coherent fit with the other material that has been previously validated by any of the other three criteria (mentioned above). If the manuscript is coherent with earlier authenticated documents, then it can also be considered as genuine.

Integrity of the Witnesses

Keeping the principles of the nature of historical evidential inquiry in mind, we will begin our assessment of the internal criteria by first testing the *integrity* of the witnesses. Our investigation will look at who these men were and what their motives were for writing about Jesus of Nazareth and claiming him to be God's Son. We will strive to test for their honesty and possible motives. The following is a list of nine of the most telling questions about the authors and their motives for writing their respective manuscripts:

1. Can any of the New Testament writers be considered as direct witnesses?

   a. Yes, most certainly. Matthew, John, Peter, James, and Jude can all be considered firsthand witnesses (John 21:24; 1 John 1:1). Mark is also considered to be a direct

---

[15] Craig L. Blomberg, *The Historical Reliability of the Gospels*, 2nd ed. (Downers Grove, IL: InterVarsity Press, 2007), 310–11.

witness, as tradition has it that he was a close associate of Peter. We know from Peter that he and others were close to Christ (2 Pet. 1:16). In other words, there were more than twelve men following Jesus as He taught.

2. What written accounts of eyewitnesses do we have?

   a. Luke writes about eyewitness accounts (Luke 1:1–4), and he is very clear about his detailed efforts in documenting the historical events as they unfolded.
   b. The author of the Gospel of John testifies that he was an eyewitness to the events and ministry of Jesus of Nazareth (John 21:24–25).
   c. Paul mentions eyewitness accounts to the disciples and then Christ's appearance to over five hundred people after the resurrection (1 Cor. 15:5–8; Gal. 1).

3. Did the early church value eyewitness accounts?

> So one of the men who have accompanied us during all the time that the Lord Jesus went in and out among us, beginning from the baptism of John until the day when he was taken up from us—one of these men must become with us a witness to his resurrection.
>
> Acts 1:21–22 (ESV)

Yes. Eyewitnesses were very important to the early church, which indicates that the church members did not rely on opinion. This is not unlike today, when if an event of any significance happens, there must be eyewitness accounts to verify the occurrence. The disciple who was chosen to replace Judas (Iscariot) and become one of the twelve was to be from among those who had been with Jesus from the very beginning of His earthly ministry (Acts 1:21–22).

   a. It was understood that there would be great judgment on those who had the privilege of learning from those who knew the Lord Jesus firsthand (Heb. 2:3).

4. Were there any eyewitnesses to Jesus's death on the cross?

Yes. There were numerous eyewitnesses to the Crucifixion. There were also several generic onlookers, along with some of the religious leaders, and a few of Jesus's faithful disciples.

   a. The Gospel of John clearly mentions Jesus talking to His mother and the disciple whom he loved (John) while suffering on the cross (John 19:26–27). This tells the readers that it was Jesus on the cross as He spoke to the people around Him with loving words that only He would have used while dying in such an excruciatingly painful way.
   b. The last words of Jesus are recorded from the cross, and these are known as the seven final sayings of Jesus (Matt. 27:45; Luke 23:43, 46; John 19:26, 27, 28, 30).
   c. There were Roman soldiers trained in the art of execution witnessing the events (Matt. 27:35, 54).

5. Did the writers make an effort to speak/write about the true facts?

Yes. There is every effort made to speak only truth. The entire testimony of Christ was relying on the true attestations of the disciples. The Bible is filled with numerous events that did not even make sense to the disciples at the time they were happening, so there was no need to embellish the marvels to which they were witness. This is not to mention that these events were being documented while the many eyewitness were still alive. If there were any exaggerations or lies, then someone somewhere would have spoken up and exposed the writers of the New Testament.

a. Luke makes it a point to tell his readers that he is documenting the true facts of the life and ministry of Christ (Luke 1:1–3).

b. Luke also makes sure to place the life of the Christ in a historical context (Luke 3:1). In this way, those of the first century could clearly relate to their own life situations in those days under Roman rule. In this verse alone, Luke makes sixteen verifiable historical references to people and political positions.

c. The apostle John makes it clear to his readers that he was there at the foot of the cross and watched as the Messiah breathed His last breath (John 19:19–35).

d. Peter announces to his readers that he and the other disciples were not exaggerating the reality of the Messiah who came in the flesh and would someday return (2 Pet. 1:16).

e. The apostle John lets his readers know that he and the other disciples were witnesses to the life and ministry of Jesus (1 John 1:1–3).

After Jesus's resurrection, the disciples slowly began to realize the significance of the events associated with Jesus, even though they had no way of knowing the enormity of it all. Even on this side of the cross, we simply cannot fully understand God's perfect justice and plan for humanity.

6. What do we know about the authors of the manuscripts that make up the New Testament?

a. All of the writers of the New Testament, with the exception of Luke (a Gentile physician) and perhaps Mark (he may not have been Jewish, as his Gospel was written in the Greek form and seemed to be directed at those who were already considered to be Christian),[16] were Jewish theists. None of them lived glamorous lives as disciples of Christ, and all but the apostle John are recorded as having died a martyr's death for their convictions that Jesus of Nazareth was/is the true Messiah.

b. The apostle Paul writes to the Corinthians to make a point that he has suffered many indignations as a result of living for Christ and making it his life's purpose to teach and share the message of the Messiah (2 Cor. 11: 22–30), as he claims his Jewish ancestry.

---

[16] Luke Timothy Johnson, *The Writings of the New Testament*, 3rd ed. (Minneapolis: Fortress Press, 2010), 144–45.

Are they Hebrews? So am I. Are they Israelites? So am I. Are they offspring of Abraham? So am I. Are they servants of Christ? I am a better one—I am talking like a madman—with far greater labors, far more imprisonments, with countless beatings, and often near death. Five times I received at the hands of the Jews the forty lashes less one. Three times I was beaten with rods. Once I was stoned. Three times I was shipwrecked; a night and a day I was adrift at sea; on frequent journeys, in danger from rivers, danger from robbers, danger from my own people, danger from Gentiles, danger in the city, danger in the wilderness, danger at sea, danger from false brothers; in toil and hardship, through many a sleepless night, bin hunger and thirst, often without food, in cold and exposure. And, apart from other things, there is the daily pressure on me of my anxiety for all the churches. Who is weak, and I am not weak? Who is made to fall, and I am not indignant? If I must boast, I will boast of the things that show my weakness. (2 Cor. 11:22–30 ESV)

7. What did the writers/witnesses have to gain from writing about the good news of the reality of Jesus as the promised Messiah? History is replete with writings about the plight of Christ followers and how they were persecuted for the first four centuries of God's revelation of the Messiah. It was not until the fourth century AD that the emperor Constantine put an end to the torturous treatment of Christians, beginning in AD 311.[17] The persecutions of those who followed the Christ began with Jesus by the Jewish religious leaders in the first century and were eventually carried out by the Roman Empire until the fourth century.

   a. From a worldly viewpoint, the writers had nothing to gain, but they had everything to lose.

   b. Jesus is quoted as warning those with Him that the world would hate them for living in obedience to Him and not compromising His Word (John 15).

   c. Paul gave up his lofty position as a Pharisee to follow the Christ and tell the world about this gift from God (Phil. 3) that brought him suffering, pain, and constant persecution.

8. Were there any adverse witnesses in the central area where Christianity began? In other words, do we have any evidence that the enemies of Jesus and His followers wrote about Him and the events surrounding His life?

   Yes. There were historical eyewitnesses who, from the very beginning, found Jesus a threat, both in the secular arena and in the Jewish community. We will take a closer look at these enemies in a later lesson.

   a. In the secular realm, it was clear that King Herod was greatly threatened by the thought of being replaced by the rightful King of the Jews (Matt. 2). The reader is also informed in this chapter that all of Jerusalem was also troubled (v. 3), which included the chief priests and scribes.

   b. Throughout Jesus's earthly ministry, the Jewish religious leaders of the day were unapologetically averse to the message of salvation that Jesus preached.

---

[17] Hans Küng, *Christianity: Essence, History, and Future*, trans. John Bowden (New York: Continuum, 1995), 176–77.

   c. After the Crucifixion, historical records maintain that those who followed Christ were constantly targeted and persecuted in and around the Roman Empire, even up to the fourth century.

9. Did the witnesses have any type of motive to embellish their stories about their knowledge and message of Christ?

No. Motivation to lie stems from the desire to profit from one of three things: monetary gain, recognition and advancement in society, and the fulfillment of lusts of the flesh. The first Christians were treated as social pariahs; this is hardly a desired situation in which to find oneself. As time went on, they were eventually kicked out of their synagogues. There is no question that many families were split by this new radical belief which became known as the Way.

   a. The only motive was the reality of a holy and transcendent God who would come again to judge the world. From all evidence provided, the writers and witnesses did their utmost to recall every detail in order to relay the message of salvation to a dying and dark world, even at great personal risk.

Something to Consider

When reading through the four Gospels, notice how all four give the same picture of Christ; His character and message are consistent and coherent throughout. Many critics of the New Testament accuse the canon of scripture to have been written well after the life of Jesus of Nazareth, and hence claim that the writers were not eyewitnesses. If this accusation were true, then why are there not as many different portrayals of Jesus as there were Christian communities? Furthermore, if the New Testament was not written by reliable eyewitnesses, then why is there a clear consistency in the Christian tradition? History should be proof enough that even with a fully developed canon, human depravity will tend to deviate from the norm while adding to and subtracting from the intended purity of the church that Christ came to build and save, which is depicted in scripture. Wouldn't we expect to see a chaotic and inconsistent formation of the early church if there were no eyewitnesses to attest to the true teachings of the Messiah? If there were no eyewitness accounts recorded, then why did Christianity decide to confine itself to only four Gospels? Wouldn't it be more convincing if there were more input of "made up" sayings that could, or would, meet the needs of individuals?

It is clear that the integrity of the witnesses who ended up writing the New Testament were reliable witnesses whose testimonies would stand in a court of law. There are no legitimate reasons not to believe that the writers were direct eyewitnesses to the life and ministry of Jesus of Nazareth. Furthermore, there is confirmation from secular sources to support the manuscripts that form the New Testament. Historical records of those who opposed the early Christian movement (such as the Jewish religious sects of the day) also reveal that what is written in the New Testament is true. Not one of the writers of the scriptures had any earthly motivation to recount the message of the Messiah, as they were all eventually tortured for their belief in the Christ. If anything, they would have been better off (in this life) if they had made up stories that compromised the Word of God (perhaps just like liberal and unbelieving "churches" do today) or had kept silent (much like the majority of professing Christians do in our own day). There should be no question that the witnesses who wrote the New Testament were reliable individuals who loved God more than they loved their own lives in this world.

Review: Internal Criterion Used to Validate Documents

Tools for Discerning Historical Relevancy

Nature of evidential inquiry is the method of approaching the truth claims made for any historical event, including those found in scripture.

Historical evidential inquiry focuses the investigative process on three principles:

1. Exclude any unfounded presuppositions.
2. Exclude any hearsay.
3. Test any claims made to see if they are able to withstand cross-examination.

Overarching criteria:

1. Multiple attestations
2. Evidences of a Palestinian environment
3. Double dissimilarity
4. Coherence

Study Questions: Validating Internal Criteria

For Review and Reflection

1. What is the best method of discovering truth, and why?

2. What are the three principles used in the investigative process of historical evidential inquiry?
   a.

   b.

c.

3. What would be the best way to begin a conversation about the historical reliability of the Bible with a friend who is a skeptic and does not believe in anything supernatural such as miracles? What points would you focus on the most, using the tools that you have just learned?

4. There are three main things that cause people to lie: sex, power, and money. Did the writers of the New Testament exhibit any of these propensities as motives for writing?

Group Discussion

1. Can you find the scripture indicating that the disciples may have had any of the three motives of sex, power, and/or money at one time? Who were they? What was Jesus's response?
2. Now that you have studied how historians test for the integrity of the witnesses (who were the writers of the New Testament), how would you respond to someone who claims that the writers of the New Testament had an agenda?
3. What proof could you provide that they did not have a set agenda? Remember, sometimes we have to step outside of scripture to make a case for the veracity of the Bible.

Key Terms

coherence: Make sure that the manuscript makes sense when compared to the material that has already been scrutinized

double dissimilarity: Since we are studying the person of Jesus as the Son of God, this criterion is used because of the extraordinary claim that Jesus is God. Historians first check to see if this man was exactly what the Jews expected in their long-awaited Messiah. Second, scholars research to find if Jesus was also what others in the Gentile realm may have expected from a Savior. In either case He did not fit into the human expectation of what people would desire from a Savior. If Jesus was too much like the human expectations, then He would most likely not truly be God in the flesh, as we are told in scripture (John 1).

evidences of a Palestinian environment: The written material should match up with the historical evidence about the culture and language of the day. It is necessary to take into consideration both the written and the oral language.

multiple attestations: Validating the manuscripts by studying the number and viability of the historical sources available that mention the event in question

Literature Cited or Recommended

Blomberg, Craig L. *The Historical Reliability of the Gospels.* 2nd ed. Downers Grove, IL: InterVarsity Press, 2007.

Moreland, J. P. *Scaling the Secular City: A Defense of Christianity.* Grand Rapids, MI: Baker Book House, 1987.

Integrity of the Witness: The Integrity of the Author

Application of Scripture: 1 and 2 Corinthians

Read 1 and 2 Corinthians.

You might be thinking to yourself, *Where does Paul fit into this idea of credible witnesses? He wasn't a disciple; in fact he persecuted the first Jewish converts to Christianity.* You are correct, Paul was neither a disciple nor (as far as we know) witness to the Crucifixion or the resurrection. So how can we believe what Paul has written? How does he qualify as a direct witness? We will explore how Paul becomes a valid witness to the life and meaning of the Christ even though the first time we ever learn of him is in the book of Acts, where he is seen as a terrorist to those who follow Jesus as the Messiah. Throughout 1 and 2 Corinthians, Paul is aware of the importance of being a direct witness to validate the message of Christ that he brings to the people of Corinth.

Revelation and Tradition

Revelation

In order to verify his credentials to the church at Corinth, Paul reminds them that although he was not one of the twelve disciples, he too was commissioned by the Lord to his role as an apostle (1 Cor. 9:1). This commissioning event changed his life and as one sent by God, he emphatically claims equal authority to the apostles to teach the Gospel to the world (2 Cor. 11:5).[18] Paul insists that he is a direct witness to the meaning and life of the Messiah because God gave him a revelation (Gal. 1:16). The very fact that Paul bends over backwards to prove to the people that he has a direct witness status is proof of the importance of eyewitnesses in giving a testimony of any kind. He wanted the Corinthians to believe that his preaching held integrity (Gal. 1:1)[19] and that the people should not listen to his opponents who challenged his authority (2 Cor. 11:5).

---

[18] D.A. Carson and Douglas J. Moo, *An Introduction to the New Testament*, 2nd ed. (Grand Rapids, MI: Zondervan, 2005), 370.

[19] Ibid.

A critical thinker will hear Paul's story about being called by God and challenge the validity of his experience because of its supernatural nature. There is no question that Paul's story is radical and hard to fathom. It is understandable why he was challenged by others, but as Bible students we cannot just ignore this dilemma and move on. There are other ways to test the reliability of Paul's writings and their authoritative nature. We know from history that Paul was a very real person who lived in first-century Palestine, which means that there were traditions, certain protocols, styles of writing, and cultural details that will show up in his letters that will tell the reader volumes about the person documenting these life events. Long before the printing press and internet, people had distinct ways of transmitting information to retain its accuracy.

Tradition

Paul is the first to admit, with gratitude, that he received his information about the life, death, and resurrection of Jesus directly from an authoritative source (1 Cor. 15:1–3). The Greek word for receive that Paul uses is *paralambanō*, "that which I also received" (NIV). This is the same as the language that rabbis used to "describe their transmission of traditions." [20] This was a technical term that carried with it the weight of authority and integrity. Paul is evoking a method of passing on information that the recipients are expected to retain and "possess."[21] This form of transmission expects active and attentive listeners, not mere passive observers. A critical scholar would look at this technical term and note if it were also used in literature outside of Paul's writings, and it was.[22] This is important because it reveals to us that Paul did not create the word in order to make an allusion to the brevity of the message that he was passing on to his audience. In fact, this was a technical term that Paul would have been familiar with because of his background as a Pharisee and student of scripture (the Old Testament).[23]

In his own defense, Paul was making it clear that there was a chain of authority when speaking about the Son of God, as he had obtained his information directly from those who knew about the life, death, and resurrection of Jesus firsthand (1 Cor. 15:5–7; Gal. 1:18). In the letter to the Galatians, we read about the time that Paul spent with Peter, who was considered the leader of the apostles, and James. It is believed that this is where Paul most likely gathered specific data about Jesus's resurrection and the way in which He fulfilled prophecy.[24] Think about it: Paul had to be accurate and honest because there were far too many people alive who would immediately expose him if he did not tell the truth. There were high expectations of integrity when delivering the Gospel message, as there should be today and in every age.

Paul's pharisaic background is central to his integrity as a witness to the reality of God's designated Messiah (Jesus of Nazareth). His rigorous training would have helped him to realize the brevity in transmitting only the truthful facts without embellishment. As noted above, the language he used was technical and loaded with meaning. The Pharisees were known to hold sacred their traditions of transmitting the Word of God from one generation of teachers

---

[20] Ibid.

[21] Richard Bauckham, *Jesus and the Eyewitnesses: The Gospels as Eyewitness Testimony* (Grand Rapids, MI: Wm. B. Eerdmans, 2006), 265.

[22] Ibid., 265, 269. See also the writings of Josephus, *The Antiquities of the Jews* 13.297.

[23] Ibid., 265, 269.

[24] Ibid., 266.

to the next.[25] The students were eventually expected to become part of the transmission, and this is consistent with Paul's expectations of the communities with whom he shared the Gospel message.[26]

Every indication reveals to us that Paul took the formal process of transmission very seriously. It is important not to forget that Paul did not work alone. He was frequently accompanied by some of the leading members of the Jerusalem church (Mark, Barnabas, and Silvanus mentioned as Silas [Acts 15:22]), who would add to his integrity as a valid messenger.[27] Paul's proclamation of his use of the *formal process* of transmitting the facts about Jesus (1 Cor. 11:23) gives us an insight into how the written and oral traditions were used to preserve the reliability of God's message of redemption. Some critics have claimed that as time went on, the message of the Gospel morphed to fit the culture in which it was proclaimed (in other words, putting words into Jesus's mouth).[28] There is proof, however, that this was not the case.

Paul is very careful to separate the words of Jesus from his own instructions to the people (see 1 Cor. 7:10–16). He clarifies to the church at Corinth that he is passing on the symbolism of Jesus and His last supper with His disciples just as it was handed down to him (1 Cor. 11:23–25). Passages like this one are also helpful when we take a look at the dating of the original writings, which we will learn more about in the next lesson. If you look through the Pauline Epistles, you might notice that this passage on the Lord's Supper in 1 Corinthians is the only passage that Paul explicitly quotes.[29] There is no doubt that Paul handles the information on the directives of Jesus with the utmost respect and care. It is important to note that as Paul transmits the truth of the Jewish Messiah, he makes sure that his readers are aware of the importance of retaining the tradition of the Christ accurately and correctly. Maintaining the integrity and purity of the Gospel becomes the responsibility of all of Paul's hearers (1 Cor. 11:2, 15:2; 2 Thess. 2:15).[30]

In an effort to capture the truth behind the person of Jesus and the events surrounding His life, biblical scholars study any documentation found outside the four Gospels where Jesus is cited (Acts 20:35; 1 Cor. 11:23; 1 Clement[31] 13:1, 46:7–8).[32] Careful attention is paid not to change what Jesus has said, nor is there an attempt to create a new tradition. The writers are reaffirming and reminding the readers of Jesus's instructions, which they would have previously learned.[33] Paul, along with the other writers of the New Testament, proves to be reliable enough that his testimony would be accepted in a court of law. Paul calls his readers' attention not only to his qualifications as an authoritative source for the truth of the Gospel (2 Cor. 10) but also to what he has been through in his efforts to teach the facts about the Christ (2 Cor. 11). He, like the other

---

[25] Ibid., 270.

[26] Ibid.

[27] Ibid., 271.

[28] Ibid., 278–79.

[29] Ibid., 267.

[30] Ibid., 269.

[31] Clement was one of the early church fathers who wrote (AD 95) about the theological significance of Jesus as the Messiah, and he quoted the New Testament writers extensively. I include him in this vain because the early church fathers realized the importance of maintaining the integrity of the writings of the eyewitnesses as they passed on the teachings of Jesus to others.

[32] Bauckham, *Jesus and the Eyewitnesses*, 279.

[33] Ibid.

writers of scripture, had absolutely nothing to gain by spreading the good news of God; on the contrary, he risked his life in so doing.

Understanding the Scripture

The Context

Biblical scholars recognize Paul's Second Letter to the Corinthians as his "most personal letter" documented for us in the New Testament.[34] Noted scholar R. H. Strachan observes that 2 Corinthians gives the reader a glimpse into Paul the man.[35] The letter reveals Paul's humanity and the lengths to which he is willing to go in his efforts to reliably teach the Gospel of the Christ. Strachan comments that this letter can be seen as an "autobiographical" sketch of the life of this determined and zealous apostle. The reader becomes privileged to share in Paul's disappointments, his courage, and the way he handles "ingratitude, and "disillusionment."[36]

Note: Just like us, Paul faced opposition when sharing the truth of the Gospel message. Much of his opposition came from the Jewish religious leaders. He also faced disappointments when the people he taught clearly did not take the Gospel message to heart and began listening to false teachers.

When was the last time that you were treated poorly or dismissed because you could see that the Word of God was being distorted? Can you share this experience with your group, and write it down in the space below?

_____

_____

_____

Paul is clearly concerned for the people of Corinth and their propensity to believe the false teachers who began to discredit Paul and the message that he brought to them (2 Cor. 10, 11). Because of the tone of the letter, scholars believe that this one was sent sometime around the fall of AD 55 or 56.[37] Literary scholars focus on the events and people mentioned in a piece of writing when dating a letter such as Paul's numerous letters that have been preserved for us in the New Testament. They seek out clues such as Paul's mention of the Macedonians (whom he mentions at least thirteen times in all of his Epistles)[38] and their apparent state of poverty, which can be checked against historical records. The church at Philippi is probably the most well-known of the Macedonian churches to those of us familiar with the New Testament. According to biblical scholar C. K. Barrett, it is suggested most possibly that there is evidence that the Macedonian churches faced poverty during this part of history because of severe persecution.[39] The reason for

---

[34] Ralph P. Martin, *Word Biblical Commentary*, vol. 40, *2 Corinthians*, ed. David A. Hubbard and Glenn W. Barker (Waco, TX: Word Books, 1986), lxiii.

[35] Ibid., lxii.

[36] Ibid.

[37] Ibid., 249.

[38] Ibid., 250.

[39] Ibid., 252.

this assertion is that historical records show that the Macedonian economy was flourishing, and therefore it is concluded that the impoverishment of the church was not the result of an overall economic depression[40] but was perhaps more central and personal in nature.

What was behind Paul's plea for a substantial collection? From scripture, we are aware that Paul had visited the "mother church" in Jerusalem prior to reaching out to the church at Corinth and the surrounding area of Achaia (2 Cor. 9:2) for funding. During his visit to Jerusalem, he promised to continue to remember the "poor" at Jerusalem (Gal. 2:10), which is what he is referring to in this current letter. Paul saw this as fulfilling God's plan for humanity, where all people (both believing Gentiles and Jews) would join together and recognize Jerusalem as the point of God's ruling authority and grace.[41] For Paul, this may have seemed like an eschatological fulfillment when "gentile believers would make their pilgrimage to Jerusalem bearing gifts" (see Isa. 2:2–5, 60:5–22; Mic. 4:1–5).[42]

Integrity of the Witness

When we are seeking intent in regard to historical figures, it is helpful to pay attention to the language used by the author. The study of the Bible is no different. In order to get a deeper understanding of scripture, you will benefit by taking note of the language that the author, in this case Paul, utilizes. Paul makes use of language that connotes "sacred acts of worship" and stems from an intimate relationship with God (the rightful object of human worship).[43] Chapters 8 and 9 are good examples of the message that Paul is trying to convey to his readers by the use of specific words. In the following space, write down the words that suggest our relationship as humans with a holy God:[44]

Chapter 8	Chapter 9
v. 1	v. 1
v. 4	v. 5
v. 4	v. 6
v. 4	v. 12
v. 6	v. 13
v. 7	v. 13

Due to the fact that terms can change meaning over time, it is helpful for the Bible student to try to find the significance of certain words used in scripture in order to grasp as much of the original intent as possible. This is also a way that scholars are able to date a literary work and place it in its historical context. We have a wonderful example of this in the tenth and eleventh chapters of 2 Corinthians. These chapters are riddled with military terminology with which the people of first-century Corinth would have been familiar. Paul alludes to "military installations"

---

[40] Ibid., 251.
[41] Ibid.
[42] Ibid.
[43] Ibid.
[44] Ibid. The words in the verses are directly pointed out.

(10:4) and to a "soldier's campaign" (10:5).[45] These are terms apparently taken from the "'wars of the Maccabees' literature,"[46] with which Paul would have been very familiar as a student of Israel's history.

There is also the mention to the building up of a stronghold (fortress) and then the demolishing of it (v. 4 and v. 8, respectively).[47] Proverbs 21:22 uses the same type of idea: "A wise man scales the city of the mighty and brings down the stronghold in which they ["they" clearly alludes to the ungodly] trust." Paul's letters also show evidence of language that would have been rabbinic in nature, which is an indication of his familiarity with the Jewish religious writings of his day and his knowledge of scripture. Paul takes his calling to its fullest as he defends his integrity and authority, not for his own edification and recognition, but because he is zealous for Christ's church. He knows the danger of deviating from the purity of the Gospel message.

The context of the first-century atmosphere into which Paul and the other faithful disciples and apostles of Christ had to speak was an incredibly complex context. Part of testing the integrity of a historical document, and therefore the writer of that document, is to note how said writer speaks to that culture. When taking the reliability of Paul's letters into consideration, it is imperative to do our best to understand Paul as he would have been viewed by his original audience. It was common for first-century Palestinian Jews to speak both Hebrew (Aramaic) and Greek, but scholars believe that there was an air of theological weightiness placed on a Jew who was fluent in Aramaic.[48]

Theological Implications

The Greek-speaking Jews were better known as Hellenists and were viewed as more on the liberal side of the theological spectrum than the stringent Palestinian Jews.[49] Scholars surmise that the Hellenists were not practicing the purity of the Jewish faith as closely as they should have and had succumbed to many of the Greek customs around them.[50] It is very important to note, however, that at this point in time with the Jewish population, the Hellenists were very aware and respectful of the guidelines set forth by the God of Israel through Jesus as they were filled with the Holy Spirit at Pentecost (Acts 2).[51] Do not make the mistake of comparing them to the nominal Christians of the twenty-first century who either have no idea what Jesus requires of them or are completely unaware of what the scriptures actually say.

The fact that Paul was a Hebrew among Hebrews (Phil. 3:5) was very important to the ministry that God had given to him. We get a glimpse of this understanding when looking at Luke's account of the angered crowd depicted in Acts 21:40–22:2.[52] When Paul spoke to the enraged crowd, they calmed down to actually listen to him when he used Aramaic to address

---

[45] Ibid., 301.
[46] Ibid.
[47] Ibid.
[48] F. F. Bruce, *The New Testament History* (New York: Doubleday, 1980), 217.
[49] Ibid.
[50] Ibid.
[51] Ibid., 218.
[52] Ibid.

them, as they expected him to speak using the Greek language.[53] When reading the Word of God, these little nuances are like gems given to us as glimpses into the past. The Lord could have chosen anyone to carry the Gospel of salvation to the Gentile populations. Why would He choose Paul?

Give two attributes of God that show up in His choice of this pharisaic Hebrew man to proclaim the good news of the Christ to the Gentile nations:

1. _____
2. _____

As a well-educated Pharisee (Acts 22:1–3),[54] Paul knew all too well the history of Israel's failings when it came to their backsliding and tendency to worship the idols around them. He knew that the nation was sent into exile and was dispersed as a people as punishment for their unfaithfulness to the God of Israel. Paul's adamancy about false teachings seeping into the church stems from his knowledge of Israel's history. The people of Corinth were allowing false teachers to sway their thinking, leading them away from the essence of the kerygma. These impostors were in effect negating God's work of redemption on the cross.[55]

Paul knew all too well how detrimental it would be for the people if they began to forget the message of the cross (even ever so slightly). The essence of the cross at its core is the result of the necessity for humanity to recognize their absolute inability to save themselves by performing a series of good works. Paul knew the words of the prophet Jeramiah as the latter lamented over the innate depravity of humankind (Jer. 17:9). Scripture is also clear that all of a person's efforts at saving himself will never achieve the perfection required of a holy God (Isa. 64:6). This is because at the heart of our good works is a selfish motivation, unless our deeds are done to please and glorify only the Lord.

Human nature has not changed since the first act of rebellion against God in the garden (Gen. 3). We have a way of deceiving ourselves and believing that we are good enough to warrant salvation. I remember seeing a clip of an Oprah Winfrey show where she challenged a member of her audience on this topic of being good enough. Oprah was most certain that good works was the gold standard for achieving a ticket to heaven. Sadly she is not alone, as this tends to be the most popular and prevalent view across the world. I was greatly disappointed when the audience participant did not know how to answer Ms. Winfrey's challenge while thousands of viewers watched.

Most devious is the heart; It is perverse—who can fathom it? (Jer. 17:9 TNK)

Another wonderful opportunity to share the message of the cross missed.

In the Old Testament, God used the prophet Hosea to speak to the nation of Israel and warn them that the people of God perish for their lack of knowledge of the Lord (Hosea 4:6). The same holds true today. All Christians are called to be ready to give an answer for our hope in Christ (1 Pet. 3:15). It should go without saying that if we are called to give a response, then we need to know why we believe what we believe, and that comes through the study of the scripture.

---

[53] Ibid.

[54] Martin, *Word Biblical Commentary*, vol. 40, *2 Corinthians*, lxiii.

[55] Ibid.

If someone were to challenge you today and ask you why it is necessary to believe in Jesus for salvation, how would you respond? Take a moment and write down your answer:

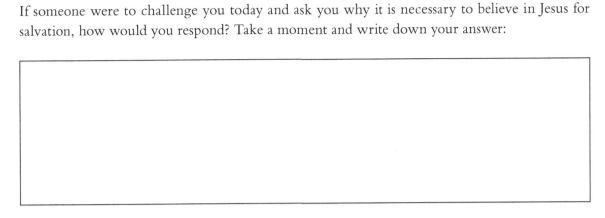

In chapters 11 and 12, Paul's concern for the people was quite justified. It was a constant battle against false messengers not only from the outside but also from the inside of the Corinthian church.[56] He employs very strong language when he vows to *avenge* (used as a forensic term) the harm done by these deceivers who have set a snare for the people.[57] These words can be taken and used to warn even the church in the twenty-first century. Anytime the purity of the message of God's Messiah is changed, even if it is changed to make the message more palatable, it not only will create friction within the church but also will set a trap for those who do not know any better. There is no question that Paul knew from Israel's broken history that any deviation from the Word of God will draw people away from the true Creator as they begin to follow a false god of their own making.

Review: Integrity of the Witnesses

Study Questions for Reflection and Theological Focus

1. What did Paul have to lose when he became an active disciple for Christ?

2. Why did Paul feel the need to compare himself with the other apostles (2 Cor. 11:5, 16–33)? (See also 2 Corinthians 11:12–14.)

3. What was Paul's purpose of taking up a collection? (See chapters 8 and 9 of 2 Corinthians, and Galatians 2:10.)

---

[56] Ibid., 307.
[57] Ibid., 306.

4. In chapter 10 of 2 Corinthians, is Paul exerting his dominance over the people? If not, what is he doing, and why? And if so, is he trying to have people fear him for the purpose of power?

5. What were some of Paul's gifts that God used to spread the Gospel to a world that did not know Him?

    a. What are your gifts, and how is God using you?

6. What is the message that Paul is attempting to convey to the Corinthians in chapter 5, verses 9–21?

    a. What are the attributes of God that you see here?

    b. How does this conflict with the image of Jesus that our culture portrays?

    c. What will you do as a result of knowing what the Bible says about Jesus?

7. What attributes of God do you find in chapter 10 of 2 Corinthians?

    a. Have you ever felt that you wanted to correct another professing Christian?

        i. What did you do, and what happened?

        ii. How does God use Paul here to tell us how to handle false teachers?

Group Discussion

1. What makes Paul a reliable witness? Make sure to use the tools that you have learned in this chapter to make your case.

2. The next time that you have an opportunity to speak to some of your skeptical neighbors or relatives, how will you use this information about Paul to help them see the significance of the reliability of the New Testament?

Key Term

kerygma: A Greek term meaning "to cry or proclaim as a herald."

God's Attributes

<u>providential</u> – God sees and knows what is ahead in our lives.

<u>sovereignty</u> – God is in control and rules over events and time.

Literature Cited or Recommended

Bauckham, Richard. *Jesus and the Eyewitnesses: The Gospels as Eyewitness Testimony.* Grand Rapids, MI: Wm. B. Eerdmans, 2006.

Bruce, F. F. *The New Testament History.* New York: Doubleday, 1980.

Carson, D. A., and Douglas J. Moo. *An Introduction to the New Testament.* 2nd ed. Grand Rapids, MI: Zondervan, 2005.

Josephus, Flavius. *The Antiquities of the Jews.*

Martin, Ralph P. *Word Biblical Commentary.* Vol. 40, *2 Corinthians.* Edited by David A. Hubbard and Glenn W. Barker. Waco, TX: Word Books, 1986.

Always remember that God gave you not a spirit of fear but one of courage and boldness in the name of Christ. Never fear that speaking Truth about discrepancies will destroy you or make you seem foolish. When you obey God's Word alone, you are abiding in the *truth*, which is the most powerful weapon in existence.

> For the weapons of our warfare are not of the flesh but have divine power to destroy strongholds. We destroy arguments and every lofty opinion raised against the knowledge of God, and take every thought captive to obey Christ. (2 Cor. 10:4–5)

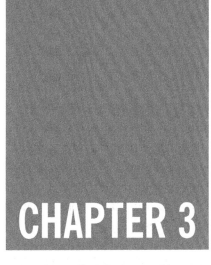

CHAPTER 3

Higher Criticism: Internal Criteria and Dating of the Originals

Dating of the Originals

Part of the practice of validating the events described in documents from antiquity is to determine when the originals were written. The fact is that the writings in the Bible have undergone far more scrutiny than any other historical document from ancient history. Granted, given the claim that the Bible makes, namely that it is the very Word of God, it should be examined to a higher degree than other historical writings. If we are going to base our eternal destiny on what we find in scripture, then we ought to make our decisions with absolute certainty that God has chosen to reveal Himself through this collection of works that we call the Holy Bible. As previously mentioned, the Old Testament is "God's Word about Christ,"[58] and the New Testament (NT) is the revelation of His Word.

Credibility

Any claim to an event in history is thought to be far more accurate the closer to those specific events that the incidents are actually formally recorded in writing. In chapter 2 we learned about the integrity of the men who recorded the events surrounding the life and death of Jesus. Although we know that we can trust the writers of the New Testament, can we also trust their memories of past events? When did they begin recording their experiences with God's Messiah? Are their views of the events and sayings of Jesus accurate enough for readers in the twenty-first century to entrust their lives to?

Liberal scholarship seems to have made a sport of discrediting the veracity of the Bible, but serious historical scholars have an overwhelming amount of evidence that should put any fallacious issues to rest. The reason why many today do not believe that the Bible is the authoritative Word of God is mostly related to its antiquity, coupled with the doubts placed on its veracity by liberal critics. Age does have its effects on things, and we will never know how many historical documents have been lost over the centuries of human history because of wars, carelessness, and

---

[58] Graeme Goldsworthy, *According to Plan: The Unfolding Revelation of God in the Bible—an Introductory Biblical Theology* (Downers Grove, IL: InterVarsity Press, 1991), 54.

natural disasters, to name a few reasons why things vanish. Fortunately for us, God made sure that His Word would forever be preserved for all of humankind. Our mission to confirm the reliability of the New Testament documents will be to first examine secular historical writings from antiquity. Second, we will compare those documents to what are known as the *extant manuscripts*, or the writings that have been discovered, of the New Testament. Third, we will date the initial source of the manuscripts.[59]

The reason why critical scholars came to unashamedly doubt the veracity of the Bible is that we do not have the original *autographs* of the writings that make up the New Testament. We do, however, have numerous *manuscripts* from which to re-create the original documents. Manuscripts are copies of the originals. It is true that when people make a handwritten copy of any document, there is always the possibility of error. When we consider the manuscripts that make up scripture, we must consider the source. Considering the attitude and context in which the disciples of Jesus lived, it is clear that the first-century church took the events surrounding the life of Jesus very seriously and that every effort was taken to ensure the accuracy of the copies made of the originals. In our investigation and defense of biblical integrity, we cannot underestimate the accuracy of the oral form of communication of that time.

What Has Survived?

It would be unrealistic to think that a piece of papyrus or vellum from the first century would still be intact, much less a group of writings. In God's perfect design, however, it was necessary for the writers to make numerous copies of their letters and books in order to have them distributed to the ever-growing church. It is not unreasonable to understand that in order for written information to spread faster, it would be necessary for someone to make copies of the original material, much like we do today. As the church grew, it makes sense that it became necessary to make duplicates of the originals so that the new disciples, like Timothy and Barnabas, could travel with them as they shared the Gospel with the world. The key is to determine how soon after the originals were the copies made. It is also helpful to accurately reconstruct the originals when we have multiple manuscripts with which to work. We will discuss this at further length in chapter 8.

Fortunately, to date, we have well over 5,686 Greek manuscripts of the original documents that now make up the New Testament from which to draw. This is more than any other historical document in the history of humanity in antiquity. Secular writings from antiquity have not fared as well. The nearest copy of an original writing that has been discovered to date is Homer's *Iliad*, which dates to 500 years after the original was written.[60] Of the manuscripts and portions of these documents, there are about 643 that can be used to reconstruct the *Iliad*.[61] The *entire* Bible was compiled in a fewer number of years than that (about 330 years after the actual historical event of the Crucifixion). Another work of historical significance, for instance, would be Caesar's *Gallic*

---

[59] Norman L. Geisler, *Christian Apologetics*, 2nd ed. (Grand Rapids, MI: Baker Academic, 2013), 343.

[60] Norman L. Geisler and Frank Turek, *I Don't Have Enough Faith to Be an Atheist* (Wheaton, IL: Crossway, 2004), 227.

[61] Ibid., 226.

War, which was written around 58 and 50 BC.[62] There are only nine or ten usable manuscripts for this historical documentation, the oldest of which is dated 900 years after the days of Caesar.[63]

Historical People and Events

There are numerous other examples of historical documentations and copies of the original documentation, but none even come close to the evidence we have for the New Testament. There are certain criteria that historical scholars take into account when working out the dates of the original written material. One of the most obvious dating criterion used is to focus on the *actual historical events* that are mentioned in the written material. Any references to *political situations* and *persons in power* are taken under investigation when determining when a historical document was written. There are numerous references to historical events and persons in power mentioned throughout the New Testament that have helped scholars date the original writings. For instance, the Gospel of Matthew mentions the death of Herod (4 BC),which precipitated the return of Joseph and Mary from Egypt (Matt. 2:19).

This is how historians have dated the birth of Jesus as having taken place at some point prior to 4 BC. There is also mention of persons holding political power in several places throughout the New Testament; one example is the Gospel of Luke, which contains no fewer than sixteen verifiable historical references in the span of two verses (Luke 3:1–2). This type of information has aided scholars in placing the Crucifixion around AD 30.[64] Documented history also confirms the expulsion of the Jews from Rome as noted in the book of Acts (18:1–2). The fact that the events and people mentioned in the New Testament are also noted in secular historical writings has been immensely helpful, not only in dating the original autographs but also in validating the veracity of the New Testament.

Another way of placing a date for the original documents is to assess the historical events that are not mentioned. Jewish historical references clearly attest to the importance of the Jewish temple. It was the center of all of Jewish life in the time of Jesus. The Jewish temple that existed in the first century was eventually destroyed in AD 70 under the rule of Flavius Sabinus Vespasianus (ruled AD 69–79).[65] This type of evidence is incredibly helpful because it lets us know that the majority of the New Testament was written no more than approximately forty years after the Crucifixion.

Consider the fact that everything sacred happened at this temple. If it were destroyed during the time when the writers of the New Testament were documenting the events of Jesus and the growth of the church, there would no doubt be some indications of its ruin. It is due to this historical event that the one Gospel that scholars suggest was written shortly after AD 70 was Matthew, with all the others having been penned prior to this historical event.[66] There are other scholars who have reason to believe that it was penned earlier, and some are certain that most of

---

[62] F. F. Bruce, *The New Testament Documents: Are They Reliable?* (Grand Rapids, MI: InterVarsity Press, 1981), 11.

[63] Ibid.

[64] Ibid., 6.

[65] Merrill C. Tenney, ed., *The Zondervan Pictorial Encyclopedia of the Bible in Five Volumes*, vol. 5, *Q–Z* (Grand Rapids, MI: Zondervan, 1977), 877.

[66] Bruce, *The New Testament Documents*, 7.

the New Testament was written prior to AD 70. This suggests that most of those who knew Jesus firsthand were still alive and could verify what was being written about the Christ.

Reality or Legend

Even if we base the late dates of the New Testament on the more liberal end of the spectrum, historians agree that these dates are much "too early to be considered" as mythical testimonies or writings.[67] According to Julius Müller's *The Theory of Myths* (1844), "The writings of the Greek historian Herodotus enable us to test the rate at which a legend accumulates; tests reveal that even the span of two generations is too short to allow legendary tendencies to wipe out the hard core of historical fact."[68] If a generation is considered to be at least forty years, then two generations would constitute, at minimum, eighty years. Considering the earliest writing from the New Testament at around AD 60 (or earlier, which we will deliberate later), fully formed myths would have begun to be established approximately by AD 140.[69] Not surprisingly, this was around the time that the "first Christian mythological material begins" to surface (the Gospel of Thomas and other noncanonical material).[70]

Dating the Material

It is not unusual for scholars to update their approximations of historical dates as new information is revealed and collected. This has been the case with setting dates for the writings of the New Testament. As time has passed and new historical information is discovered, the approximate dates for the original documents has continued to narrow, and at the same time become earlier than previously believed. We will now focus on some of the latest findings by Roman historians who are trained to test the authenticity of existing evidence for events during the Roman Empire of antiquity. Noted Roman historian and scholar Colin J. Hemer has given very early dates for the documentation found in the Gospel of Luke and the book of Acts. Hemer's research is well respected and markedly in depth.

External Clues

Secular Writings

It is well-known that Luke is the author of both the Gospel that bears his name and the book of Acts. Scholars recognize that Luke's book of Acts was written shortly after the Gospel of Luke. Hemer gives several reasons why he believes that (without going into great detail here). Because of the fact that James was still alive when Acts was written, it was most likely penned prior to AD 62. Hemer bases this understanding on secular historical documentation that mentions that the death of James (Jesus's half-brother) took place in AD 62 (Josephus's *Antiquities* 20.9.1).[71] With this

---

[67] Geisler, *Christian Apologetics*, 352.

[68] Ibid., 352. Cited from William Lane Craig, *The Son Rises* (Chicago: Moody, 1981), 101.

[69] Ibid.

[70] Ibid.

[71] Ibid., 353.

fact in mind, he is certain that the Gospel of Luke was written no later than AD 61.[72] These are very early dates considering that Jesus's crucifixion happened around AD 30. This places these two major historical documents as having been written within thirty years after the death and resurrection of Jesus! With this in mind, it is helpful to remember that the book of Acts includes the majority of Paul's missionary journeys.

Why are outside sources so valuable to the reliability of the New Testament?

_____

_____

_____

Archeological Evidence

Even more encouraging is that twentieth-century historical scholarship dates Mark and Matthew as having been written before the Gospel of Luke, possibly as early as the fifties.[73] Dr. Luke was such an accurate historian that modern-day scholars have been known to use his documentation in the book of Acts as a way to locate historical sites and verify archeological locations. The discovery of the Dead Sea Scrolls revealed fragments of what are believed to have come from Mark, Acts, Romans, 1 Timothy, 2 Peter, and James. These were discovered in a cave that contained items that were dated between 50 BC and AD 50.[74] This is wonderful news because the fragments of these manuscripts indicate a very early date for the documentation of the events surrounding the life of the Christ and the life of the early church. Archeological finds such as the caves at Qumran gave reason to scientists such as William F. Albright of the twentieth century to declare, "In my opinion, every book of the New Testament was written by a baptized Jew between the forties and the eighties of the first century AD (most likely between about AD 50 and 70)."[75]

How are discoveries important to the reliability of the New Testament?

_____

_____

_____

Who Was in Power?

It is also well attested that Paul's Epistles were written within this early time frame and certainly prior to his death. Paul's death is documented for us in the writings of the early church fathers. They record for us that Paul was executed under the rule of Nero, whose leadership was terminated in AD 68.[76] Some of Paul's writings are known to predate the fifties. His letter to the Galatians, for instance, is believed to have been penned in or around AD 48, only eighteen years after the death and resurrection of Jesus. Historians also take note of internal clues that will aid

---

[72] Ibid., 352.

[73] Ibid.

[74] Geisler and Frank Turek, *I Don't Have Enough Faith*, 225–27.

[75] W. F. Albright, "Toward a More Conservative View," *Christianity Today* (January 18, 1963): 3.

[76] Geisler and Turek, *I Don't Have Enough Faith*, 240.

in placing a date on other writings in the New Testament. What this means is that when scholars look for consistency and continuity in the Gospels and Epistles, they take note of the continuity between the writings.

Internal Clues

Where Did He Get That?

What is the author repeating? Where did he get his material? Why is it important enough to document? The answers to these questions are all clues as to what was going on either in the culture or within the community that the writer is describing. Paul's letters to the various churches reveal practices that were already established early on in the first-century church. Scholars reveal that Paul appears to be quoting directly from the Gospel of Luke when he imparts information about the practice of the Eucharist (1 Cor. 11:23–25).[77] The passage in 1 Corinthians is very similar to the version found in the Gospel of Luke (Luke 22:19–20).[78] There is reason to believe, however, that since Paul's First Letter to the Corinthians was written prior to the Gospel of Luke, this tradition came from an earlier source.[79] What this reveals is that the early church was already practicing the Eucharist tradition as a way of remembering the sacrificial death of the Lord.

Keep in mind that the First Letter to the Corinthians is dated between AD 55 and 56, seemingly prior to the documentation represented by the Gospel of Luke (AD 61 or before). We also know that in his letter to the Galatians (AD 48), Paul states that he had visited with Peter and James (Jesus's brother) for fifteen days, three years after his conversion. This is where biblical scholars believe Paul "received" the understanding that Christ was sacrificed for our sins (1 Cor. 15:3–8). It is also believed that Paul most likely learned of the tradition of the breaking of the bread and the sharing of the cup in remembrance of God's substitutionary atonement during this visit. What this tells an historical sleuth is that the institution of the Lord's Supper was in practice very early on in church history.

Well-known resurrection specialist and biblical scholar Gary Habermas is not alone when he states that the practice of breaking bread to remember the resurrection and its significance dates as far back as "eighteen months to eight years after" the resurrection.[80] He also notes that there are other reasons to believe that this institution began even prior to eighteen months after the resurrection.[81] This is very exciting news, as many skeptics accuse the church of inventing this tradition long after the first century. Considering the Lord's Supper has been practiced since the days of the disciples, there is no way that the resurrection can be considered a legend, since it "goes right back to the time and place of the event itself."[82] Always remember that life is not two-dimensional but rather multidimensional; therefore, examining history means it is necessary to focus on what was going on in the culture in which the writers had to live.

---

[77] Richard Bauckham, *Jesus and the Eyewitnesses: The Gospels as Eyewitness Testimony* (Grand Rapids, MI: Eerdmans, 2006), 267.

[78] Ibid.

[79] Ibid.

[80] Geisler and Turek, *I Don't Have Enough Faith*, 242.

[81] Ibid.

[82] Ibid.

Think about It

If the early church was already recognizing the Lord's Supper for the purpose of remembering the significance of the resurrection soon after the event in Jerusalem where Peter and James were when Paul came to them, then if Jesus did not resurrect and His body was indeed buried somewhere, the Romans would certainly have been happy to produce the body and make a public display of it.[83] The tension between the Roman Empire and the Jews was very high, and the Roman officials recognized those who followed the Christ as just another extension of Judaism. They would have been more than pleased to put a stop to the turmoil caused by this new sect of Judaism and the Jewish leaders. As it was, they did not have the body to display, nor did the Jews; therefore, the practice of remembering the sacrifice for atonement continues to this day.

Early Church Fathers

Aside from comparing historical events and cultural trends to the information written in the New Testament documents in an effort to date their origin, historical scholars seek out other material outside of the New Testament writings that may relate to the existing manuscripts. We know from the evidence that within the early church movement, there was a great deal of documentation in the form of letters to churches and individuals being written and shared. Scripture reveals that many people were being transformed and converting to the Way of Christ (Acts 2:38–47) during this early period. The disciples were raising disciples, and it was from this flock that the second wave of writers arose. This next generation of church leaders has come to be known as the Apostolic Fathers, and they began to write between AD 90 and 160.

Three of the better-known very early church leaders were Clement of Rome, who wrote in AD 95; Ignatius, who wrote from Smyrna in Asia Minor around AD 107; and Polycarp, who also wrote from Smyrna in Asia Minor in about AD 110.[84] All of their writings were based on the documentation found in the New Testament. Why is this important? It is important to us because it shows that the writings of the New Testament were already circulating by this time, which means that the New Testament was written well before these dates and had become common knowledge to the growing church. We must also take into consideration that both Polycarp and Ignatius (who were disciples of the apostle John) were hundreds of miles away from the origin of the New Testament documents. Historical investigators surmise from this fact that realistically it took time for documents to travel from one part of the continent to another, strongly suggesting early dates for the original writings.[85]

Considering the fact that the early church fathers' writings have been found in various locations apart from Jerusalem and Rome, what can we learn about the spread of the Gospel message?

_____

_____

_____

---

[83] Ibid.

[84] Ibid., 236.

[85] Ibid., 242.

Between the first and fourth centuries there was a great deal of persecution and turmoil surrounding those who followed the Way of Christ. It is certain that countless documents and manuscripts were destroyed in the Roman raids conducted during the reigns of the Roman emperors who wanted to do away with Christians altogether (Nero and Domitian, to name two). If it were not for the prolific writers of this time period, we would not have the treasure trove of citations that we hold today. In addition to the three early church fathers aforementioned, there were numerous others who also began to write liturgical and public material,[86] citing in their works nearly every single verse in the New Testament with the exception of eleven verses! The evidence for early dating of the original autographs is undeniable.

Even the well-known atheist John A. T. Robinson, initiator of the "Death of God" crusade, wrote that the evidence for the New Testament documentation reveals that "most of the New Testament books, including all four Gospels, were written sometime between AD 40 and 65."[87] Even the Gospel of John, which everyone has historically given a late date, was completed by AD 69 according to Robinson's *Redating the New Testament* (1976).[88] We will end our lesson on the dating of the original autographs with a word from the late scholar and manuscript expert the late Sir Frederic Kenyon:[89]

> The interval then between the dates of the original composition and the earliest extant evidence becomes so small as to be in fact negligible, and the last foundation for any doubt that the Scriptures have come down to us substantially as they were written has now been removed. Both the *authenticity* and the *general integrity* of the books of the New Testament may be regarded as finally established.[90]

Part of the process of dating any work from history is to validate the time in history from which it originated. In other words, it is important to study the customs of the people of that time period to compare those practices with what the author is actually saying. True historical works will match with the documentation on cultural trends and the norms of that day. If they do not, then there is reason to question the validity of the manuscript under investigation. The scripture reading for this chapter is Paul's letter to the Galatians. We will take a critical view of this letter with the intent of searching for the historical clues that will help date and validate Paul's written account.

Who were the addressees of Paul's letter to the Galatians? Numerous scholars over the centuries have made their contributions to the context and intent of this Epistle to the churches of Galatia. Much like all of the Epistles of the New Testament, Paul's letter to the Galatians is a realistic snapshot of the early church and the obstacles faced by these fledgling Christians. There is no question that to fully understand why people behave the way they do, one must understand their past. When dealing with an entire civilization, the scholar will find it most beneficial to study the movements of a society in its own context. Any given culture will tend to be multifaceted, containing layers of traditions; therefore, it is necessary to take a close look at the complexity of the proposed community to better comprehend its mind-set.

What sort of background did these people whom Paul was so concerned about in Galatia

---

[86] Hans Küng, *Christianity: Essence, History, and Future* (New York: Continuum, 1995), 132.

[87] Geisler and Turek, *I Don't Have Enough Faith*, 243.

[88] Bruce, *The New Testament Documents*, 15.

[89] Ibid.

[90] Ibid., 15. Citing Kenyon's *The Bible and Archeology* (1940), 288–89.

have? In order to get an idea of how the recipients of this letter may have understood what Paul was conveying to them, we will focus on the aspect of the *slavery* and *inheritance* language he uses. It appears that there is an underlying assumption that the addressees are familiar with not only slavery but also the rights of being an heir. It is imperative to impress upon the postmodern mind that the connotations of slavery and inheritance must be understood in their historical context and not to impose a seventeenth- or eighteenth-century understanding onto the text. This is necessary in order to get a true picture of how the language the author uses is taken as either literal or allegorical, which could suggest that those receiving the letter were from various backgrounds. There is no question that to better understand how scripture remains relevant for all time without becoming subjective, it is imperative to comprehend the past.

Review: Internal Criteria Used to Validate Documents

Tools used for dating documents are as follows:

1. Focus on actual historical events.
2. Pay attention to references of political situations.
3. Notice who were those people in positions of power.
4. Notice events that are not mentioned.
5. Historians study the evidence that has survived.
6. Investigate the written material found outside of the New Testament, and compare its consistency with the documents that make up the NT.

A basic outline to follow when determining the date for the documents is as follows:

1. Examine the secular historical writings of that time.
2. Compare the events, people, and political atmosphere to the extant manuscripts.
3. Date the initial source.

Study Questions

For Review and Reflection

1. What constitutes the credibility of a historical written document?

2. What major event is not mentioned in the majority of the New Testament writings?

   a. Which Gospel may make an allusion to this event?

   b. What does this mean for the dating of this Gospel?

3. Can you name two outside sources used to calculate when the documents of the New Testament were written?

a. _____

b. _____

4. How long does it take for a fully formed myth to be established?

_____

5. How have the writings of the early church fathers helped to date the manuscripts and original writings?

Group Discussion

1. If a skeptical friend were to suggest that the practice of the Eucharist was a fabrication of the Roman Catholic Church, how would you respond?

Key Terms

autographs: The original writings.

extant manuscripts: The documents that have been discovered and used in reconstructing the New Testament.

manuscript: A document.

Literature Cited or Recommended

Albright, W. F. "Toward a More Conservative View." *Christianity Today* (January 18, 1963).

Bauckham, Richard. *Jesus and the Eyewitnesses: The Gospels as Eyewitness Testimony.* Grand Rapids, MI: Eerdmans Publishing Co., 2006.

Bruce, F. F. *The New Testament Documents: Are They Reliable?* Grand Rapids, MI: InterVarsity Press, 1981.

Geisler, Norman L. *Christian Apologetics.* 2nd ed. Grand Rapids, MI: Baker Academic, 2013.

Geisler, Norman L., and Frank Turek. *I Don't Have Enough Faith to Be an Atheist.* Wheaton, IL: Crossway, 2004.

Goldsworthy, Graeme. *According to Plan: The Unfolding Revelation of God in the Bible—an Introductory Biblical Theology.* Downers Grove, IL: InterVarsity Press, 1991.

Küng, Hans. *Christianity: Essence, History, and Future.* New York: Continuum, 1995.

Tenney, Merrill C., ed. *The Zondervan Pictorial Encyclopedia of the Bible: In Five Volumes*. Vol. 5, Q–Z. Grand Rapids, MI: Zondervan, 1977.

Dating the Originals
The Date and Authorship of Galatians

Application of Scripture: Galatians

Read Galatians.

Biblical scholars agree that Paul is indeed the author of the letter to the Galatians.[91] The significance of the North or South Galatia debate will determine the cultural context of the addressees, as the cultural mind-set (and heritage) between North and South were vastly different. The research available suggests a people group with a variety of backgrounds that would represent the southern parts of Galatia. The majority of scholars believe that this was indeed a circular letter that was directed at several churches in the Roman province of Galatia. From a Southern Galatian stance, it appears that the letter was written around the time of the Jerusalem Council meeting in AD 49 or 50, either just before or just after. Due to the fact that the majority of scholarship tends to lean toward a Southern Galatian audience, we will focus most of our study based on this view as well.

Paul's Argument

In order to best understand the reasoning behind Paul's words to the churches in Galatia, it is necessary to build a frame of reference based on the letter as a whole. To begin, notice how the author seems to dispense with his traditional somewhat lengthy greetings of gratitude and jumps right into the heart of the matter. His tone is one of anger and defensiveness, as he deems it necessary to lay out his extensive credentials in order to get the attention of his audience. The first three chapters are clear admonishments of the church's lapse of faith in the Way of the Christ, as follows:

- 1:1–5—Letter heading and greetings.
- 1:6–7—Deserting to a different Gospel, one preached by humankind.
- 2:1–10—Even Titus was not forced to be circumcised before the Jerusalem leaders in
- the faith.
- 2:11–14—Ritualistic behavior is not acceptable as it nullifies God's work on the cross.
- 3:1–18—Foolish Galatians! It is either by faith or works that one is saved, but not both.
- 3:19–24—The law was added because of sin, which kept people captive.

The last set of verses in chapter 3 is where we begin to see the language of *captivity* associated with slavery, which will later lead into the language of family and the understanding of adoption into

---

[91] Richard N. Longenecker, *Word Biblical Commentary*, vol. 41, *Galatians*, eds. David A. Hubbard and Glenn W. Barker (Dallas, TX: Word Books, 1990), lvii.

the family (vv. 26–29). Chapter 4 is where we find Paul softening his tone slightly in an effort to engage his addressees through examples to which they will be able to relate.

Here is where Paul begins to inferentially exhort his intended audience:

- 4:1–2—An heir is no different than a slave, but there is an expectation of an inheritance at maturity for the heir.
- 4:3–5—As children we were enslaved to the elements of the world. Those who were born under the law were also enslaved. But in God's timing, He had a plan to set us free from these bondages.
- 4:6–7—God's plan included the adoption of all who would receive this gift as sons and daughters and hence heirs to the kingdom. This adoption frees one from slavery forever.
- 4:8–9—Why would you continue to desire slavery by serving false gods while you have been offered this sonship from the one true God?

We learn in the book of Acts that Paul is a well-educated and well-versed individual who is noticeably aware of the importance of speaking to his audiences at their respective levels of understanding (Acts 17). When addressing the churches of Galatia, Paul repeatedly refers to being enslaved, suggesting perhaps that they were personally familiar with the concept of slavery.

Paul also speaks of being adopted into a family, which in most instances represents inclusion, even though a family frequently embodies exclusive boundaries in some form. He speaks of this adoption, however, in a very positive and liberating sense. Studies have shown that the people of Galatia were not a homogenous group, that their heritages were varied, and Paul necessarily had to choose his language carefully when exhorting his addressees. History and archeological evidence reveal that the Gauls, who were originally from Europe, were invited to inhabit the area known today as Galatia in 278–277 BC.[92] They kept to their Gaulish language and religious practices and eventually imposed these on the local inhabitants.[93]

These were *polytheistic* groups who saw nothing contradictory about adopting the religious practices of the local inhabitants. The Gauls were successful warriors and dominated the existing population of the land (the Phrygians), who were seen not only as "slavish" but also as an "inferior caste."[94] Eventually these Phrygians were only thought of as slaves by the Greeks and others who came to dominate them. Even Socrates quipped that they were suited as slaves.[95] This is important to us because these were people who were part of Paul's audience in Galatia.

---

[92] W. M. Ramsay, *Galatia*, accessed July 6, 2015, http://www.biblestudytools.com/encyclopedias/isbe/galatia.html.
[93] Ibid.
[94] Ibid.
[95] W. M. Ramsay, *A Historical Commentary on St. Paul's Epistle to the Galatians* (Grand Rapids, MI: Baker Book House, 1965), 32.

There is evidence that the residents in the south were beginning to be aroused by the attractiveness of both Greek Hellenism and the grandeur of the Roman Empire.[96] It makes sense that Paul would remind his addressees of the freedom and familial inclusion offered through the Christ in light of their sense of inferiority in their culture (Gal. 4:3–5). The late well-known archeologist and scholar W. M. Ramsay suggests that Paul is attempting "to strengthen their weaknesses and to make their minds harmonious and well-balanced, so that they may judge truly and wisely."[97] The Jews, on the other hand, held a status of distinction granted to them by the *Seleucid* rulers.[98] They were given special privileges that enabled them to become wealthy business owners.[99] These special rights included the right to practice their religion along with all of its customs.[100] In 25 BC when Galatia became an official province of Rome, it was these various people groups and cultural influences that were deeply embedded in this Galatian society to which Paul wrote.

---

[96] Ibid., 443.

[97] Ibid.

[98] Ibid., 189.

[99] Ibid., 190.

[100] Ibid.

Kathryn V. Camp, D.Min.

Constructing the Historical Context

External Sources

When dating any historical document, it is greatly beneficial to reconstruct the culture of that time period in history by using reliable secular sources. Part of the reconstruction is to take into account the lifestyles of the people and the cultural influences that affected their daily lives. This is important because if actual historical evidence does not reflect what is found in the New Testament writings, then there is reason to believe that the manuscripts are not historically reliable. If the Epistle to the people of Galatia and the surrounding areas is historically accurate, it should reflect how the individuals lived within the societal norms of the first century. The letter to the Galatians places a great deal of importance on the family. When secular historical records are studied of that region, however, we begin to understand why Paul uses the terms that he uses and why he appeals to the readers as passionately as he does.

The readers and hearers of Paul's letter were clearly diverse in their own cultural contexts. The main governing groups by the first century AD were the Romans, the Greeks, and the Jews. All three were to affect the way the society understood the act of adoption and the notion of being an heir. Since adoption is a familial concept, as is the idea of inheritance, it will be helpful to take a closer look at how the family systems worked within these cultures. This will aid us in understanding the historical context into which Paul appealed to those who were marginalized in Galatia.

Slavery was also a fact of life for many of the citizens of Galatia. It appears that the various governing groups held to their own customs of how slaves were viewed and treated. The underlying element to the complexities within any cultural framework will be the religious customs of that particular people group. A culture's religious beliefs will not only determine its familial structure within a society, but also the way the individual relates to others within the community, including slaves.

Family Structure

Roman

History reveals that at the time that Paul wrote his letter to the Galatians, Rome was making some headway within the culture of southern Galatia as to their customs and their skills of organizing a society.[101] More than likely the customary law that governed the family had also begun to be impressed upon the population. Roman law gave the father, as the patriarch of the family, "absolute power" over everyone who resided in his household.[102] *Patria potestas* according to Roman law was not much different for the household than slave ownership was.[103] Adopting a child would have been much like claiming a piece of property.[104] Those adopted children

---

[101] Ibid., 183.
[102] James D. G. Dunn, *The Epistle to the Galatians: Black's New Testament Commentary*, ed. Henry Chadwick (Grand Rapids, MI: Baker, 1993), 210.
[103] Ibid.
[104] Ibid.

50

(including the heirs) under the rule of the head of the household (the father) would have been much like slaves and not allowed to own anything, thus not able to enjoy any future inheritance until the appointed time.[105]

According to historical records, by the first century when Paul wrote to the Galatians, the Roman idea of adoption was no longer associated with inheritance. The Roman father was free to leave his property to anyone whom he so desired.[106] In essence, the father of the household was not obligated to ensure future security to those living under his roof. This, undoubtedly, lies in contrast to the promise of family security in God's kingdom as offered through the Christ (Gal. 3:26–4:7). On the other hand, the Greek way of life and understanding of adoption and that of inheritance was quite different from what was customary to the Romans.

Greek

The Greek influence on the family system appears to be more prevalent at this time in history for these Galatians. This does not negate, however, the fact that there was an understanding of the implications of Roman laws and customs, which were beginning to influence some of the citizens. Unlike the Roman law and its familial structure, the Greeks did not consider the father to hold unconditional power over his children.[107] It is known that the Greek form of a will was not revocable while the testator was alive, but it was amendable. The emendation, however, could not revoke any of the inheritance previously promised.[108] Likewise, the adoption of a son was usually for the purpose of a continued family legacy. The adopted son became a legal heir to the family inheritance and was assimilated into the family as much as possible.[109]

Although the Greek will may seem noble to the outside world, the underlying premise for the need to have a will in the Grecian culture was to "carry on the family and the family religion."[110] The idea of passing on the family religion was of such importance to the Greek way of life that if an individual died intestate, the state would appoint an heir so that the family gods would continue to be worshipped.[111] In essence, the idea was that if an individual (son) was adopted, he was naturally expected to inherit the family's religious traditions and carry on the family name. This idea of family gods undoubtedly made it very difficult for those who were raised in this culture to break free without severing family ties.

Jewish

For the Jews, an heir had to be of blood lineage in order to benefit from any family inheritance. This is why the idea that a Gentile sinner would be adopted as an heir of Abraham's seed was indeed "abhorrent."[112] It is well-known that if a man died without an heir the Levirate law was

---

[105] Ibid.

[106] Ramsay, *A Historical Commentary*, 354–55.

[107] Ibid., 132.

[108] Ibid., 351.

[109] Ibid., 337–43.

[110] Ibid., 340.

[111] Ibid., 339–40.

[112] Ibid., 342.

enacted to ensure an heir to a man's estate.[113] The inheritance for the Jew was clearly tied to the land that was promised in the Abrahamic covenant (Gen. 12:1–9).[114] For the most part, the Jews seemed to keep to their own traditions, and likewise the family was held together by the law laid out for them by their patriarch Moses. That is not to say, however, that all Jewish people held to their own group of people. There is historical evidence that clearly shows how many of the Phrygian Hebrews assimilated into the culture and intermarried with the rest of the population.[115]

Slavery

Slavery was simply a fact of life in the Roman Empire as slaves were seen as a necessity.[116] Roman law considered slaves to be the property of the lord of the household under whom they worked.[117] Not surprisingly, the majority of those living in slavery were either the descendants of prisoners of war or were working off debt.[118] Slaves in the Roman province were not allowed to hold citizenship, which kept them from the protection and rights held by Roman citizens.[119] In fact, freed criminals had more rights than a slave in the Roman Empire.[120]

There were slaves who were not tied to a life of servitude and were given the opportunity to work their way out of slavery to become a class known as freedmen.[121] Historical records reveal that by the first century AD, slavery was a way to gain Roman citizenship, as slaves were intentionally trained in Roman customs and were allowed citizenship upon being freed.[122] The theological parallel would have meant that accepting Christ represented immediate spiritual freedom (Gal. 4:6–7). It would also mean a transfer of loyalties to and status in God's kingdom.

The Jewish customs of slavery, on the other hand, were laid out in the law of Moses (*Pentateuch*). The Pentateuch regulated the treatment of those who lived in servitude with a family. The law stated that no one should be kept as a slave for more than six years (Exod. 21:2) unless such a request was made by the slave. Even though most slaves of the Jews were domestic servants, the Levitical law allowed for the slave to begin a life out on his or her own after the obligatory six years. For the Jew, the burden of the law could have resounded with them as being a slave to the law of Moses (Gal. 3:19–24) with the added religious obligations imposed upon them by the religious rulers of the day (Matt. 23:1–7).

---

[113] Merrill C. Tenney, ed., *The Zondervan Pictorial Encyclopedia of the Bible in Five Volumes—Vol. 3, H–L* (Grand Rapids, MI: Zondervan, 1977), 912.

[114] Dunn, *The Epistle to the Galatians*, 211.

[115] Thomas A. Rand, "Set Free and Set Right: Ritual, Theology, and the Inculturation of the Gospel in Galatia," *Worship*, no. 75 (September 5, 2001): 455, cited from *Celts and the Classical World*, accessed through American Theological Library Association Serials (ATLAS), July 6, 2015.

[116] Mark Cartwright, "Slavery in the Roman World," *Ancient History Encyclopedia*, last modified November 1, 2013, accessed July 6, 2015, http://www.ancient.eu /article/629/, (1).

[117] Simon Hawthorne, *Rome, Ancient Rome: The Roman Republic—Rise of the Roman Empire and Roman History, Introduced*, 2nd ed. (Simon Hawthorne, 2015), Loc 709 of 1139, Kindle.

[118] Ibid.

[119] Ibid.

[120] Cartwright, "Slavery in the Roman World, (3).

[121] Hawthorne, *Rome, Ancient Rome: The Roman Republic*, Loc 806 of 1139.

[122] Merrill C. Tenney, ed., *The Zondervan Pictorial Encyclopedia of the Bible in Five Volumes—Vol. 5, Q–Z* (Grand Rapids, MI: Zondervan, 1977), 458.

> Formerly, when you did not know God, you were enslaved to those that by nature are not gods. But now that you have come to know God, or rather to be known by God, how can you turn back again to the weak and worthless elementary principles of the world, whose slaves you want to be once more? (Gal. 4:8–9 ESV)

Religion

There is, however, a slavery of another kind that is not so obvious; a culture's religious beliefs can indeed hold people in a state of bondage. Therefore, it behooves us to research what sort of religious customs the people of Galatia held to and how they, in turn, related to Paul's language in his Epistle. The Celts (who lived in the northern parts of Galatia), like the Greeks and the Romans, kept to their own religious practices and saw nothing wrong with assimilating other religious traditions into their own.[123] Historical scholar and writer H. D. Rankin suggests that tradition reveals that the Celts worshipped the natural forces of nature and did not hold to the machinations of the Greco-Roman gods that one would find in the Pantheon.[124] It is well-known, however, that eventually the Celts accepted the worship of the goddess Cybele as the goddess of wild nature, and by the first century AD this Phrygian goddess was well embedded in the Galatian culture.[125]

The Greeks integrated Cybele into their pantheon of gods around the fifth century BC. The Romans eventually assimilated her into their vast assortment of gods around the latter part of the third century BC.[126] Cybele gained official recognition in the Roman Empire during the reign of Claudius (AD 41–44).[127] There is no question that Cybele was a very attractive deity as she represented the basic livelihood of the people. Cybele was the goddess of the harvest and a protector of the society, she in essence watched over every aspect of an individual's life. There was always a temptation to bow down before an idol in the hopes of prosperity and well-being. This was a threat to fledgling Christians in the first century, and Paul was directly addressing these practices.

Attis was known as the male counterpart to Cybele and was considered a resurrection god representing the annual "rebirth of vegetation."[128] Legend had it that in a moment of insanity he castrated himself and then committed suicide, but myth goes on to tell how Zeus granted that Attis's corpse not decay, but would regenerate every spring. In a religious effort to reenact this self-mutilation, those who followed the cult were known to work themselves into a frenzy, ending in seriously cutting themselves.[129] It was also the custom for the priests who served at Cybele's temple to be castrated.[130] The cult grew in popularity throughout the Roman Empire and was

[123] W. M. Ramsay and James Orr, eds., *International Standard Bible Encyclopedia* (1915), s.v. "Galatia," accessed July 6, 2015, http://www.biblestudytools.com/encyclopedias/isbe/galatia.html.

[124] Rand, "Set Free and Set Right," 454.

[125] Donald L. Wasson, *Ancient History Encyclopedia*, s.v. "Cybele," accessed July 6, 2015, last modified February 4, 2015, http://www.ancient.eu /Cybele/.

[126] S. R. F. Price, *Rituals and Power: The Roman Imperial Cult in Asia Minor* (Cambridge, England: Cambridge University Press, 1987), 53–54.

[127] Ibid.

[128] Price, *Rituals and Power*, 53–54.

[129] Ibid.

[130] Ibid.

celebrated every spring, complete with sacrifices, fasting, and purification ceremonies, followed by feasts and a day of blood symbolizing the castration of Attis.[131]

Eventually, Claudius found it necessary during his reign to make a law stating that one would not be allowed to maintain his Roman citizenship if he were to castrate himself.[132] By the time Paul was writing to the people in Galatia, there was a wide range of religious beliefs, which included *animism*[133] and the worship of cosmic forces. This may sound foreign and ignorant to modern ears, but without God in our lives, we too will not feel fulfilled and must continue to add to our array of flesh-driven trappings to fill the void.

List three things that people fill their lives with that do not include God:

1. _____
2. _____
3. _____

All of these rituals and others like them are recorded in historical sources outside of scripture. They provide a wealth of information about the cultural norms of the people to whom Paul was appealing. The historical documentation of these various religious practices aids in placing this letter, and others like it, within an actual time frame of history. When we have a clearer understanding of the cultural realities of the first century, we are better able to comprehend the author's fervency when he addresses the people. Paul clearly knew the danger of people being led astray by false gods and unnecessary cultic practices.

Accordingly, Paul was concerned with the array of belief systems at work and embedded in the Galatian culture. The meaning of the "elemental forces" (Gal. 4:3) has been the discussion of many biblical scholars over the years as the meaning could have meant anything from the worship of the cosmic forces (like the Celts practiced) to the worship of the variety of religions to which they (Greeks, Phrygians, and Romans) were exposed.[134] In order to better understand Paul's concerns, it is necessary at this stage to study the meaning of the expression "under the basic principles of the world" or, in other translations, "elements." Biblical scholar Richard Longenecker suggests that in context, the Greek word used would most likely have been "derived from a military term."[135] He asserts that the term insinuates a "row," "rank," or "line" type of reasoning, a sort of series of elements.[136]

> In the same way we also, when we were children, were enslaved to the elementary principles of the world. But when the fullness of time had come, God sent forth his Son, born of woman, born under the law.
>
> Gal. 4:3 (ESV)

The Greek term in question can be used in a variety of ways, but in the Greek terminology, the common understanding would have been along the lines of "the basic materials of which

---

[131] Wasson, s.v. "Cybele."

[132] Ibid.

[133] Ibid.

[134] Dunn, *The Epistle to the Galatians*, 212–13.

[135] Longenecker, *Word Biblical Commentary*, vol. 41, *Galatians*, 165.

[136] Ibid.

everything in the cosmos, including man, is composed."[137] This would include the elements of the earth such as the air, water, and fire.[138] Scholars believe that Paul adds the phrase of "the world" (Gal. 4:3) to the "first principles" in a fleshly sense instead of a spiritual sense due to his Jewish ancestry. The Jews in the audience would have understood this reference as an allusion to the Mosaic Law and the physical sanctuary that was originally represented by the tabernacle in the wilderness.[139] God clearly used Paul's background and intellectual skills to speak at various levels, enabling him to reach his intended audience.

This analogy would have been not only upsetting to the Jewish crowd but also insulting, as they had a difficult time of letting go of the physical and ritualistic nature of the temple and Jewish traditions (Gal. 2:11–14, 3:1–18).[140] This was a continual point of contention between Jesus and His followers and the Jewish authorities. Scripture records how Stephen was stoned because his plea to his fellow Jews clearly implied that the temple and the law were merely stepping-stones to understanding the fullness of God's plan (Acts 6:13–15). This is part of what the Jews saw as blasphemous, that those who followed Jesus stressed the outdatedness of the ceremonial law and the use of the temple. Paul, who at that time was known as Saul, was one of those who condemned Stephen for this very reason. This steadfast holding on to tradition, however, came with its own set of shackles, as its staunch adherents could not break free of the traditionalism in which they had become entrenched over the centuries (Gal. 4:3–5). The external sources from history are evidence of the ritualistic behaviors of the pagans, as well as the religious traditions of the Jews noted in their own sources, and both provide a snapshot of the tense atmosphere into which Paul was called to operate.

Can you think of some church traditions that have nothing to do with salvation, on which people place a great deal of value? Write about them here.

_____

_____

Internal Sources

Whereas the external sources verify the historical accuracy of cultural norms and events of the first century, the internal sources represent all the scriptures that make up the biblical canon. Due to the fact that the Bible not only reflects human history but also reveals the nature and character of the Creator of the universe, it must be theologically consistent and coherent to be set apart as a reliable source for truth. If the New Testament does not reveal a consistent picture of God, then we cannot claim it as the Word of God. What you will find as you read through scripture is that there is not one word wasted, and every detail points back to an immutable and loving God. The letter to the Galatians is a perfect example of how God chose to use Paul to speak to the various people groups with their diverse backgrounds and intellectual abilities.

---

[137] Ibid.

[138] Ibid.

[139] Ibid., 167–68.

[140] Jerome H. Neyrey, "Bewitched in Galatia: Paul and Cultural Anthropology," *The Catholic Biblical Quarterly*, no. 50 (1988): 76, accessed through American Theological Library Association Serials (ATLAS), July 6, 2015.

The Addressees

Martin Luther points out that simple minds need simple analogies in order to help them understand what is being said.[141] In an effort to reach his audience in Galatia, Paul did not use the type of arguments that he posed to the intellectual elite who were his audience on Mars Hill (Acts 17). To the Galatian church, his analogies include family situations with which his addressees would have been familiar, such as heirs and family inheritance. Based on the external sources mentioned earlier, we learn how impressionable the Phrygian portion of the population were as they were just beginning to enjoy some of the fruits of the influences of the Greek culture and its focus on education and personal freedoms.[142] Careful observation discloses that Paul's language reveals an ethnically integrated church, as his speech is analogous and would have meaning to either the Jews or the Gentiles in the church, albeit at different levels of understanding. An ethnically diverse church is consistent with the actual population based on historical records for first-century Galatia.

Teaching and Exhorting Freedom

Paul's concern for the addressees is that they would once again begin to enslave themselves (Gal. 4:3) with religious customs, which would only nullify God's work on the cross (Gal. 2:11–14). The Phrygian Galatians would in essence regress to a mind-set of slavery from which their ancestors could not seem to break free. As to his Hebrew audience, his desire was to impress upon them that the law of circumcision was only meant to be temporary and that they were now free in Christ and no longer enslaved to rituals. This message of bondage was imperative as there was also the threat that the Gentiles would leave the church if circumcision was required because there was the potential that it would cause them to lose their much cherished status as part of the Roman Empire.[143]

> And because you are sons, God has sent the Spirit of his Son into our hearts, crying, "Abba! Father!" So you are no longer a slave, but a son, and if a son, then an heir through God.
>
> Gal. 4:6–7 (ESV)

Principles of Adoption

Paul's Gentile audience would have understood the "Spirit of his Son" as the witness to the adoption into the family of the Father (Gal. 4:6),[144] the former of whom would have been required for this act to be legal and binding. The deeper theological consequences of this passage for the Jewish addressees would have clearly implied that the Spirit of the Son was the same as the Spirit of God, which not only would begin to solidify the reality of Jesus as Divinity but also would end in the eventual parting of the ways between Judaism and Christianity.[145] For the Gentile, the adoption into the family of Israel was binding, which would give them the full status of a legal

---

[141] Martin Luther, *Galatians: The Crossway Classic Commentaries*, ed. Alister McGrath and J. I. Packer (Wheaton, IL: Crossway Books, 1998), 195.

[142] Ramsay, *A Historical Commentary*, 180–83.

[143] Rand, *Set Free and Set Right*, 460.

[144] Dunn, *The Epistle to the Galatians*, 219.

[145] Ibid., 221.

heir with the benefits of the family inheritance more akin to the Greek understanding and unlike the laws of humankind[146] as such was understood under Roman law.[147] In contrast to the fickleness associated with the Roman form of adoption, the God of Israel's promise is not revocable (4:4–7). It is possible, nevertheless, for an heir to choose to leave the family of God by turning back to her old ways, but it is the choice of the individual, not of the Father (4:9).

Attitude toward Religion

The Jews were well versed in the Law of Moses, which states that it would always hold the natural Hebrew as an heir to the kingdom, but that blatant acts of disobedience would be subject to discipline (Deut. 28:15–68). The point was that disobedience was on the part of the individual and a choice to leave the security that the God of Israel has to offer (much like Jesus's message of the prodigal son [Luke 15:11–32]) was an exercise of the individual's free will and not of the Father's doing. Nevertheless, Paul attempts to help the Jews understand that even though the Torah could not be abrogated, it must now be viewed in light of God's revelation through His Christ.[148] He does this by associating the Torah with the child who is under the control of the father until the time appointed by the father to claim his inheritance (Gal. 4:1–2, 3–5). The idea that Paul is conveying by analogizing the law to a figure of authority who rules over an individual is that the Torah represents a symbol of the religious rituals by which the God of Israel intended to separate those who belonged to Him from the rest of the world (Lev. 20:26).

> This is religion; when humanity seeks a salvation on its own terms through a system of works.

With the advent of the Christ, however, the rituals that are represented in the Torah are no longer needed. They are found to be obsolete because the long-awaited Messiah perfectly fulfilled the otherwise unattainable requirements and became the substitutionary atonement for all of humanity. Jesus of Nazareth would now be the symbol that would mirror the Torah. The fullness of God was found only in this Jesus (Gal. 3:13–41; Col. 2:9), and through Him the temple gates that separated the Jew from the Gentile would become obsolete (Gal. 3:28–29). Only those who refuse to recognize the Christ for who He truly is would remain outside of the family.

For the Jews this was a difficult and gradual (for many, but not all) shift in trust and understanding of God's revelation. As for the Gentiles, however, the temptation to revert to the empty and vacillating religious practices of their ancestors would prove to be a constant lure. There is within humankind a great desire to regress to a system of works, as opposed to uphold the foundational terms of a true faith (Gal. 3:1–8). This is religion, when humanity seeks a salvation on its own terms through a system of works. Consequently, those who were Gentile by birth in Galatia would have either been drawn to the desire for the freedom that Christ offers, even if it meant being circumcised, thus distorting the true freedom and familial inclusion that comes from the God of Israel, or they would reject circumcision because of their status of being a Roman citizen and thus leave the church. Either way, this works-based demand would distort God's intended relationship with the people. Paul's teaching is consistent with the rest of scripture

---

[146] Ramsay, *A Historical Commentary*, 338–39, 350.
[147] Dunn, *The Epistle to the Galatians*, 222.
[148] Gordon, "The Problem at Galatia," 39.

as there are many instances in the Old Testament where God tells the Hebrews that He would rather have their obedience than their rituals (1 Sam. 15:22–23; Ps. 40:6; Hosea 6:6).

Historic Context of the Addressees of Galatians

Freedom in Christ

Paul is addressing a Gentile population that has long been considered ignorant and treated as outcasts of society. There is a great desire to be included. The fact that Paul stresses freedom would no doubt strike a chord with this sector of the population. As previously mentioned, Martin Luther noted that Paul's speech was not intellectually subtle, but instead he painted pictures of life circumstances with which his audience would have been familiar.[149] Paul is beseeching a group that has not been a notable part of society to recognize the freedoms and familial inclusion that they have never enjoyed in their culture.

On a different level, his language speaks directly to the Jews. They understand clearly the secession of the Abrahamic Covenant and the seed that would at some point inherit the kingdom of God. They would not have been as vulnerable to the surrounding religious cults, but they would, no doubt, have been susceptible to reverting to a mind-set of superiority through the practice of their rituals laid out in the Torah. Even so, the threat to the Gentiles was greater, as the Hebrews were respected. One commentator noted that the Phrygians may have wanted to be included at the table of Israel to the extent that they would have been willing to be circumcised.[150] Throughout Paul's ministry he is called to reach a population that is not familiar with the God of Israel. Yet through it all he never compromises the Gospel or the Hebrew scriptures to make it easier for the people or for himself.

Numerous religious cults today are filled with people who are seeking to be included because they have never known a true sense of family. How will you make a difference to such people?

_____

_____

_____

Religious Influences

Paul was well aware of the syncretistic tendencies of the Gentile nations. Therefore, he used simplistic language to clarify that Jesus and the God of Israel were in no way to be understood as an addition to the various religious idols to which these Gentiles had been so accustomed for centuries (Gal. 3:19–20). There is no question that the threat of syncretism was very real, as Cybele was the goddess that controlled all of nature and fertility, and the God of Israel was the God who created the cosmos and everything in it. Attis was to the people a resurrection god, and the Jesus Paul preached had resurrected from the dead to give life and freedom to all. This

---

[149] Luther, Galatians, 195.
[150] Rand, *Set Free and Set Right*, 457.

is the atmosphere in which Paul had to interject not only the promises of freedom from slavery but also the exclusivity of the Christ amid a morass of religiosity.

Review: Dating the Originals
Study Questions

For Reflection and Theological Focus

1. Why does ritualistic behavior nullify God's work on the cross? Can you think of any rituals that people participate in today that are done to secure salvation?

2. Where in scripture do you find that works are not good enough? List at least two.

3. What was the Roman family structure?

    a. Can you think of any other cultures today where the man of the household has complete authority over everyone?

    b. Can you find in scripture God's idea of the family?

    c. How would use the knowledge of this freedom in Christ to help someone in a faith that keeps the family in bondage?

4. What were the benefits of adoption into a Roman family, and how did it differ from adoption into God's kingdom?

5. In regards to emperor worship, how would Paul have been a threat to the Roman Empire?

6. Can you explain how the myth of the regeneration of the god Attis would be confusing to new Christians?

    a.   If someone were to tell you that there are plenty of myths out there that refer to the resurrection of a god that brings new life, how would you engage this person in a conversation about what makes Jesus different from a mythological god like Attis?

7.   Can you explain why circumcision would misrepresent God's work on the cross?

Group Discussion

1.   Review each question in the foregoing section and discuss how these customs were practiced in the first century and how each of these behaviors is important to establishing the date of the original document.
2.   Aside from verifying the customs of family life, what has been the main reason that biblical scholars have dated the letter to the Galatians to around 48 AD?
3.   How will you use this information when discussing the historical reliability of the New Testament documents?

Key Terms

animism: The belief that objects house a "spirit" or a "soul." Many of the societies that believe in these spirits believe in at least two types: ancestor spirits and nature spirits. In order to keep these spirits on good terms with the community or household, they are paid homage to and worshipped.

patria potestas: Refers to the complete power that the father as the head of the household held over those dependent on him.

Seleucid: A ruling power in Syria and Babylonia that began shortly after the death of Alexander the Great in 323 BC. The Seleucid dynasty spanned a period of about 258 years, from the rule of Seleucus to his successor's end in 65 BC. The book of Daniel, 11:5, speaks of Seleucus as the "prince of the king of the South." He eventually won Asia Minor in 281 BC, and the Seleucid dynasty ran its course in history.

God's Attributes

grace – God extends grace to all without compromise.

love – All love extends from God. When we set our hearts toward God, our lives will begin to exhibit the true love that comes directly from God, not the shallow feelings that the world offers.

sovereignty – God's plan has always included people all over the world.

Spirit – God is Spirit. The Spirit of God gives true life to the believer. When a person lives in the Spirit, that person's life will reveal the character of the Creator.

Literature Cited or Recommended

Cartwright, Mark. "Slavery in the Roman World," *Ancient History Encyclopedia*, last modified November 1, 2013, accessed July 6, 2015, http://www.ancient.eu /article/629/.

Dunn, James D. G. *The Epistle to the Galatians: Black's New Testament Commentary.* Edited by Henry Chadwick. Grand Rapids, MI: Baker Publishing Group, 1993.

Gordon, T. David. "The Problem at Galatia," in *Interpretation*, 32–43. Accessed July 6, 2015 through American Theological Library Association Serials (ATLAS).

Hawthorne, Simon. *Rome, Ancient Rome: The Roman Republic—Rise of the Roman Empire and Roman History, Introduced.* 2nd ed. Simon Hawthorne, 2015, Kindle.

Longenecker, Richard N. *Word Biblical Commentary.* Vol. 41, *Galatians.* Edited by David A. Hubbard and Glenn W. Barker. Dallas, TX: Word Books, 1990.

Luther, Martin. *Galatians: The Crossway Classic Commentaries.* Edited by Alister McGrath and J. I. Packer. Wheaton, IL: Crossway Books, 1998.

Neyrey, Jerome H. S. J. "Bewitched in Galatia: Paul and Cultural Anthropology." *The Catholic Biblical Quarterly* 50 (1988): 76. Accessed July 6, 2015 through American Theological Library Association Serials (ATLAS).

Price, S. R. F. *Rituals and Power: The Roman Imperial Cult in Asia Minor.* Cambridge, England: Cambridge University Press, 1987.

Ramsay, W. M. *Galatia.* Bible Study Tools. Accessed July 6, 2015. http://www.biblestudytools. com/encyclopedias/isbe/galatia.html

Ramsay, W. M., and James Orr, eds. *International Standard Bible Encyclopedia*, 1915, s.v. "Galatia." Bible Study Tools. Accessed July 6, 2015. http://www.biblestudytools.com/encyclopedias/ isbe/galatia.html.

Ramsay, William M. *A Historical Commentary on St. Paul's Epistle to the Galatians.* Grand Rapids, MI: Baker Book House, 1965.

Rand, Thomas A. "Set Free and Set Right: Ritual, Theology, and the Inculturation of the Gospel in Galatia." *Worship*, no. 75 (September 5, 2001): 453–68. Accessed July 6, 2015 through American Theological Library Association Serials (ATLAS).

Russell, Walt. "Who Were Paul's Opponents in Galatia?" *Bibliotheca Sacra* (July–September 1990): 329–50. Accessed July 6, 2015 through American Theological Library Association Serials (ATLAS).

Schürer, Emil. *History of the Jewish People in the time of Jesus Christ.* 2nd ed. Second Division. *The Internal Condition of Palestine, and of the Jewish People, in the Time of Jesus Christ.* Vol. 2. Translated by Sophia Taylor and Rev. Peter Christie, 1890. Reprint, Peabody, MA: Hendrickson, 2014.

"Slavery in Ancient Rome, 170 BC." 2010. EyeWitness to History. Accessed July 6, 2015. www. eyewitnesstohistory.com.

Tenney, Merrill C. ed. *The Zondervan Pictorial Encyclopedia of the Bible in Five Volumes—Vol. 3, H–L*. Grand Rapids, MI: Zondervan, 1977.

———. *The Zondervan Pictorial Encyclopedia of the Bible in Five Volumes—Vol. 5, Q–Z*. Grand Rapids, MI: Zondervan, 1977.

Wasson, Donald L. *Ancient History Encyclopedia*, s.v. "Cybele." Last modified February 4, 2015. Accessed July 6, 2015. http://www.ancient.eu /Cybele/.

CHAPTER 4

Higher Criticism: Internal Criterion Used To Validate Documents

Accuracy of the Witnesses

I have often been asked to explain, how certain preachers can come to the theological conclusion that the pressing cultural issues of our day should vaguely be addressed, if at all. Not to mention the fact that many churches choose to accommodate the cultural issues at hand while turning a blind eye to the logical consequences of their decisions to do so. There is no question that there is a human tendency to avoid controversial issues and just try to get along with everyone, especially in the church. This is why when advocates for social change become incredibly powerful and pushy, through political pull, use of the media, and use of the education system, the tendency in the church is to begin to compromise the basic tenets of the Judeo-Christian faith to keep the peace. Unfortunately, *that* "peace" will come with its own set of consequences (Jer. 23:14, 16–22).

The consequence of compromising God's Word is death (James 1:12–15). So, how do the religious leaders in the church end up comfortable with compromise? In a previous lesson we briefly touched on the cultural shift in the West (during the seventeenth and eighteenth centuries) that began a trend that would eventually cause the majority of the world to distrust the Bible and question its authority over the lives of human beings. This is why we see churches all over the United States proclaiming a "Gospel Lite," as opposed to the unamended Word of God. Many, if not most, churches are set more on providing a feel-good atmosphere than serving as a place to find absolute Truth.[151] The twenty-first century is witness to the end result of a culture that has rejected the Word of God as it is written for well over one hundred years.

Regular church attendance is less than 17 percent of the population on any given Sunday, and the number of unchurched has never been higher.[152] We live in a time where speaking Truth is offensive no matter how gently and lovingly it is delivered. This paradigm shift all began with the seeds of doubt and suspicion. Suspicion eventually gave root to skepticism and critical analysis during the nineteenth and twentieth centuries, the consequences of which we are living through in the twenty-first century. A branch of *literary criticism* (which is the study of how a piece of

---

[151] Michael Horton, *Christless Christianity: The Alternative Gospel of the American Church* (Grand Rapids, MI: Baker Books, 2008), 29–64.

[152] George Barna and David Kinnaman, eds., *Churchless: Understanding Today's Unchurched and How to Connect with Them* (Austin, TX: Tyndale, 2014), 13–32.

literature was written and why) is known as *form criticism*; this is where we will begin our study for this chapter in our quest to find out the accuracy of the writers of the New Testament (NT).

Form criticism is one of the tools that was developed and used to establish the validity and the accuracy of the witnesses (writers) of the New Testament. This type of critical scholarship was spearheaded by three Germans in the early 1900's.[153] Their contributions became incredibly influential in academia and eventually trickled down through the churches and into society. If you recall from chapter 2, the way an individual approaches an investigation will determine the outcome (this is the *nature of evidential inquiry*). The men who developed this method for critiquing the writings of the New Testament, Karl Ludwig Schmidt, Martin Dibelius, and Rudolf Bultmann, approached their inquiries from the belief that the Gospels were written by the church leaders in an effort to preserve tradition to suit the needs of the culture, while interjecting their own theological bent.

This approach neglected to take into consideration that the eyewitnesses were the actual authors of the writings which make up the New Testament. Their accusations basically attack the literary integrity of the New Testament's record of the life of Jesus and the events surrounding His life on earth. These scholars believed that what we hold today in our Bibles represents a documentation that was relevant for the church in its own historical context. The question is, how did they come up with this evaluation? The answer lies in a tool used in form criticism known as *redaction*. You will probably never encounter this word for anything you will do, but I need to address the basic premise from which these individuals were approaching their presuppositions in order to clarify why so many religious leaders of our day do not regard the Bible as the absolute authority.

Redaction suggests that a finished work came together as a result of several individuals who specifically selected, edited, and reworded the sources that they had in order to highlight a certain style and theological belief. This sort of critical scholarship presupposes that the writers of the Gospels not only compiled a specific *tradition* but also purposely left out any material that did not fit in with their beliefs or agendas. The result of this way of looking at the Gospel material assumes that these writings from history can be studied and viewed merely as a set of techniques that were used in shaping the oral and written traditions of the day. Although the reasoning behind form criticism has since been successfully refuted and shown to be terribly flawed, much of New Testament academic inquiry continues to reflect this way of thinking.[154] It is through academia that this and other outdated literary criticisms have filtered into society through seminaries and secular educational institutions alike.

Name two things that the idea of redaction presupposes about the way that the New Testament was formed:

1. _____
2. _____

---

[153] Richard Bauckham, *Jesus and the Eyewitnesses: The Gospels as Eyewitness Testimony* (Grand Rapids, MI: Eerdmans, 2006), 242.
[154] Ibid., 242

We will briefly look at three major assumptions made by critics that lack sufficient evidence to be considered as relevant historical criticisms on the accuracy of the writers. Redaction proponents assert the following points, which are followed by my indications of the assumption and possible response:

1. That the Gospels reflect certain classifiable segments or types of forms. This is related to the idea that the thought of writers of the early church wrote them to support the needs of their communities. For instance, redactionists claim that the Gospel of Mark used a set of already existing *oral traditions*, or history that is passed on long after the people involved have died, in ancient Palestine to produce the text that we hold today.[155]

   - **Assumption:** What is recorded in the Gospel(s) did not truly happen in the way in which it has been delivered.[156] The contexts in which the events and sayings of Jesus are assumed to have been "determined by topical and other non-historical considerations."[157]
   - **Response:** It is misleading to suggest that the form of a piece of literature will determine its historical accuracy.
     - The form that a tradition takes should tell us how history has been preserved for us, but this fails to prove how the material was created.
     - It is very possible that Jesus taught in a variety of formats that would help His audience to remember what He communicated to them. He very well may have taught in segments to make it easier for people to understand—we cannot say for sure.
     - Jesus was always very serious when it came to speaking the Word of God as He spoke with authority and expected His disciples to listen and to remember what He was teaching them (Luke 4:32; John 14:25).
     - Jewish oral traditions, which we learned about in an earlier chapter, go against this idea, as do the Gospels.

2. There is no way to discern fact from fiction in the Gospels because we cannot presume that people were sophisticated enough to discern reality from superstition.

   - **Assumption:** People living in antiquity were not interested in facts, and therefore they were not able to tell the difference between fact and folklore and included everything in their traditions about the Christ.
   - **Response:** This view would negate all historical writings. What the evidence proves is contrary to this assumption about the nature of historical documentation from antiquity.
     - The evidence reveals that the Jews, the Romans, and the Greeks all valued eyewitnesses and precise reporting.

---

[155] Ibid.
[156] Ibid.
[157] Ibid.

- Scripture reveals that the witnesses did indeed concern themselves with reality and factual recollection of events and sayings (Luke 1:1–4; John 21:24; Heb. 2:3–4; 2 Pet. 1:16).
- This view fails to recognize the seriousness and accuracy of Jewish oral tradition when passing on information about the God of Israel (Deut. 4:2, 18:14–22).
- It assumes a large time span between the event surrounding the life of Jesus of Nazareth and the documentation of said events. "The time span between Jesus and the Gospels is much shorter than the periods of time spanned by the traditions studied by the folklorists."[158]

3. The Hellenistic Jesus of the Gentile populations served different purposes than the Jesus who served the Palestinian community.[159] In other words He was a Jesus who was contemporary and fictionalized to serve the needs of the community. This Jesus is said to have spoken to the community through appointed prophets.[160]

- **Assumption:** This critique assumes that the Christian communities were not concerned with the facts about Jesus but were content to have a godlike figure in which to believe. The supposition is also based on the belief that there were prophets who gave words and mannerisms to Jesus whom the people could emulate and worship as well as relate to, both of which eventually made it into the Bible that we hold today.
- **Response:** There is no evidence of any appointed prophets who spoke the dictums of the Jesus of history.
  - The writers (witnesses) of the Gospels were very careful to separate their own narration of the life of Jesus from the words attributed to Him (Acts 20:36; 1 Cor. 7:10, 12, 25).
  - Any literature outside of the Gospels that remotely began to document the sayings of Jesus was written much later in history than the Gospels (second-century writings such as the Infancy Gospels of James and Thomas).
  - The Gnostic writings of the second century did not attribute any sayings to Jesus.
  - The historical authenticity of the book of Acts is well attested to, and this book is where we can find biographical details that are consistent with the Gospels.
  - It is not only arrogant but also ignorant to suggest that the early Christians would not have desired to know everything that they could learn about this Son of God. In fact, it is due to this curiosity that apocryphal and Gnostic material began to flood the culture during the second century.
  - There is a complete disregard and refusal to acknowledge the work of the Holy Spirit in the lives of the witnesses to the life of the Christ (John 14:25–26).

These and other like assumptions are reluctant to recognize any supernatural activity in the lives of the New Testament writers. Scholars note that while form criticism has the potential

---

[158] Ibid., 247.
[159] Ibid., 245.
[160] Ibid.

for providing an understanding and basis to begin a historical critical analysis, it should not be understood *as* historical criticism.[161] We must keep in mind that while certain aspects of form criticism may have their place in paving the way to begin a historical analysis, a good writer may deliberately chose to write in a certain literary form for a specific purpose. "But he will make them his servants, not his masters."[162]

It was during this movement and idea development of form criticism that critics began to "classify the Gospels as folk literature."[163] The aforementioned critical assumptions, and others like them, basically demolish the entire understanding and historical reliability of the actual events found in the New Testament. The reality of form criticism is that it is a tool that can tell us about the assumed form, but it is an insufficient tool for determining "the origins or relative ages of traditions."[164] It is as if form critics take a preconceived hypothesis of the form and purpose of various sections of scripture and force this into their predetermined mold even if it does not make sense to do so. There is no reason to believe that some of the traditions found in the church did not previously exist even prior to the Crucifixion. There are many Jewish customs that naturally assimilated into the Christian ways of worship.

Redaction as a literary tool can be both positive and negative.

1. How can redaction be used in a helpful way?

    _____

    _____

2. Name the biggest problem that you see as a use of redaction as a tool:

    _____

There are traditions recorded in scripture that were already common to the Jews, such as the breaking of the bread and giving thanks to God. Not to mention the tradition and symbolism of baptism (a practice used to initiate Jewish converts and symbolic of true repentance). The fact is, history can be and has been accurately preserved by individuals who give, or gave, a great deal of significance to the events of the day. When all is said and done, it is helpful to keep everything in perspective. The assumptions that form critics are making about how the Bible was written are just that, assumptions. For a more in-depth analysis on the insufficiency of form criticisms, see J. D. G. Dunn's "Altering the Default Setting: Re-envisaging the Early Transmission of the Jesus Tradition" in *New Testament Studies* (2003).[165]

The vast majority of biblical and historical literary scholars agree that Paul's letters reveal that there was indeed a reliable system of transmission in place to ensure that the traditions of the life and events of Jesus were accurately handed down.[166] Scholars point out the language that Paul used to

---

[161] Ibid., 247.
[162] Colin J. Hemer, *The Book of Acts in the Setting of Hellenistic History*, ed. Conrad H. Gempf (Winona Lake, IN: Eisenbrauns, 1990, 2008), 35.
[163] Bauckham, *Jesus and the Eyewitnesses*, 244.
[164] Ibid., 247.
[165] Ibid., 248.
[166] Ibid., 264.

show his readers the careful attention paid to the transmitting of accurate information. He used very technical terms for "handing on information" and the "receiving of information."[167] For example:

- Passing on a tradition = *paradidōmi* (Greek) and *māsar* (Hebrew)
  - 1 Cor. 11:2
- Receiving a tradition = *paralambanō* (Greek) and *qibbēl* (Hebrew)
  - 1 Cor. 15:1
  - Gal. 1:9
  - Col. 2:6
  - 1 Thess. 2:13, 4:1
  - 2 Thess. 3:6

These are terms that were used in Greek schools and were found in Jewish Greek material, which would have been very familiar language to both Paul's Greek and Jewish audiences.[168] Paul also very astutely mentions that the Jesus traditions that he is transmitting to the people came from careful, faithful observation in order to preserve the truth about the Messiah.

For various reasons the Letter to the Ephesians is believed to have been written by Paul therefore, we will focus on his character and ability to convey truth without embellishments. To do this, it is important to remember who Paul was in order to gain a better understanding of his ability and intent for transmitting reliable and verifiable historical facts. To begin, it is important to recognize that he was trained as a Pharisee under the tutelage of Gamaliel (Acts 22:3), who was a well-respected teacher and leader (Acts 5:34) of the Pharisees. What this reveals to us about Paul is that he was very aware of the law and the importance of handing down the Jewish traditions based on the God of Israel. In essence, Paul was an attorney and was very adept and precise with the language he used. Whereas the Pharisees were preoccupied with the traditions of the law (the first five books of the Old Testament), the Sadducees, who were the other Jewish ruling party, were consumed with the political affairs of the Jewish people and the temple (they were equivalent to what we in the United States know as the Senate).[169]

Chain of Succession

The Jewish historian Josephus reveals that because the Pharisees (who added endless rules and regulations to the existing law) and the Sadducees did not agree fully on what constituted the law for the people of God, their disagreements provided for a system of checks and balances for the people (*Antiquities* 13.297). However, in his documentation of their disagreement on these issues, Josephus mentions how the Pharisees handed down their traditions to the next generation by using the phrase *diadochē*.[170] This phrase is important because it was also used by "the Hellenistic schools of philosophy."[171] The indication is that those who received the traditions from their

---

[167] Ibid.
[168] Ibid.
[169] Merrill C. Tenney, ed., *The Zondervan Pictorial Encyclopedia of the Bible in Five Volumes—Vol. 5, Q–Z* (Grand Rapids, MI: Zondervan, 1977), 212–13.
[170] Bauckham, *Jesus and the Eyewitnesses*, 270.
[171] Ibid.

predecessors were not just the general public but also those individuals who comprehended their role as preserving the understandings of the "master's original philosophy,"[172] or traditions as in the case of the Jews and followers of Jesus.

Each culture and civilization in history has its own reasons for preserving history and its cultural traditions. The most prevalent form for the transmission of information in the first century was oral which is important to remember in the search for the accuracy of the New Testament writers. Scholarly observations have revealed that oral societies, more often than not, were very careful to distinguish between their legends and folklore from valid historical accounts.[173] Given the fact that the writers were actual eyewitnesses, or their contemporaries (Luke), we are dealing with witnesses within living memory of Jesus of Nazareth. This means that the New Testament was first transmitted and then written down according to oral *history* (which is the conveyance of knowledge while there were firsthand witnesses still alive), as opposed to oral *tradition* (which is the passing on of information after the living memory, in this case of the Christ).[174]

> Since the writers of the New Testament wrote while Jesus's contemporaries (including His family) were still living, what do you think would have happened if they began to embellish their stories to fit their personal agendas?

The first-century Jewish converts were not just following a charismatic leader named Yeshua (Jesus); they clearly saw Him as the Savior for all of humanity. This was not the same as the Roman emperor type of savior, but a Redeemer in continuity with Israel's God, and their long-awaited Messiah. Jesus's life was history in the making within the context of the promises of the God of Israel (Yahweh) (Acts 5:35–39). Every indication for the intentions of every writer of the New Testament was one of relaying a message of salvation. Not one writer ever wrote for self-aggrandizement purposes. The fact is that the numerous historical references are all verifiable as historical facts. It is evident that the writers (witnesses) made every effort to convey factual evidence to their intended audiences, as follows:

- Luke makes it a point to tell his readers that he is documenting the true facts of the life and ministry of Christ (Luke 1:1–3).
- Luke also makes sure to place the life of the Christ in a historical context (Luke 3:1). In this way, those of the first century could clearly relate to their own life situations in those days under Roman rule.
- The apostle John makes it clear to his readers that he was there at the foot of the cross and watched as the Messiah breathed His last breath (John 19:19–35).
- Peter announces to his readers that he and the other disciples were not exaggerating the reality of the Messiah who came in the flesh and would someday return (1 Pet. 1:16).
- The apostle John lets his readers know that he and the other disciples were witnesses to the life and ministry of Jesus (1 John 1:3).

---

[172] Ibid.
[173] Ibid., 272.
[174] Ibid., 276–77.

Review:

Tools for Validating the Accuracy of the Witnesses

1. Understand the value of the *diadochē*, or the chain of succession.
2. Know the difference between oral *history* and oral *tradition*.
3. Consider the character of the eyewitnesses who are attributed as being the authors of the New Testament documents.

Form Criticism

Form criticism is a branch of literary criticism that is characterized by the following:

- It fails to recognize eyewitnesses as the authors of the New Testament.
- It uses the tool known as redaction, which suggests that the writers compiled specific traditions and edited facts to fit an agenda.
- Its redactionists assume historical writings must be viewed as a set of techniques. However, redaction has been successfully refuted as a flawed tool when determining the historical authenticity of a document. Not only does redaction fail to recognize any supernatural activity, but also it is insufficient for determining origins or relative ages of cultural traditions.
- Redaction can be used to provide an understanding of what literary forms were used in a particular time period in history. These observations can be used to begin an historical, critical analysis of literary forms.

Study Questions: Internal Criteria Used to Validate the Documents

For Review and Reflection

1. Name two ways that historians study the accuracy of the writer:

2. Why is the character of the writer so important?

3. Can you see a parallel in taking the character of a witness (or writer) into account when studying the accuracy of a person who authored the New Testament documents and a person giving a testimony about a past event on the witness stand in a court of law? How?

4. Name at least three instances in scripture that lead us to believe that the authors of the New Testament were not interested in proclaiming a personal agenda:

_____

_____

_____

5. Is the New Testament written based on oral tradition or oral history?

  a. Why is this important in discerning the historical accuracy of the writer?

6. How is the redactionist's view that there is no way to tell historical fact from fiction flawed reasoning?

Group Discussion

1. Do you see the redactionists' approach being played out in the understanding of the historical relevance of the New Testament in our world today? Where?

2. Knowing what you know now, how will you approach a person who disregards the historical value of the Bible because his or her views have been shaped by a redaction approach to form criticism?

3. What is the danger in viewing the Bible as a book from history that has been redacted?

Key Terms

form criticism: A branch of literary criticism that attempts to define how a piece of literature was written and why. It categorizes the various passages of scripture according to literary type.

oral tradition: The transmitting of information about an event or person long after those involved have passed away.

redaction: The art of reducing a piece of literature to manipulate its content in an effort to advance an agenda or set of beliefs.

Literature Cited or Recommended

Barna, George, and David Kinnaman, eds. *Churchless: Understanding Today's Unchurched and How to Connect with Them.* Austin, TX: Tyndale, 2014.

Bauckham, Richard. *Jesus and the Eyewitnesses: The Gospels as Eyewitness Testimony.* Grand Rapids, MI: Eerdmans, 2006.

Hemer, Colin J. *The Book of Acts in the Setting of Hellenistic History.* Edited by Conrad H. Gempf. Winona Lake, IN: Eisenbrauns, 1990, 2008.

Horton, Michael. *Christless Christianity: The Alternative Gospel of the American Church.* Grand Rapids, MI: Baker Books, 2008.

Tenney, Merrill C., ed. *The Zondervan Pictorial Encyclopedia of the Bible in Five Volumes—Vol. 5, Q–Z.* Grand Rapids, MI: Zondervan, 1977.

Accuracy of the Witness
Understanding the Context

Application of Scripture: Ephesians

Read Ephesians.

The letter to the Ephesians is said to be one of Paul's least pastoral letters to the churches. But I view this Epistle as one of the most spiritual in nature and filled with emotion and knowledge of the culture that Paul is so well-known for. It also has many of the same themes as the letter to the Colossians. The writer of this document is said to have most likely intended it to be a circulatory letter to the churches in Asia (Colossae, Laodicea, Ephesus), but it was taken to Ephesus at the hand of Tychicus (6:21). Paul is a master at meeting people at their level of understanding in order to effectively get his message across, and the letter to the church in Ephesus is no different. Asia, like other areas, was a polytheistic and superstitious culture.

Although much of the material that we covered in the first part of this lesson was a bit technical, we need to keep in mind that the whole purpose of seeking the importance of how accurate the writer of the document was, is to bring others to a better understanding of God's Word. As you learn, you should also begin to see the beauty in the way that God has preserved a picture of Himself for us through His chosen witnesses. While reading through this Epistle, continue to seek the nature of God and to document your thoughts in the space provided at the end of this lesson. Our main objective is always to know God above all else while reading scripture; however, in our current lesson we will also focus on the accuracy of the witness (the author, Paul). In order to accomplish this, we need to grasp what it meant to be a Gentile in the first century to the best of our ability.

In other words, does Paul's letter match up to the historical context in which these people were actually living? Comparing a document's claims with factual evidence from history is one of the best ways to test for the integrity of any document. Previously we focused on the letter to the Galatians, and we learned how important it was for Paul to stress the freedom and inclusion that his readers would have in the Christ on account of the various cultural backgrounds of these

Gentiles and Jews. While the Epistle to the Galatians focused on the cultural nuances of family life and what they understood of adoption and slavery, the letter to the Ephesians places more of an emphasis on the nature of being a non-Jew. There was a definitive sense of exclusion and inferiority among these Gentiles, so Paul encourages these people by assuring them of the security of their salvation, which God has provided through His gift of grace in Jesus (Eph. 2:4–10). This is the first (in the canon) of the prison Epistles (Philippians, Colossians, and Philemon), as when incarcerated Paul had time to think and write to the churches.

This lesson will concentrate mostly on chapters 2 and 3 of this Epistle as it gives the reader some insight into the historical context in which the recipients were living. As you read through Paul's writings, notice how he does his utmost to speak to his audience in the language that he chooses and the mannerisms that they will best comprehend (1 Cor. 9:19–23). This is a perfect example of how we as disciples of Christ should also reach out to those around us. Just as Paul could not change the fact that he was a Jew trained in the law, we should not try to change who we are. Instead, Paul used his in-depth knowledge of God from the Jewish perspective to bring outsiders into a better comprehension of the living God of Israel. Your knowledge of God will not go to waste unless you keep it all to yourself and never intentionally reach out to others.

> When you read this, you can perceive my insight into the mystery of Christ, which was not made known to the sons of men in other generations as it has now been revealed to his holy apostles and prophets by the Spirit.
>
> Eph. 3:4 (ESV)

Scholars note that in chapter 3 Paul uses Jewish terminology to explain the *eschatological* significance of the indwelling nature of God's Christ.[175] He speaks of a mystery that has now been made known to the spiritual realm that was once hidden (Eph. 3:4–5). Paul has used this type of terminology before in 1 Corinthians 2:7–10 and Colossians 1:26. 27, and it is seen in other parts of scripture, such as 1 Peter 1:20.[176] This is a helpful piece of information because if the reader happens to be a Jew, he or she would understand the significance of God's self-revelation in the chosen Messiah. The Jewish people were (as some continue to be to this day) expecting this long-awaited Messiah to appear in the last days. Scholars further note that this sort of *apocalyptic* language had become rather common in the writings of early Christianity.[177] This fact in itself reveals that the first disciples and witnesses clearly comprehended the eschatological nature of God's revelation to them. In other words, this was not a later fabrication of the church, which is the accusation of critical scholarship. The Jewish understanding of the end times not only included shalom, but also a world without wars and turmoil, because all the nations would recognize the God and King of Israel as ruler (Isa. 11:1–9), but also one of the results, namely that there would be true *shalom*. The Jewish understanding of peace is shalom, which includes a sense of wholeness and well-being. This peace will stem from the knowledge of God and the assurance of salvation.[178]

There can only be true peace when there is no alienation, that is, no alienation between the individual and the Lord, God, and also no alienation between each other as people. Prior to the Crucifixion, there were two classes of humanity: those who had access to the God of Israel (the Jews) and those who did not (everyone else, the Gentiles). Shalom is seen as a gift from God and

---

[175] Andrew T. Lincoln, *Word Biblical Commentary*, ed. Bruce M. Metzger, David A. Hubbard, and Glenn W. Barker, vol. 42, *Ephesians*, ed. Ralph P. Martin and Lynn Allan Losie (Grand Rapids, MI: Zondervan, 1990), 170.

[176] Ibid.

[177] Ibid.

[178] Ibid., 140.

is a key element in Israel's eschatological expectations.[179] Paul's words of encouragement suggest that a time has come when there will be a unity between Jews and Gentiles (Eph. 2:12, 13), when this gift of well-being and salvation can be accessed by all of humanity.

> There shall come forth a shoot from the stump of Jesse, and a branch from his roots shall bear fruit. And the Spirit of the Lord shall rest upon him, the Spirit of wisdom and understanding, the Spirit of counsel and might, the Spirit of knowledge and the fear of the Lord. And his delight shall be in the fear of the Lord. He shall not judge by what his eyes see, or decide disputes by what his ears hear, but with righteousness he shall judge the poor, and decide with equity for the meek of the earth; and he shall strike the earth with the rod of his mouth, and with the breath of his lips he shall kill the wicked. Righteousness shall be the belt of his waist, and faithfulness the belt of his loins. The wolf shall dwell with the lamb, and the leopard shall lie down with the young goat, and the calf and the lion and the fattened calf together; and a little child shall lead them. The cow and the bear shall graze; their young shall lie down together; and the lion shall eat straw like the ox. The nursing child shall play over the hole of the cobra, and the weaned child shall put his hand on the adder's den. They shall not hurt or destroy in all my holy mountain; for the earth shall be full of the knowledge of the Lord as the waters cover the sea. (Isa. 11:1–9 ESV)

Biblical scholars suggest that it is conceivable that a Jewish person could have possibly understood this peace as a time when all of the world would recognize, obey, and worship the God of Israel (Isa. 2:2–4 and Mic. 4:1–4).[180] Paul emphasizes this peace as realized in the person of Christ (Eph. 2:14), as opposed to being a mere concept of peace.[181] These theological presuppositions of shalom and unity are where we will begin to do some historical research to learn about the writer's accuracy. What was going on historically to suggest that there was no unity? Would the reality of the historical context cause unrest between the Jews and the rest of the world (Gentiles)? Does history concur with what Paul is saying to the Ephesians and the other churches in Asia?

Israel's Privilege

To begin, we will consider how Israel was privileged over the other nations of the world. Israel's history is recorded for us in the pages of the Old Testament, various rabbinic writings, and notations found in ancient documents from other people groups. The seeds for the nation of Israel were clearly formed in the Pentateuch. God's intention was to build a nation from one man so that all of humanity would find salvation (Gen. 12:1–3). It was because God chose the decedents of Isaac (Gen. 17:19) that the Hebrew race benefited from the supernatural blessings that allowed them to prosper and grow even in the midst of great adversity (Deut. 7:1–9, 9:5–6). Although God has always cared for all of His creation, His redemption and focus would come through the children of Israel.

> Now the Lord said to Abram, "Go from your country and your kindred and your father's house to the land that I will show you. And I will make of you a great nation, and I will bless you and make your name great, so that you will be a blessing. I will bless those who bless you, and him who dishonors you I will curse, and in you all the families of the earth shall be blessed."
> Gen. 12:1–3 (ESV)

---

[179] Ibid.

[180] Ibid.

[181] Ibid.

It was this race that would be privileged enough to hear the voice of God and live (Deut. 4:33, 5:26). The God of Israel was clear from the very beginning that His people would not behave like the rest of the nations (Lev. 18:1–5). They would be a holy people because God is holy (Exod. 19:5–6). The Hebrew understanding of the word *holy* is very important not only to our research but also for our understanding of God's profound gift of grace to us as Christians. *Qādôš (qadosh)* is the Hebrew word for holy; it means "to be singled out or separated from the rest." God is separate from His creation, and when He chose the Hebrews to represent Him to the world (Isa. 11:10; Mal. 1:11), He was singling them out and separating them from everyone else on the planet.

When you came to Christ, you were singled out to commune with God. It was nothing you did on your own (John 6:44, 65; Eph. 2:8). It was the same with Abraham and his descendants; God chose them because He wanted to (Deut. 9:5–6). The Jews saw the rest of the world as unclean and sinful because they knew that they had been chosen by God to be different (holy). Gentiles were never allowed to enter the inner courtyard of the temple and were contained in a separate outer area (Eph. 2:2–13). There were physical signs that were clearly posted around the entrances to the temple that restricted the Gentiles from going beyond the wall of separation. We will discuss this in more detail in chapter 8, when we cover archeological evidence for the New Testament. This was the way that the Creator set it up, and it remains this way today. It is in Christ alone that now the Gentile nations had the opportunity to enjoy the salvation and shalom that God offered to the nation of Israel (John 14:6). Paul's mention of separation between the Jews and the Gentiles is another testament to his accuracy about the cultural tensions that existed in the first century.

The Jews, however, were not ready to let go of their long-held customs that revealed their relationship and piousness to the God of Israel. One of the greatest obstacles for the Jews was God's requirement of circumcision (Gen. 17:9–14) for His covenant people. During the *intertestamental period*, the Greco-Roman world began to push its customs onto its conquered regions, with Jerusalem being one of those provinces. History informs us of the turmoil and struggle for Israel to remain a distinctive people amid the Gentiles and their heathen ways of life. Historical records reveal that as Hellenism encroached Jerusalem, their ways were threatened as the Seleucid rulers changed the Israelites' constitution.[182]

Eventually the new constitutions and laws began to take away any distinctiveness that the Jews had as a nation, uniqueness such as recognizing the Sabbath and honoring their food laws and their custom of circumcision.[183] The Maccabees wrote about the ridged and gruesome enforcement by the rulers to keep the Jews from circumcising their boys (1 Macc. 1:14–15).[184] It was these very atrocities committed against the Jewish people that not only precipitated the Jews to rebel (167–141 BC), but also eventually prompted the rise of the religious

> Not because of your righteousness or the uprightness of your heart are you going in to possess their land, but because of the wickedness of these nations the Lord your God is driving them out from before you, and that he may confirm the word that the Lord swore to your fathers, to Abraham, to Isaac, and to Jacob. "Know, therefore, that the Lord your God is not giving you this good land to possess because of your righteousness, for you are a stubborn people."
>
> Deut. 9:5–6 (ESV)

---

[182] Luke Timothy Johnson, *The Writings of the New Testament*, 3rd ed. (Minneapolis: Fortress Press, 2010), 20–22.

[183] James D. G. Dunn, *The Parting of the Ways: Between Christianity and Judaism and Their Significance for the Character of Christianity*, 2nd ed. (London: SCM Press, 2006), 39.

[184] Ibid.

leaders known as the Pharisees. The ritual of circumcision was an outward sign that revealed to the world their distinction as God's covenant people and their separation from the rest of the world, which they fought to retain and were not ready to give up so freely.

This was a sign that clearly indicated that they were citizens of Israel (God's chosen people). Circumcision of a male's foreskin notwithstanding, the God of Israel spoke through the prophet Jerimiah and told the people that He preferred their hearts to be circumcised (Jer. 4:4), meaning that God wants our hearts to be sensitized to His promptings and set on obedience through love for Him. He was pruning His people to wean them from a works-based system of atonement (Amos 5:21–27) because He had something far more lasting in mind. Due to humanity's ruptured relationship with the Creator, there was no way that humankind could ever be "good enough" to stand before a holy God (Isa. 64:6). It is in this passage that God warns the people through the prophet Isaiah that everyone is unclean, no matter what righteous deeds they perform.

The goal, to show if Paul was accurately speaking to the context of the day, should be very evident. There is ample evidence outside of the New Testament to reveal to any historian that there was a true sense of separation between the Jews of the first century and the Gentiles. This division between the people groups did cause turmoil and confusion. Paul was walking a very fine line between the freedom that Christ offered and the historical covenantal rituals instituted by the God of Israel. "What was at stake was the *essence* of *Judaism* in which" Paul had been raised.[185] The beauty of Paul's ability to communicate with people of all walks of life was that he knew that the message of Christ would bring true freedom, yet he never compromised or veered from his stance as an Israelite. Paul did his utmost to ensure that the Jews knew they had not lost their place in God's plan of redemption.

> Are there traditions in your church which keep you from leaving, even though the message being taught is not completely in line with the Bible?

Works-Based Religion

Paul was not only raised as a Hebrew among Hebrews (Phil. 3:3–6), he was also educated in the customs and philosophies of the Gentile nations (Acts 17). He was well aware of the religious practices of the people in Ephesus. To this very day, anyone outside of Christ believes that somehow they are able to be good enough or to perform enough good deeds in order to find salvation of their soul after death. There is ample evidence throughout human history of the temples built all over the globe used to perform all sorts or rituals to a multitude of gods. The first century was no different. There is evidence of various types of temple worship to the gods in Ephesus, and Paul was well aware of how difficult it was for people to let go of rituals and traditions, even if they were unhealthy practices.

[185] Ibid., 196.

Gentile Religious Practices

It is well-known that the Gentile nations were *polytheists* and worshipped many gods and goddesses. The people's devotion to the pantheon of gods through daily offerings is well-documented in history.[186] It is known that many of the images used in festivals were part of the Artemis cult in Ephesus.[187] By the first century, the practice of emperor worship was also well established, and Paul knew the dangers of how luring it would be to the Gentiles to simply add the Christ on to their long list of gods on whom they depended for life and prosperity. You too may know people who claim to be Christian yet believe people of all religions will achieve salvation and go to heaven.

Among other architecture in the city of Ephesus were four very prominent imperial temples, an altar, four gymnasia, and an imperial portico all "associated with the emperor"[188] and veneration thereof. This was the comfort zone for the Gentiles, the place where they felt a part of the culture. These are important historical evidences that reveal Paul's accuracy as he speaks to a pagan culture and teaches them about the freedom found in the Christ.

Paul knew this and was continually reassuring these new Christians that they did belong to the citizenry of Israel through Jesus (Eph. 2:11–13) and did not need to depend on other gods. It makes sense then, in light of what we know from historical evidence, that there was a danger to the Ephesians if they began to fall back onto the practices of worshipping the gods with which they were familiar. In addition to their superstitions, there was also cultural and political pressure to offer sacrifices to the gods, as well as to the emperor.[189] Anyone not offering these customary sacrifices was deemed atheistic and seen as a disruptor of the peace and an enemy of the empire.[190] The reality of the polytheistic practices of the Gentiles is yet another testament to Paul's accuracy, as he admonishes the people by telling them that there is only *one* God, not many (Eph. 4:4–6). What is even more disturbing than a Gentile falling back onto his or her customs of idol and emperor worship is the evidence revealing that the Jewish population in Ephesus was guilty of participating in imperial worship along with the pagan culture around them.[191]

Do you fully trust God? Or do you hang on to a system of doing "good works" to check off a list? What steps can you take today to trust God more?

_____

_____

_____

---

[186] S. R. F. Price, *Rituals and Power: The Roman Imperial Cult in Asia Minor* (Cambridge, England: Cambridge University Press, 1984), 189.

[187] Ibid.

[188] Ibid., 135.

[189] Ibid., 209.

[190] Ibid.

[191] Ibid.

Jewish Religious Practices

In the Diaspora, the tendency for the Jewish population was to loosen their devotion to the God of Israel because they were far away from Palestine and the regulations placed on the population by the religious leaders.[192] It was bad enough in the Diaspora, but there is historical evidence that the Jews were even allowing emperor worship through sacrifices given at the temple in Jerusalem.[193] The Greek way of life had a far-reaching influence throughout areas in Asia Minor and down into Egypt. The Jewish population struggled to harmonize their Jewish customs with those of the Hellenized culture around them, but in the end the distance from Jerusalem caused them to further compromise the way in which they observed their faith.[194] There is evidence, nonetheless, that there were numerous synagogues throughout Asia Minor and Greece as Paul frequently mentions his visits to the local synagogue in the towns where he teaches.[195]

We know from the book of Acts that there was at least one synagogue in Ephesus and perhaps more (Acts 18:19, 26, 19:8).[196] The Jewish historian Josephus also concurs that there were synagogues scattered throughout the Diaspora,[197] which further proves Paul's accuracy in his letter to the Ephesians. One other thing we can know about the fact that there were synagogues in Ephesus and other parts of the Diaspora is that the law and the Prophets were read on the Sabbath in these foreign lands just as they were in Jerusalem. We can safely surmise that the Jewish inhabitants were at least fairly familiar with their heritage and the significance of the God of Israel. This would be a necessary factor for Paul to confer upon them the importance of the realization that Yahweh's Messiah had indeed arrived.

Part of their heritage was based on the meaningfulness of the annual pilgrimages made to the temple in Jerusalem for the traditional Jewish festivals. History records for us that even those in the Diaspora in Egypt felt the need to make the pilgrimage to Palestine in observance of the Jewish holy days, so it would not be unusual to consider that those in Asia Minor also made the trek at least once, if they could, either by land or by sea.[198] Josephus records that the population of Jerusalem would expand to about 2,700,000 inhabitants during these high holy days.[199]

Paul's letter to the Ephesians was undoubtedly filled with words of encouragement to the Jewish people in the Diaspora as well as to the Gentile converts. Ephesus was a long way from the Jewish roots so evident in Jerusalem, and the farther away the people were geographically, there was a tendency to lose touch with the culture and meaning of the purity of the Jewish tradition. This can happen to us as Christians as well. When we are not tapped into a Bible-believing church, we will slowly begin to drift from the purity of God's Word that nourishes our lives. When we are distanced from the centrality of the faith, the tendency is to also find ourselves compromising in order to be at peace with the world around us. The Jews in the Diaspora were

---

[192] Emil Schürer, *History of the Jewish People in the Time of Jesus Christ*, 2nd ed. Second Division, *The Internal Condition of Palestine, and of the Jewish People, in the Time of Jesus Christ*, vol. 2, trans. Sophia Taylor and Rev. Peter Christie, 1890. Reprint (Peabody, MA: Hendrickson, 2014), 281.

[193] Price, *Rituals and Power*, 209.

[194] Schürer, *History of the Jewish People in the Time of Jesus Christ*, 282.

[195] Ibid.

[196] Ibid.

[197] Ibid.

[198] Ibid., 290–91.

[199] Ibid.

no different. The geographical distance of Asia Minor from Jerusalem and the historical evidence of the tendency to compromise the Jewish faith both reveal the author's accuracy of life in the Diaspora for both the Jews and new converts.

Internal Conflict

During the intertestamental period there was an incredible amount of social and political pressure to participate in emperor worship. For the Gentile pagans, imperial worship was not a problem, but for the Jews it was deadly and could be seen as idol worship. Interestingly enough, however, history records that Gentiles were allowed to bring sacrifices to the Jewish altar.[200] Even so, they were only allowed to make what were known as freewill and vow offerings, but not offerings that pertained to sin atonement.[201] Although the Jews allowed the Gentiles to make sacrificial offerings, the latter were still excluded from the most sacred promises offered through the God of Israel for repentance of sins. Paul was well aware of this exclusion, and his words to these new Christians would have been welcome words of inclusion and comfort. Yet again, we find historical documentation that serves to authenticate Paul's letter as to his purpose in writing to the Ephesian community.

Paul and the Temple

Paul could not emphasize enough the unity that was offered only through Jesus as God's Christ. The Gentiles were now a part of the Jewish family, and there was no longer a wall of separation between the two people groups (Eph. 2:11–13, 19–22), which invariably caused conflict. Jesus had offered the final sacrificial atonement for the sins of all of humanity (Eph. 2:14–18), deeming the temple unnecessary. Paul's message to both the Jews and the Gentiles was multidimensional in nature. On the one hand, everyone was aware that the Jews offered sacrifices to the emperor, which undoubtedly caused an internal conflict for the Jewish covenantal people.

> Remember that you were at that time separated from Christ, alienated from the commonwealth of Israel and strangers to the covenants of promise, having no hope and without God in the world. But now in Christ Jesus you who once were far off have been brought near by the blood of Christ.
> Eph. 2:12–13 (ESV)

For the observing new Christian it would serve to create confusion and a sense of duplicity. The Gentiles were used to worshipping and sacrificing to numerous gods, which meant that as it appeared on the outside, the Jews were also participating in polytheism. This is why Paul was so adamant about impressing upon the Gentiles that there is only *one* God who offers salvation and peace (Eph. 4:4–7). On the other hand, Paul expounded upon the fact that the Jews no longer had an obligation to make their daily sacrifices. The fact that the temple sacrifices were no longer necessary for either the Jew or for these new Christians was seen as an attack on the most sacred of customs handed down to the Israelites through Moses.[202] Paul not only inadvertently threatened the Jewish way of life but also was seen as standing in direct opposition to the Roman Empire, as

---

[200] Ibid., 300.

[201] Ibid.

[202] Dunn, *The Parting of the Ways*, 157.

Christians were not to worship anything or anyone other than Jesus (as God).[203] The Jews could not begin to tolerate this message of relinquishing the temple sacrifices, much less accepting the Gentiles to enter beyond the wall of separation to worship the God of Israel; it was too much (Eph. 2:12–13). The whole idea of Jesus being accepted as God in the flesh was difficult enough without the expectation that their long-held customs would have to change. As for the secular realm, God's people would now have to fully trust in God for salvation, not humankind. Paul was despised and in prison as a traitor and a god-hater (Eph. 3:1).

What could he do? Paul found himself in a very precarious position. If he compromised and allowed the Jews to continue their harmless customs, they would continue leading lives without the recognition of God's unparalleled grace and freedom offered through the Messiah. If he allowed the Gentiles to continue worshipping other gods, they also would never truly understand the fullness of salvation, peace, and inclusion that the God of Israel had to offer to them. Either way he would be guilty of the blood of all those with whom he had influence because they would never come to a saving faith in Christ (Ezek. 3:16–21). Paul faced a very real dilemma, as history reveals the tensions between the Jews and those who chose to follow the Christ and the adversity between the Christian and the Roman Empire. It is very important to recognize the reality of the layers of complexities that Paul faced as he wrote to encourage those in Asia Minor to remain steadfast even amid great opposition.

> Are there people in your life who seem like good people but do not know the God of the Bible? How will you make a difference, even if it means that you might be persecuted for speaking the truth?

Review: Internal Criteria Used to Validate Documents Study Questions

For Theological Reflection and Assessing Historical Accuracy of the Witnesses

Theological Reflection

1. Where can you find Jesus mentioning the "last day" in the Gospels? When does He tell us these last days will begin?

    a. As disciples of Christ, why is this important to us?

    b. Why was it important to Paul?

---

[203] Ibid.

2. Can shalom be attained through the efforts of humans? If so, how? If not, why not?

3. According to Ephesians 2:12, 13, how is the peace and wholeness granted by God revealed in Jesus?

   a. Why does Paul find it necessary to stress this truth to the recipients of the letter?

4. What does it mean to be holy?

   a. Would the Jews in the audience have understood the significance of this very unique concept?

   b. Would the Gentiles have understood what Paul was talking about? Why would this be a very important concept for the author to stress with these newly converted Christ followers?

   c. What does the historical evidence reveal about both these people groups and the importance that the call to holiness would have on their lives? Use scripture and historical context to reflect on your response.

   d. What does the call to be holy mean for your life in the society in which you live today?

Group Discussion

Historical Accuracy

1. Are Paul's concerns for the people of Ephesus and their polytheistic practice of worshipping other gods in line with the historical evidence?

2. What historical evidence is available to prove that the people of Asia Minor were worshipping all sorts of deities?

3. When Paul wrote to the people at Ephesus and the surrounding area, he wrote in a way that would speak to both the Jews in the Diaspora and the Pagan Gentiles who knew very little, if anything, about the God of Israel and His Messiah. Could he have effectively addressed the issues of both cultures if he did not have an intimate knowledge of both diverse people groups and their customs?

   a. Discuss at least three issues that Paul addresses to his audience and their importance to their understanding of God's plan of redemption.

   b. Discuss what was at stake.

4. From what you have read and researched online or elsewhere, is there any discrepancy between the issues that Paul brings up in his letter to the Ephesians and the historical facts?

5. How would you engage a skeptic on the topic of the New Testament writers' historical accuracy?

Key Terms

apocalyptic: The unveiling or the revealing of eschatological secrets referring to the last days. A type of literature written to convey hope for a better world in the future not yet realized.

polytheists: Those who believe in the existence of more than one god.

shalom: The Jewish understanding of peace, which includes not only a sense of peace but also the realization of well-being and the wholeness that is lacking without God in one's life.

God's Attributes

grace – God includes all people in His plan of redemption.

omniscience – Only God knows the heart of humankind. He gave the writers of scripture great discernment in how to appeal to humanity with words of encouragement and caution.

shalom – Only God can provide true wholeness.

transcendence – God's plan of redemption far exceeds what humans alone can accomplish, and His plan has been in place from the beginning of the world.

Literature Cited or Recommended

Dunn, James D. G. *The Parting of the Ways: Between Christianity and Judaism and Their Significance for the Character of Christianity.* 2nd ed. London: SCM Press, 2006.

Johnson, Luke Timothy. *The Writings of the New Testament.* 3rd ed. Minneapolis: Fortress Press, 2010.

Lincoln, Andrew T. *Word Biblical Commentary.* Edited by Bruce M. Metzger, David A. Hubbard, and Glenn W. Barker. Vol. 42, *Ephesians.* Edited by Ralph P. Martin, and Lynn Allan Losie. Grand Rapids, MI: Zondervan, 1990.

Price, S. R. F. *Rituals and Power: The Roman Imperial Cult in Asia Minor.* Cambridge, England: Cambridge University Press, 1984.

Schürer, Emil D. *History of the Jewish People in the Time of Jesus Christ.* 2nd ed. Second Division. *The Internal Condition of Palestine, and of the Jewish People, in the Time of Jesus Christ.* Vol. 1. Translated by Sophia Taylor and Rev. Peter Christie, 1890. Reprint, Peabody, MA: Hendrickson, 2014.

CHAPTER 5

Higher Criticism: Internal Criterion Used To Validate Documents

Accuracy of the Documents

Up to this point, we have taken a close look at four very important ways that have been used to test the veracity of the New Testament. We have looked at the importance of recognizing the nature of evidential inquiry and the integrity of the witnesses in chapter 2. We have taken a close look at how the experts date historical documents, a process that has validated the dating of the New Testament manuscripts and the original autographs in chapter 3. Then in chapter 4 we completed our study of how we can determine the accuracy of the witnesses who wrote the Gospels and the Epistles that are included in the New Testament, as we focused on Paul's letter to the Ephesians. This fifth chapter brings us to our final internal criterion for validating the scriptures: the process used to substantiate the accuracy of the documents that have been included in the New Testament.

The study of chapter 4 revealed the care that the writers took to be faithful to the actual historical accounts, and the accuracy of the documents depends heavily on this understanding. The two modes for transmission of historical information in the first century were oral and written. We have already studied how the distinction between oral tradition and oral history were viewed in the first century. Scholars clearly note that the preservation of a text, either written or oral, was dependent not on the mode of transmission "but [on] a prior attitude towards its nature and authority which dictated that it should not be changed."[204] There is no indication in scripture that would lead us to believe that the writers had any reason to tamper with the historical facts that surrounded the Gospels or the letters that were passed from one church to another as Christian communities began to form.

In fact, every indication would suggest the opposite of any intentional development of a man-made agenda designed to benefit the church. One of the main accusations faced by the New Testament is the claim that it was designed and written for the advancement of the church. This claim is wrought with problems of both a historical and theological nature. Why would the church write to advance itself? This accusation is entirely inconsistent with history and ignores

---

[204] Richard Bauckham, *Jesus and the Eyewitnesses: The Gospels as Eyewitness Testimony* (Grand Rapids, MI: Wm. B. Eerdmans, 2006), 273.

the context in which the writers and witnesses lived and documented events. The allegation made that the New Testament is comprised of man-made ideals and is not the result of the Holy Spirit moving in the hearts and minds of the writers directly challenges the revelation of God's plan for the redemption of humanity (Acts 1:16; 2 Tim. 3:16; 2 Pet. 1:20–21).

To accuse the writers of the New Testament of deliberately plotting out an agenda designed to benefit humanity's ideal of the church not only challenges God's supernatural revelation but also fails to reflect historical accuracy. Such a deliberate act of deception seems to stem from an ignorance of historical fact. The Christian church did not ever intend to become institutionalized the way it ended up being after the fourth century. Although the church was relieved of a great deal of persecution at the rise to power of the emperor Constantine, once the Roman Empire took it under its wings, the hierarchy within the church began to distance itself from the average person.[205] However, the separation and formation of the Catholic Church as an institution did not begin until the middle of the fourth century; well after the New Testament documents were written.

External Evidence

Historical Accuracy

It is true that once a hierarchy at any level begins to form, there will inevitably be individuals who will stop at nothing to be placed in positions of power. As we take the hierarchy of the church into consideration, we will study the historical background and beginnings of the role of the *bishop*. Studies of the early organization of Christian communities in the first and second centuries do not mention the office of bishop.[206] *Ignatius of Antioch* appears to be the only reference to any sort of mention of this hierarchical office in a letter written to the churches in Asia Minor around 110.[207] There is no reference to any such office in Rome, however, until around the middle of the third century.[208] A historical reference to the position of bishop is important to us for the reason that it was at this stage when those who were considered the authoritative voices in the church began to become detached and distanced from the communities in which they originally served.[209] Once the monarchial bishop hierarchy established itself in the West, the quest for control and power began to shape what was to form the church as an institution.

Those skeptical scholars who suggest that the scriptures were written to benefit the church more than likely have this institutionalized-church era in mind. Although God had always intended for order in His community, those placed in positions of authority were always meant to serve and live among God's people, not above them (John 13:12–17). Once we understand the order of events in history, it should become clear that the witnesses who wrote scripture had no other agenda than to accurately record the life and events surrounding God's Messiah and to spread the good news of salvation to as many people as possible in obedience to Christ (Matt.

---

[205] Hans Küng, *Christianity: Essence, History, and Future* (New York: Continuum, 1995), 127–78.

[206] Ibid., 127.

[207] Ibid.

[208] Ibid.

[209] Ibid.

28:18–20). These were men on a mission to save the souls of the lost, not on a campaign to garner power and notoriety.

General Test for Accuracy

Aside from a focus on the accusations made against the writings of the New Testament that fail to recognize the historical context in which they were written, there are two other considerations scholars study when testing for the accuracy of the documents used in the New Testament. It is helpful to think through the historical relevancy and the general message of scripture, as well as to take a close look at the small details mentioned in the writings while comparing them to actual historical events and dates. When studying the accuracy of any medium that portrays a moment in history, one needs to check for the relevancy that it had for the people of that time period, as well as for cultural accuracy. Think about it: when you are watching a movie about a time in the past (say, from the 1960s genre), if you were to spot a laptop or cell phone in one of the scenes, it would not make sense, would it?

Writing Style Accuracy

The same premise stands when we evaluate the writings in the New Testament. How accurate is the written material? Is it realistic? Does it appear to have been written in the first century, or the second century, or later? There is a type of fictional writing that we are familiar with today called *historical narrative fiction*. Many skeptics have accused the Bible of being a piece of literature that represents this type of writing style. Unfortunately for these skeptics, history does not reveal this style of literature at any point prior to the first century, nor does it show this method of writing until centuries later. Their accusations are historically unfounded. The Gospel of Luke and the book of Acts have been scrutinized by numerous scholars who have found these documents to be so accurate that even secular historians agree that they are valid and authentic works from history.

Biblical scholar and emeritus professor at Sheffield University in the United Kingdom Loveday Alexander has made an exhaustive study of Luke's writings (Luke and Acts). She concludes that although Luke's works are indeed historically accurate, he does not seem to have been writing in an effort to place himself in history as a historian, but instead he seems to have been writing to record the facts just as he claims (Luke 1:1–4).[210] Alexander's research revealed that Luke's preface is similar in writing style to the more technical writings of the day, to documents such as medical journals.[211] We know from scripture that Luke is indeed a physician (Col. 4:14), so it would make perfect sense that his style of writing would lean toward the more technical and exact type of record keeping which he was professionally used to. It is important to note that, although the study of the various forms in which ancient literature took shape are indeed relevant to the validity of the New Testament documents, one should judge the veracity of a writer by what he is saying rather than by the way he proclaims it.[212]

---

[210] Bauckham, *Jesus and the Eyewitnesses*, 118.
[211] Hemer, *The Book of Acts—in the Setting of Hellenistic History*, 35.
[212] Ibid.

What are three of the external evidences that historians seek in order to verify the historical accuracy of a document?

1. _____
2. _____
3. _____

Internal Evidence: Fact or Fiction?

What Is Being Said?

If the New Testament were being written to advance the agenda of the church (which it was not), then we would have to ask why the authors would have left in embarrassing details about Jesus and the disciples. Jesus did not hold back when claimed in many ways to be God in the flesh. If the church were fabricating its idea of a perfect God, then why would they include material that could place the God of peace in a bad light? Consider the following:

- People called Jesus a "drunkard" (Matt. 11:19).
- They said that He was possessed by a demon (Mark 3:22; John 7:20).
- His family thought He had lost his mind and wanted Him to come home (Mark 3:21, 31).
- He ignored His mother (Matt. 12:46–50).
- The people of Nazareth tried to murder Him (Luke 4:29–30).
- His own family thought of Him as a fraud (John 7:5).
- He was thought of as a deceiver by His own people (John 7:12).
- He told the people that they would have to eat His flesh and drink His blood (John 6:53–54).

These are all very difficult to explain and would not make sense if they were written with an agenda to advance the church for the purpose of garnering power over people. In fact, it was Jesus's very demand that those who wished to have eternal life would have to drink His blood and eat His flesh (John 6:51–56) that caused the early church a tremendous amount of difficulty. The first- and second-century Christians were actually being accused of cannibalism because of their understanding of the Eucharist as the blood and body of the Christ.[213]

Can you think of any other unflattering things that were said about Jesus? Write them down here, and back it up with scripture.

The writers of the New Testament also included many incriminating particulars about themselves that would not have done any good to advance a power agenda, as follows:

---

[213] Hans Küng, *Christianity: Essence, History, and Future*, 131.

- Jesus called Peter "Satan" (Mark 8:33).
- Thomas would not believe his friends when they all testified to the resurrection of Jesus (John 20:25).
- The disciples could not even stay awake after Jesus asked them to pray with Him twice (Mark 14:32–41).
- The disciples were not able to exorcise a demon-possessed boy because they did not believe strongly enough (Mark 9:14–29).
- After all of Jesus's instruction and examples that He set for the disciples, they were still concerned about their own positions of power in the coming kingdom (Mark 9:33–37).
- The women were given credit for braving it out as they went to the tomb as soon as it was legally acceptable to go at the break of the Sabbath (Luke 24:1–12).

Women held a lower status in the first and second centuries than did the average male, yet they were the ones who were always found ministering to Jesus. Why would the writers include women in this way if their goal was to establish an institution that only recognized men as the authority in the church? Other internal factors that attest to the accuracy of the documents that make up the New Testament would be the following:

- Many of the writers claimed to be eyewitnesses to the events surrounding the life of Christ or else wrote after hearing the testimonies of the actual witnesses (Luke 1:1–2; John 21:24–25; 2 Pet. 1:16–18).
- The authors invited the readers to cross-examine their written claims by checking around with those who were witnesses to Jesus's miracles and ascension into heaven (Acts 2:22; 1 Cor. 15:6).
- The writers stood the risk of great persecution from the religious leaders of the day as well as the political authorities (Acts 4:1–21, 6:8–7:60, 12:1–3, 18:1–2).
- The authors were very careful to distinguish Jesus's words from their own narrative.
  - He used terms not found elsewhere in scripture: "Abba," "which of you," "have you not read," "I tell you the truth," "how foolish you are and slow of heart," "amen."
  - Jesus's sayings are written in a form easy to remember.
- Much of the material in the New Testament reveals controversies that would have been irrelevant to the church, as follows:
  - Difficulties between the Pharisees and the Sanhedrin (Matt. 26:60–61)
  - Jesus's reprimand to the religious leaders for their misuse of the corban (Mark 7:9–13)
- Other material did not relate to issues faced by the institutionalized church, as follows:
  - Circumcision
  - Dietary restrictions
  - Missions to the Gentile nations
  - Cleanliness rituals

A close and objective look at the historicity of the manuscripts, along with the various careful studies that have been made, reveals an authentic group of documents that make up the New Testament. Every indication is that not one of the New Testament authors was concerned about his social recognition.[214] To the contrary, all of their documentation is centered on the eschatological reality of salvation found only through Israel's Messiah, Jesus of Nazareth.[215]

Specific Test for Accuracy

The scriptures speak for themselves that the whole of the New Testament is based on a thoroughly Jewish understanding of the God of Israel and His promise for the redemption of humanity through His chosen Vessel. For the skeptic who needs more evidence than what is provided by a general observation of the writings and how they are relevant to history, we can offer a more specific look at the internal evidence. The New Testament is wrought with historical references that can be verified by outside historical sources, so we will take a quick look at a few of them. The book of Acts is the perfect place to begin when helping others understand the historical value of the New Testament. The late and famed archeologist Sir William Ramsay is said to have claimed to be a skeptic who set out to disprove the validity of the scriptures, only to end up using the book of Acts to help him identify the ancient sites of Palestine, as well as other "antiquities, and societies of Asia Minor."[216]

Evidence for Historical References

<u>People and Dates</u>

The book of Acts not only coincides with the Gospel of Luke but also provides information on the missionary journeys of Paul. As both are the contributions of the physician Luke, it is not surprising to find his dedication to detail in both works. Embedded in the Gospel of Luke we find a wealth of historical material that is addressed in accurate chronological form. For instance, Luke 3:1–2 contains no fewer than sixteen references to historical figures who can be verified through either Jewish or secular historical documents. These mentions are significant because they place the events of the Gospel in real-time history. What is more helpful still is that Luke gives the reader an approximate age for Jesus as He began his ministry in connection with these political figures (Luke 3:23). It is here where the historian is able to begin to match up the dates for these high-profile political officials and then place Jesus and His disciples into their historical context.

Can you find the sixteen historical references?

In the fifteenth year of the reign of Tiberius Caesar, Pontius Pilate being governor of Judea, and Herod being tetrarch of Galilee, and his brother Philip tetrarch of the region of Ituraea and Trachonitis, and Lysanias tetrarch of Abilene, during the high priesthood of Annas and Caiaphas, the word of God came to John the son of Zechariah in the wilderness. (Luke 3:1–2 ESV)

---

[214] Bauckham, *Jesus and the Eyewitnesses*, 277.

[215] Ibid.

[216] Geisler, *Christian Apologetics*, 2nd ed., 259–60. Citing William M. Ramsay, *St. Paul the Traveler and the Roman Citizen* (London: Hodder and Stoughton, 1865), 8.

A historian will also take the names of other people noted in the documents, like Luke's mention of Gamaliel as Paul's mentor (Acts 22:3), and research such individuals to see if they actually existed and if they adequately fit into what is written. The Bible student may also be able to find clues about the individual specified, in other parts of the scripture or perhaps even within the same book. For example, Gamaliel is first mentioned in Acts 5:34. A little research will also reveal that he was a prominent figure amid the religious leaders of the first century. Noted Roman historian Colin J. Hemer places Gamaliel in history as the grandson of Hillel,[217] who was a Jewish scholar (ca. 60 BC – AD 20).[218] These are the types of references on which honest critical scholars would be focused. Hemer places Paul's tutelage under Gamaliel before AD 32, which gives the reader and the skeptic a time in history that certainly fits the events in the New Testament.

Another religious leader mentioned in scripture who is identified as a high priest, Ananias (son of Nedebaeus) in Acts 23:2, can also be traced in Jewish history. According to the writings of the Jewish historian Josephus, we know that Ananias was appointed to his position by Herod of Chalics around AD 47.[219] We are also able to trace his trial before Claudius to around AD 52 as a result of the record keeping of Tacitus, a historian for the Roman Empire in the late first and early second centuries.[220] According to Josephus's documentation, in his *Antiquities* (*Ant.* 20.9.2.206–207), we also learn of Ananias's brutal character.[221] This trait is in agreement with scripture as it also records his violent tendencies. He has Paul struck in the mouth as the latter stood before him during his trial in Palestine before the Sanhedrin (AD 57).

There are numerous other people mentioned in scripture who can be and have been verified in non-Christian writings, which further serves to validate the authenticity of the New Testament documents. Aside from the verification of the existence of individuals, historians also research events mentioned in a document. According to Acts 11:28 there were famines during the reign of Claudius (41–54). Secular historical notations record two distinct famines in Rome, one in 42 and one in 51.[222] It is even known that the famines were not the result of a harvest failure in the crop-producing nations but rather the result of failure and "difficulties" at the local level that priced the less fortunate out of reach of food affordability.[223] In order to determine an event such as a famine in the past, scholars trace the geographical and economic "outworkings" noted in history.[224] Egypt was a major source of grain supply for the area, and Egyptians kept records of their crops and the prices. Therefore, a careful study of these historical records would allow us to trace economic and geographical fluctuations.

---

[217] Hemer, *The Book of Acts*, 162.

[218] Merrill C. Tenney, ed., *The Zondervan Pictorial Encyclopedia of the Bible in Five Volumes—Vol. 3, H–L* (Grand Rapids, MI: Zondervan, 1977), 159–60.

[219] Hemer, *The Book of Acts*, 170.

[220] Ibid.

[221] Ibid., 171.

[222] Ibid., 164.

[223] Ibid., 165.

[224] Ibid.

Accuracy of Geographical Locations and Cultural Customs

As mentioned previously, Luke records a great deal of Paul's missionary journeys in the book of Acts. The cities and villages where Paul evangelized are all recognizable places that can be mapped out or traced back in history. This is very important when discussing the validity of scripture. There are times when a modern-day reader of scripture is not able to relate to some of the apostle Paul's urgency. Fortunately it is possible to study some of the ancient customs and the rituals associated with certain cultures. An understanding of the ancient customs helps the reader to better comprehend why Paul was so insistent and at times vehement about the way in which he spoke to the different communities to whom he wrote.

We know from the book of Acts that Paul had contact with the Ephesians many times (18:19, 19:1), which informs the reader of the relationship that Paul had with the people of that region. Critical historical scholars focus on the language used in a passage to determine geographical routes, such as mentioned in Acts 19:1. The term that Luke uses to indicate Paul's journey to Ephesus is said to suggest that he traveled through the "hilly overland," which was a direct route on the interior to get there.[225] From this information scholars surmise that this could explain why Paul did not spend time in Colossae according to his letter to the Colossians (2:1). These are all clues that help to reconstruct the early growth of the Gentile church and to keep everything in its historical context.

Evidence for Cultural Distinctions

Aside from geographical indicators, the New Testament includes a glimpse into the cultural tensions that followed Paul and the other authors of the New Testament. The book of Acts records a very tense situation that seems to have prompted Paul's departure from Ephesus (Acts 19:23–20:4). The second part of this lesson will delve deeper into the culture and its influences on the people of Ephesus. The purpose of having a deeper understanding of the societies in which the apostles were sharing the Gospel is to help us (and then others) see how what is written in the New Testament is relevant to the real-life dilemmas faced by the people of antiquity. Once we are able to put the events of the New Testament into context, we will begin to see parallels to the dilemmas we all face when confronting our culture with God's Word. The encouraging piece to all of the scriptures is that God promises to remain faithful to all who are faithful to Him (Matt. 28:16–28; John 10:28–29; Rom. 8:28).

> I give them eternal life, and they will never perish, and no one will snatch them out of my hand. My Father, who has given them to me, is greater than all, and no one is able to snatch them out of the Father's hand.
>
> John 10:28–29 (ESV)

Living in obedience is to trust that God is going to be there when we step up as true disciples of God's kingdom.

---

[225] Ibid., 187.

Review: Internal Criteria Used to Validate Documents

Tools Used to Validate the Accuracy of the Documents

The following is a list of criteria that is used to validate the historical accuracy of a document:

1. External validation: seeking evidence outside of the New Testament

   - Church records based on writings of the early church fathers and mention in secular history
   - Details mentioned as to historical context, which is then verified with secular historical documents
   - Identifying the author's style of writing while comparing it to other writings in the same time period

2. Internal validation: looking for clues within the text to validate facts as they coincide with historical accuracy of the evidence

   - Focus on what is being said.
     Writers left in embarrassing details.
     Women are given credit for their ministry to the Christ.
   - Writers claimed to be eyewitnesses.
   - Writers risked persecution.
   - The controversies mentioned in the New Testament are irrelevant to the institutionalized church that was eventually run by non-Jewish believers.

Study Questions: Accuracy of the Documents

For Review and Reflection

1. What is the New Testament about?

   a. Why is this important when discussing the accuracy of the documents?

2. Why is it significant that Luke is so careful to document historical political figures that coincide with Jesus's ministry?

3. How can you use the above information when discussing the accuracy of the New Testament documents?

4. How do historians place individuals mentioned in the New Testament in real historical time? Can you give an example?

5. How are events mentioned in the New Testament verified? Can you give an example?

Group Discussion

1. Now that you know the process that literary scholars have used to test the historical accuracy of the New Testament documents, how will you use this information when discussing the historical reliability of the New Testament?

Key Terms

bishop: Stems from a Greek term *episkopos*. It is used in the New Testament five times when referring to those who oversee the care of others. The official office of an episkopos, or bishop as we know it today, did not take root until at least the third century. The word is used in 1 Peter 2:25 when recognizing Jesus as the Shepherd of our souls.

Ignatius of Antioch: One of the early church fathers.

Literature Cited or Recommended

Bauckham, Richard. *Jesus and the Eyewitnesses: The Gospels as Eyewitness Testimony.* Grand Rapids, MI: Eerdmans, 2006.

Geisler, Norman. *Christian Apologetics.* 2nd ed. Grand Rapids, MI: Baker Academic, 2013. Citing William M. Ramsay, *St. Paul the Traveler and the Roman Citizen.* London: Hodder and Stoughton, 1865.

Hemer, Colin J. *The Book of Acts: In the Setting of Hellenistic History.* Edited by Conrad H. Gempf. Winona Lake, IN: Eisenbrauns, 1990, 2008.

Küng, Hans. *Christianity: Essence, History, and Future.* New York: Continuum, 1995.

Tenney, Merrill C., ed. *The Zondervan Pictorial Encyclopedia of the Bible in Five Volumes—Vol. 3, H–L.* Grand Rapids, MI: Zondervan, 1977.

Accuracy of the Documents
Does Scripture Reflect Historical Reality?

Application of Scripture: Ephesians

Read Ephesians.

Paul's letter to the Ephesians was intended to be a circular letter and provides an insightful picture of the historical context for Asia Minor in the first century. The author is focused on the influences that the Greco-Roman culture had on the people in that area. One of the author's main concerns was the family structure and how it was to mirror God's relationship to His church. God's ideal for the family stood in stark contrast to the rest of the world, and it remains that way today. It appears that there was a culture clash between those who would live as Christians and the surrounding society. This should not come as a surprise to anyone participating in this Bible study, since God's ways have always been higher than our ways (Isa. 55:9). Historical evidence that reveals cultural and societal behaviors is helpful to determining the accuracy of the New Testament documents. Therefore, not only will we look at the cultural atmosphere of the city of Ephesus and the surrounding areas, but also we will compare the terminology found in this letter to other literature of the same time period.

Correctly Interpreted: Based on Historical Facts

Paul spends quite a bit of time addressing the family structure and the expected behavior of these new Christians. Part of the reason we do not live as we should is sin, and another is because scripture is misinterpreted. Much of the reason for interpretive difficulties in our day is due to the effects of critical liberal scholarship, teachings that have incrementally eroded the validity of the Bible in the eyes of society through academia. This letter is a very good example of how parts of scripture can be terribly misinterpreted. There are those who claim that the Bible may have been valid and meaningful in antiquity but is no longer relevant for those living today in our modern world. When we place it in its historical context, however, the author's message becomes timeless. A little research reveals that the people of Asia Minor needed correction just as we do in our own day.

Addressing the Culture

Paul begins by directing Christians as to the lifestyle that is expected by God for holy living. Recall that the God of Israel called all that would be His to be holy (meaning separate), because He is holy (Lev. 20:26). Even though the author is addressing mostly Gentiles, he has not deviated from God's requirements and is passing on these important values to the people who are only beginning to know God. As modern-day readers, we are also privileged to know a little bit about the people of Ephesus as we study the book of Acts. The reader is told that the atmosphere in Ephesus was anything but friendly to Paul and the Gospel message (Acts 19:23–41).

You shall be holy to me, for I the Lord am holy and have separated you from the peoples, that you should be mine. (Lev. 20:26 ESV)

There was a great deal of tension between the prevailing culture, who regularly worshipped numerous gods and goddesses, and the Christian community, who was called to worship only *the* one true God. He was the one God who had nothing to do with the central goddess figure known as Artemis. Artemis was such a central symbol throughout the region that historical records show that she was worshipped in at least thirty-three known places.[226] There is also archeological evidence that even well after Paul established the church at Ephesus, the cultic practices of Artemis were alive and well. Historical records reveal that a certain Roman official presented a silver statue of the goddess to the people of Ephesus to be placed at the open-air theater (seating about twenty-five thousand people) between AD 103 and AD 104.[227] The battles we face today may not include allegiance to a particular statue, but they do pertain to the ethical and moral dilemmas of our time. If we are not subject to the absolute moral authority of God, then we are relegating our worship to the mandates made by volatile humanity.

> When considering the hostile climate toward Paul and the message of Christ, do you find historical evidence to back up Paul's concern for the battle of the hearts and minds of the people of Ephesus? Can you explain?

The Battle Rages On

The battle to remain faithful to God is not any easier today than it was in first -century Asia Minor. In reality, wherever we have a civilization with active trade and commerce, we have a government to contend with. Ephesus was no insignificant place; it was the "greatest commercial city of Asia Minor."[228] Although it is located seven miles inland today, there is geographical evidence that reveals that Ephesus was situated on a harbor, which gave people access to commerce both by land and sea.[229] Aside from being perfectly positioned for successful trade, the city was politically influential and was "on one of the main routes from Rome to the eastern imperial frontier."[230] Paul's message directly threatened the livelihood of those who benefited from cult worship. The challenge for Christians is somewhat the same today; wherever there is a group that stands to gain either financially, politically, or in the realm of other fleshly desires (1 John 2:16), there will be a violent push to silence any form of absolute Truth. For Christians, it becomes a challenge to stand for an absolute ultimate Being who requires faithfulness to His moral code of conduct.

---

[226] Bruce, *New Testament History*, 329.

[227] Ibid., 328.

[228] Ibid., 319.

[229] Ibid.

[230] Ibid.

Historical Context

Chapter 6 of Ephesians is one of the biblical texts that is frequently misquoted and, thus, misinterpreted. Many have used this passage to point to and claim that the Bible approves of slavery. To the contrary, as outlined in chapter 3 of this workbook, which discusses the letter to the Galatians, slavery was simply a part of everyday life, and we cannot compare it to the slavery of the eighteenth and nineteenth centuries. Paul is teaching these fledgling Christians how they are to treat others. As a Pharisee, Paul was very familiar with God's command to those who had slaves; they were to treat them

> Rendering service with a good will as to the Lord and not to man, knowing that whatever good anyone does, this he will receive back from the Lord, whether he is a bondservant or is free.
> Eph. 6:7 (ESV)

fairly (Lev. 25; Deut. 15). With the advent of the Christ, however, there would be new expectations for both slaves and their masters (Matt. 20:20–28). There would be a new hierarchy, one of serving each other just as one would serve the Lord (Eph. 6:7–8).

Naturally, this is a concept that must recognize that no matter what position God has placed us in, there is always the reality that we must answer to God as the ultimate authority. Jesus is quoted as telling a parable about an unforgiving servant in an effort to teach the importance of humility (Matt. 18:21–35). The point He makes is that God has placed us in various positions of power over others, but in the end we are all equal as we are all ultimately sinful and in need of forgiveness (Eph. 6:9). God's economy will not ever be realized until all people recognize God as the ultimate authority over their lives and thus treat others with the love and respect given to us as humans by God. In real-life circumstances, this is much more difficult when we are dealing with ruthless individuals who do not recognize the God of the Bible.

Unfortunately, we do live in a fallen world, and as Christians we are called to be patient with the ignorant and to walk away from those who vehemently refuse to honor God (Matt. 10:11–15; 2 Cor. 6:14). Paul knew full well that some would reject the message of the Gospel and that others would be drawn to the promise of a better way of life. He was therefore always aware of his audience, and he frequently spoke at various levels, carefully choosing his words. He knew that the people of Asia Minor were not thoroughly familiar with Jewish laws and customs, so he was patient with them in many respects. He was teaching them how to live as those who had now been grafted into the family of Israel's God. The author also understood the dangers that they would face as they lived in an atmosphere that was hostile to the God of Israel and His chosen Messiah.

When we take all of the historical evidence of the cultural and societal norms into consideration, it is not difficult to understand why the author chose to focus on the topics of family, slavery, and spiritual warfare. The historical backdrop is useful in validating the accuracy of the documents.

Communicating on Various Levels

Paul knew that his audience in Asia Minor also included Diaspora Jews; therefore, the language that he used to warn them of how to handle the hostility toward the Way of Christ took shape on two different levels. Ephesians 6 is filled with *apocalyptic* terminology with which the Jews would have been intimately familiar.[231] To the Jews, there was an understanding that the God of Israel would intervene in human history in the end, and that He would triumph over evil and save His people. Ancient Jewish literature is filled with apocalyptic references from which historians can draw to see where Paul likely formed his understanding of God's ultimate rule (a heavenly and spiritual realm).[232] To the pagan Gentiles, they would have been familiar with the battles fought by the Roman Empire and the surrounding nations (earthly realm).

> Finally, be strong in the Lord and in the strength of his might. (Eph. 6:10, ESV)

There are many examples of this type of imagery in the Old Testament where there are spiritual battles being waged in the heavenly realms as God intervenes with humanity (2 Kings 6:17; Dan. 10–12). Apart from scripture, however, scholars have found the same type of material in some of the documents discovered in the Dead Sea Scrolls and in sections of *1 Enoch*.[233] Historians claim that this type of literature presented itself when there was great tribulation for the people of Israel by outside oppressors (imperial rulers).[234] What the literature reveals is a view of the tension that has existed between the "Western empires and the social and political forms that they imposed on subject people."[235] This is the very same struggle we see in the letter to the Ephesians.

Cultural Values

Paul recognizes that the people in Asia Minor are faced with a value system within their given societies that is antithetical to God's values. He reminds his readers that there is more to life than the here and the now (otherwise known as secularism). Paul calls his readers to stand firm and to be strong in the Lord (Eph. 6:10). This is language also found in Joshua 1:6, 7, 9, as well as in documents from the Qumran community: "Be strong and valiant; be warriors! … Do not fall back (1QM 15.6–8).[236] There is a deliberate focus on an eschatological outlook on life with which the Jews would have been familiar, as they were expecting great tribulation in the last days.[237]

Level of Comprehension

The author used the imagery of military armor to depict the serious nature of the battle that all Christians must be ready to contend with. On the earthly physical level, most, if not all, of the recipients of the letter would have been familiar with Roman armor. The Greek historian Polybius, from antiquity, mentions the sword, the shield, armor that is attached below the knees, and the breastplate, along with other pieces of equipment, in his writings (6.23.2).[238] Paul uses

---

[231] Richard A. Horsley, ed., *Paul and Empire: Religion and Power in Roman Imperial Society* (Harrisburg, PA: Trinity Press International, 1997), 144.

[232] Ibid., 143–45.

[233] Ibid., 144.

[234] Ibid., 145.

[235] Ibid., 146.

[236] Lincoln, *Word Biblical Commentary*, vol. 42, *Ephesians*, 441.

[237] Ibid., 435.

[238] Ibid.

the same types of terms to describe the well-known military armor (Eph. 6:10–18).[239] He also clearly draws from the Hebrew scriptures when he calls the people to recognize that God and His Messiah are in control (Ps. 35:1–3; Isa. 42:13).

Write some parallels to the armor mentioned in the Old Testament the armor which Paul uses: How many parallels can you find?

Isaiah 49:2:_____ = Ephesians _____
Isaiah 52:7:_____ = Ephesians _____

Christians are to live in the world but not to be seen as a part of the world system (John 15:19, 17:14–16). We are to have a sense of the future kingdom, and it is in this vein that Paul draws from the book of Daniel (Dan. 12) to convey the eschatological outlook that is imperative for survival in this battle. He was well-known for this sort of imagery in his correspondence to the churches, as he was all too aware of the antagonism shown toward Christians (1 Thess. 5:8; 2 Cor. 6:7, Rom. 6:13, 13:12). Believe it or not, we face the same battles today when we stand for God's unadulterated Word. Life is a constant struggle, and much like the first-century Christians, we need to be prepared for battle. Although the military terms used were familiar in the secular and the Jewish theological realms, they were also recognized and used by those in the mystery cults, by the philosophers, and by the orators of the day.[240]

Two schools of philosophical thought known as the *Stoics* and the *Cynics* emphasized that the battle was waged on the philosophical wisdom of the individual, suggesting that the person had to be self-sufficient.[241] The idea that life was a battle was not a foreign one to the people of the first century. What placed the Christ followers apart from all the rest of the populace (even the Qumran community) was a total dependence on God and His redeeming work on the cross. Although the Qumran community was devoted to Israel's God, and although their literature included the Lord's messengers fighting alongside them, they expected to be actively physically fighting with the armor mentioned in their own writings.[242] This is not the intent of the author. The language that he uses is written in the passive form.[243] In other words, those who follow Christ will face fierce spiritual battles and are called to draw "strength" from and to be empowered by God's Messiah (Eph. 3:16). This is not a battle that can be won on our own strength.

> David was in great danger, for the troops threatened to stone him; for all the troops were embittered on account of their sons and daughters. But David sought strength in the Lord his God.
>
> 1 Sam. 30:6 (TNK)

Here again, we see Paul using terminology found in the Old Testament (1 Sam. 30:6). It is beneficial to note that although documents outside the New Testament also call for facing battles using military terminology, there is an expectation of self-sufficiency. The focus on the individual as the determinate factor in the outcome of a war lies in stark contrast to the total dependence on God during battle on which the Christian is called to rely. The Christ follower is expected to

---

[239] Ibid.

[240] Ibid., 437.

[241] Ibid., 438.

[242] Ibid.

[243] Ibid., 441.

take full advantage of the gift of Christ while praying for protection from the forces of evil (Eph. 6:18–20). In reality, Paul reminds the churches that although the Christ has triumphed over the powers of evil, these forces remain active on this earth (Eph. 1:21, 3:10).

Indeed it is encouraging to know that at the Second Coming of Christ, the dark forces will be permanently expelled and a new era will begin for those who are faithful to God (Isa. 65:17; 2 Pet. 3:13; Rev. 21:1). Until that time, however, the battle that rages around us is very real. The fact that Paul calls for the Christian to put on the "full armor of God" is a cry to all of those who follow Christ to be prepared to engage in this battle on a daily basis (Eph. 6:18). There are no bystanders in this war. Satan loves bystanders because they are not a threat to his kingdom (Eph. 2:1–2). Those who are satisfied to stand by in silence have made their decision to help Satan and ignore God.

We are all called to engage in this battle for the souls of those living around us. But, as Paul warns, if we do not "suit up" with the whole armor, we will not be ready when the opportunity to bring God glory arises. First Peter 3:15 states that we should be ready to tell people about the hope that lives within us. Every day that we are given the breath of life is an opportunity to bring glory to God by finding ways to share the Gospel of Truth with our *words* and our actions. Do not be fooled by Satan's lie that by simply being nice to others, you are doing your part in sharing the love of Christ with others.

> But in your hearts honor Christ the Lord as holy, always being prepared to make a defense to anyone who asks you for a reason for the hope that is in you; yet do it with gentleness and respect.
>
> 1 Pet. 3:15 (ESV)

God's aid is eternal, and when we begin to take advantage of the gift of power that God has given to us through Christ, we begin to harness the spiritual forces around us as we become a very real threat to Satan's kingdom. Becoming a threat to Satan is very real, and this is why Paul warns the church to live in a state of preparedness and alertness (Eph. 6:18). Although when seeking to historically validate the documents of the New Testament, we usually search for similarities in other period literature, or the validation of societal conditions in which first-century people lived, we also seek the way Christians are called to think. Christians are to seek God's guidance in all situations (John 14:23–24; 2 Cor. 10:5), recognizing that behind the flesh-and-blood opposition to us is a spiritual battle (John 14:30) that can only be won on our knees. The author does not step out of the consistent theological theme found throughout scripture, which is another way that we can validate Paul's words to these new converts.

Accuracy

> Praying at all times in the Spirit, with all prayer and supplication. To that end keep alert with all perseverance, making supplication for all the saints, and also for me, that words may be given to me in opening my mouth boldly to proclaim the mystery of the gospel, for which I am an ambassador in chains, that I may declare it boldly, as I ought to speak.
>
> Eph. 6:18 (ESV)

At this stage, it is beneficial to recognize that at every point of historical cultural understanding with reference to the norms of these societies, and that in light of the purpose for the apocalyptic and the eschatological terms used, there are no contradictions in genre. The first-century church to which Paul was writing faced very real dangers. They were faced with moral and ethical dilemmas just as we are today, which makes this and the other writings in the New Testament timeless. The military terms that the author uses were clearly understandable as they were familiar to his audience on several levels. This document has proven to be highly accurate in every way, and there is no reason to doubt its authenticity or veracity.

Holy One of Israel, instill in me a heart that desires to serve You as a faithful disciple. Prepare me each day for any battles that I may face while witnessing for Your kingdom. Grant me the wisdom that I will need when engaging my culture with Your Truth. Lord, bless me with opportunities to serve You as a messenger of Your Word. Amen.

Review: Does Scripture Reflect Historical Reality Study Questions

For Focus and Theological Reflection

1. What was the city of Ephesus like in the first century? Name three historically reliable facts that describe this city:

    a. _____

    b. _____

    c. _____

2. How do we know that Ephesus had a seaport in the first century?

    - Why is this important to the historical accuracy of the documents?

3. What are the outside sources that have been discovered that relate to Paul's apocalyptic terminology?

    - Why is this relevant to the historical accuracy of this document?

4. What other historical sources use the same military terminology that Paul uses?

- Considering all that you have learned up to this point, how is this detail important to validating the historical accuracy of this document?

- Although the author's language does mirror that of other historical sources from antiquity, how is Paul's call to battle different from that of the other literature? Why is this important to Christian theology?

Group Discussion

1. Does Paul's apocalyptic language make sense in the historical context of first-century Asia Minor? If not, why not? If so, how?

2. What would the author's words have meant to these people?

3. How does the language that the author uses help us determine the accuracy of the documents?

4. Try to address both 1 and 2, above, in your reflection.

5. Many people in Westernized societies do not agree with physical violence and may take issue with the Bible because of some of the military language that it uses. How would you explain to the modern-day reader what Paul is actually saying and why he uses the language that he does?

6. Once you've explained why military terms are used, how can you segue the conversation into how this very language is the way that historians validate the accuracy of the documents?

Key Terms

1 Enoch: This is an apocalyptic piece of literature written sometime between 163 and 80 BC.

Stoicism: This is an ancient Greek philosophy developed by a Greek philosopher known as Zeno of Citium around 300 BC. The philosophy teaches that the way to ultimate freedom is to distance oneself from all worldly pleasures through a focused effort of self-control.

Cynicism: A school of philosophical thought in ancient Greece that came to be noticed in the fifth century BC. It was made popular by a student of Socrates named Antisthenes (445–365 BC). Its adherents were taught that a virtuous life and true freedom came from living a life of poverty and rebuking any worldly wealth. Virtue could be attained through a life that was in harmony with nature. Many skeptics of the Christian faith inaccurately believe that Jesus was a first-century Cynic. Although this is an ignorant statement to make, it stems from a clear misunderstanding of the long history of the Judeo-Christian faith.

God's Attributes

protectiveness – He promises to protect those who rely on him.

sovereignty – God knows what is going on in the spiritual realm and seeks our trust.

Literature Cited or Recommended

Bruce, F. F. *New Testament History*. New York: Doubleday, 1969.

Detzler, Wayne. *Living Words in Ephesians*. Welwyn, Hertfordshire: Evangelical Press, 1981.

———. *Daring the Devil: Spiritual Warfare*. USA: Wayne A. Detzler, 2011.

Horsley, Richard A., ed. *Paul and Empire: Religion and Power in Roman Imperial Society*. Harrisburg, PA: Trinity Press International, 1997.

Lincoln, Andrew T. *Word Biblical Commentary*. Edited by Bruce M. Metzger, David A. Hubbard, and Glenn W. Barker. Vol. 42, *Ephesians*. Edited by Ralph P. Martin and Lynn Allan Losie. Grand Rapids, MI: Zondervan, 1990.

CHAPTER 6

Is History Knowable?

Up to this point we have been using specific literary tools that aid in assessing the validity of historical documents. The type of investigation we have been using is known as *higher criticism*, which uses tools that take a close look at the source of the text. You have successfully studied the means by which historical specialists assess the internal criteria of a document. Scholars who seek to answer questions that will validate the authorship of a document, when the document was originally dated, how authentic the document is, and the reliability of the material written use these tools. Have you wondered why all of this is necessary? This lesson may come as a surprise to you, but there is an entire school of thought that doubts that there can be any knowledge about history. This is important to us as Christians because the Judeo-Christian faith is rooted in history. If we cannot know history, then the implication is that we cannot be assured of the veracity of scripture.

This is not a new phenomenon. In fact, it began around the 1400s, when scholars commenced to investigate the study of history, otherwise known as *historiography*, or how history is studied, and basically this is what you have been doing in the last four chapters. When we look back in time, we discover that between the fifth and eleventh centuries there was a period of great cultural and intellectual degeneration in the West (AD 600–1200).[244] The majority of the populace was considered to be illiterate during this time, and the intellectual elite were the religious leaders of the day. History reveals that there was an intellectual and cultural revival in the eleventh and twelfth centuries, but by the thirteenth century the writing of history began to fall by the wayside.[245] This falling out of favor of the intellectual elite was largely due to an insistence upon eyewitness accounts in order to validate the events in question.[246]

The problem seemed to stem from the fact that those who compiled historical events based on the testimony of the authorities were eventually copying these historical events written by others over time.[247] This method came under suspicion because historians became critical of the sources from which they drew information about the past.[248] In other words, they began to mistrust the

---

[244] William Lane Craig, *Reasonable Faith: Christian Truth and Apologetics*, 3rd ed. (Wheaton, IL: Crossway, 2008), 208.
[245] Ibid.
[246] Ibid.
[247] Ibid.
[248] Ibid.

validity of the historical sources available and felt that events could be interpreted subjectively, thus compromising the actual historical facts. This suspicion of historical documents had a definitive impact upon the way a Christian was able to explain the historical validity of the Bible. The obvious problem with this scenario is that now the only way to explain the existence of God would be through a moral argument for God, the factoring of *a priori*, or innate knowledge, type of reasoning, or through an emotional experience (which is highly subjective).

Christian Claims and History

At this stage of our study, you realize how the reliability of historical facts is highly instrumental to a deeper comprehension of the biblical narrative. History is important to the Christian faith because Christianity is "not a code for living or a philosophy of religion; rather it is rooted in real events of history."[249] What does this mean for the Judeo-Christian faith? It means that the truth of particular historical facts are interwoven with the truth claims of God's revelation of the Christ and His work amidst humanity.[250] Scholarly skeptics realize this fact and seem to strive to discredit the historical claims made throughout scripture by placing suspicion on the historicity of the narratives. If history is unknowable, then the Bible would be left to one's own interpretation of the facts.

The wonderful thing is that God has made sure that His unique stamp on the creation of His nation would forever be wound up in history. Both the Jewish faith and the Christian faith are tightly woven into the fabric of actual historical events. At every turn of historical criticism, God has made certain not only that his fingerprints are on the events in the lives of His chosen people, but also that the historical documentation of the rest of humanity also testifies to the happenings of those who worship the God of Israel. God is so awesome; you have nothing to fear when sharing the reliability of the Bible with others. God has you covered!

A Philosophical Framework

The thirteenth century brought with it a more sophisticated way of approaching the veracity of the Judeo-Christian faith with the aid of philosophical arguments.[251] Many theologians throughout history have used various techniques to share the truths of scripture and the Truth of God. Fourth-century theologian Saint Augustine defended the Christian faith through the *moral argument* (without a basis for good, there can be no basis for evil) and the argument from observation of the miracles that fulfilled prophecy in the Bible. Granted, Augustine lived in a time when there was not as much intellectual skepticism as there came to be in the later centuries. Eleventh-century Anselm of Canterbury made a defense for the existence of God using what is known as an *ontological* argument based on a priori reasoning. His objective was to work around the historical skepticisms of his day by basing his defense for the existence of God on the idea of God itself, in other words, "God is that than which no greater can be conceived."[252] The basic

---

[249] Ibid., 207.
[250] Ibid.
[251] Ibid., 209.
[252] Khaldoun A. Sweis and Chad V. Meister, eds., *Christian Apologetics: An Anthology of Primary Sources* (Grand Rapids, MI: Zondervan, 2012), 23.

premise for this argument is that if God is the greatest thing that can be conceived, then God must have within Him all properties known and unknown; and "since existence is a property, God exists!"[253]

By the thirteenth century, however, scholars were finding fault with Anselm's argument and began to demand external signs for the existence of God. This was the era of one of the greatest minds of all time, Thomas Aquinas. Thomas was a brilliant thinker, theologian, and scholar who synthesized the understanding that faith and reason must work together. For Thomas, the proof for the existence of God could be confirmed mainly through the miracles found in scripture.[254] These were outward and attested-to signs as well as the fulfillment of written prophecies. Aquinas's focus eventually led to the study of *epistemology*, or the study of how we know what we know.

His arguments dealt more with the philosophical and theological tenets of understanding the Judeo-Christian faith than with historical evidences. There are, however, always many layers that make up time in history, and the thirteenth century was no different. Although Aquinas's arguments opened new possibilities for defending the faith tenets of Christianity, historical skepticism remained throughout academia and among the intellectual elite. But his thought process was so philosophically sound and intellectually intact that he made it possible for future generations to build valid arguments based on historical evidence, and therefore avoiding any *circular reasoning*, which is the process of using the Bible to validate the Bible.

Modern Critical History

The Italian Renaissance brought with it the rise of the science of modern historical study.[255] There was a great deal of enthusiasm at this time for the study of and search for ancient manuscripts.[256] During this time the academic pursuit of the study of Latin and Greek manuscripts swept through Germany—and then France in 1494.[257] This academic fervor eventually led to the Protestant Reformation, where curious theologians began to seek out the ancient manuscripts from the *patristic* era. Their search led them to the translation of documents that revealed the unscrupulous claims made by the Roman Catholic Church.[258]

As a result of exposing the Catholic Church to the public at large through the efforts of men like Jon Hus and Martin Luther, there was enormous interest in the truth behind historical claims.[259] Reading history became hugely popular with a society that was slowly becoming increasingly literate.[260] There was such a great awareness of historical evidences that history reveals that "every class of European society took interest in the new historical scholarship and sought to use it to support its own point of view."[261] By the 1600s historical scholarship had clearly taken

---

[253] Ibid.

[254] Craig, *Reasonable Faith*, 209.

[255] Ibid., 210.

[256] Ibid.

[257] Ibid.

[258] Ibid., 211.

[259] Ibid.

[260] Ibid.

[261] Ibid.

root. In other words, people began to realize that if they took the time to pick and choose from events in history, they could interpret the facts subjectively in order to rewrite history to make a point that suited their own needs.

The nineteenth century ushered in new guidelines for historical scholarship that led to an objective form of historical study. The purpose was to keep the biases of the historian out of the "historical equation."[262] It was in this scholarly advancement that people would once again be able to trust what they read about historical events. Even though the intent of objective historical reporting made complete sense for accurate transmission of the facts, there arose another school of thought in the late nineteenth and early twentieth centuries. The "school of historical relativism" felt that objectivity was naive at best.

The Rise of Historical Relativism

Those who remained negative toward any objectivity in the historical sciences refused to acknowledge that it was possible to simply report the factual evidences found. They believed that it was up to the historian to interpret those facts, thus once again leaving history up to subjective interpretation. It did not take long for this sentiment to make its way through the halls of academia. The idea of relativism that began in the 1800s had infiltrated every aspect of society by the mid-1900s. Relativism is now deeply rooted in every facet of culture in Westernized civilizations across the globe.

This has not merely been a secular trend; the ideology of relativism has pervaded the campuses of seminaries for nearly the last one hundred years. It started as a seed of thought in some seminaries and has blossomed to the extent that it is difficult in postmodernity to find a training facility for ministers that remains faithful to the inerrancy of scripture. What did this mean for the Christian faith? It meant that the historicity of the Bible was now up to the interpretation of the person doing the research of biblical facts.

What is the biggest problem with this understanding of how to interpret history or historical literature?

_____

_____

_____

In a culture that demanded that everything be witnessed at the risk of having an event fall into question, the reality of the miracles of Jesus was now to be discounted from explaining the historical figure of Jesus. The result of this dilemma ended up, in many cases, in the situation that in the search for the historicity of the real Jesus, He began to take on the image of the person doing the research. How is the theologian or scholar to get around the problem of the lack of the need for direct access to firsthand witnessing of any events from the past? In an effort to answer this dilemma, we need to understand what the relativist's arguments are.

The argument for subjectivity remained, as follows:

---

[262] Ibid., 216.

1. The historian interpreted the facts through his or her own personal understanding.
2. There is no way to accurately test a historical hypothesis or any given historical fact.
3. Scientific research is not neutral but subject to the bias of the one conducting the test.

With these arguments alone facing the sciences, the question came to be, how can anyone know anything at all? What is being questioned here is the ability to gain any knowledge from the past or any other type of scientific inquiry. If we look at this statement critically, however, we notice that the relativist is posing the reality of a historical event against a subjective version of the actual event. For example, the statement "Historical statements or claims about the past are not objectively true or knowable,"[263] once stated, is itself a past statement and thus is self-destructive. The point is that even if everyone were to forget the Holocaust, for instance, it would not cease to be a historical fact.

Getting Around the Claims for the Lack of Objectivity

The important thing to keep in mind is that a historical fact does not cease to be a fact based on what sociological ideologies surround the historian.[264] It is possible to test historical evidence and any hypothesis drawn by the historian. Objectivity of historical truths is attainable. While many individuals may have their own agendas, it is possible to use the science of critical analysis to test the validity of historical claims. There are three distinctive elements to objective historicity, as follows:

1. "A common core of indisputable historical facts exists."[265]
2. "It is possible to distinguish between history and propaganda."[266]
3. "It is possible to criticize poor history."[267]

Comprehending the fact that history is knowable is the first step to identifying true historical elements in a document. Then it is possible to assess how much is objective fact and how much is subjective. When studying the historical events surrounding the life of Jesus and His disciples, it is imperative that we take note of what presuppositions the historical writer may hold. Is the writer predisposed to a worldview of naturalism or supernaturalism? The historian's worldview will undoubtedly color the way that he or she eventually interprets the historical finding, but it will not change the reality of the discovery. Those who approach the historical evidence for the life of the Christ from a naturalistic point of view will find it necessary to explain the supernatural events (miracles) by some form of natural phenomenon.

---

[263] Doug Potter, "Problem of History: Is History Knowable?" (lecture, Southern Evangelical Seminary, Charlotte, NC, September 2013).

[264] Craig, *Reasonable Faith*, 234.

[265] Ibid., 235.

[266] Ibid.

[267] Craig, *Reasonable Faith*, 234.

Can you give an example of a presupposition that would affect the way a person viewed the historicity of the Bible?

_____

_____

_____

Changing the Face of Christ

A Christ without miracles becomes an extraordinary man in history who had many profound things to say for the people of the first century. A Christ who performed miraculous deeds while fulfilling scripture is recognized as the Son of God who was far more than an extraordinary man. He is the timeless and long-awaited Messiah who would reconcile the world to a holy God. It is through His acts in history that we are confronted with our own sinful nature, which makes many, if not most, people uncomfortable. In reality, if the historian does not hold to a theistic worldview, he will not have all of the intellectual tools necessary to comprehend God's supernatural intervention. This is where a naturalism bias will affect the historian's interpretation of the facts.

For our purposes as students of God's Word, it is best to follow the guidelines of historical scholarship when assessing the validity of anyone's interpretation of the historical facts based in scripture. Scholars accept the reliability of primary and secondary sources. Primary sources are the types of documents that we have been discussing in the last four chapters. A primary source is a document produced by someone from the time of the events in question.[268] It is not necessary that the document be the actual original, as a copy of the original is legally acceptable. That is why we study the validity of the manuscripts that we have from antiquity that make up the scriptures.

Professional historians have accepted the historical validity of the New Testament documents. It is those critical liberal scholars, however, who remain as some of the most negative and vociferous people against the historical reliability of the Bible.[269] Ironically, Roman scholars have long accepted the historicity of the book of Acts and take it for granted that it is a valid assessment of life in first-century Palestine.[270] The critics who remain skeptical are those who continue to base their skepticism on prearcheological evidence (prior to the 1950s).[271] In other words, their arguments are based on presuppositions that have long been disproven. Historiography is a science, and when we are called to make a defense for the reliability of the Bible, the tools used to validate what we hold as sacred are based on what centuries of historical scholarship accepts as valid ways to test for factual evidence.

The two main sets of tools used are known as lower and higher criticism. "Higher Criticism examines the source of the text."[272] The questions asked in higher criticism are those on which we have been focusing: who wrote the original, when was it written, is the content reliable, is

---

[268] Potter, "Problem of History: Is History Knowable?"

[269] Geisler, *Christian Apologetics*, 2nd ed. (Grand Rapids, MI: Baker Academic, 2013), 360.

[270] Ibid., 353, 357–60.

[271] Ibid., 360.

[272] Potter, "Problem of History: Is History Knowable?"

it authentic, and so on.[273] Lower criticism takes a close look at the text itself.[274] The questions asked are what are the available manuscripts that have been used in the reconstruction of the New Testament and what types of attempts have been used in the reconstruction. In the second part of this lesson, we will take a look at the writer's purpose as we study the letters to the Philippians and the letter to the Colossians.

Review:

Tools Used to Study Historical Accuracy

1. Higher criticism examines the source of the text:
   - Nature of evidential Inquiry
   - Integrity of the witnesses
   - Dating of the originals
   - Accuracy of the witnesses
   - Accuracy of the documents
   - Study of secular claims made
   - Study of archeological evidence
2. Lower criticism examines the text itself:
   - Study of the quality of manuscripts that exist
   - Study of the reliability of the manuscripts used to reconstruct the originals

Study Questions: Is History Knowable?

For Review and Reflection

1. What is the first step to identifying true historical elements in a document?

2. On what do the majority of skeptical scholars base their disbelief in the historical reliability of the New Testament documents?

3. What does higher criticism examine? What questions does higher criticism seek to answer?

---

[273] Ibid.

[274] Ibid.

4. What is lower criticism? What does this tool seek to find?

Group Discussion

1. How will a worldview based on evolution affect the way a person thinks about the historicity of the biblical facts?

   a. How will it affect their view of Jesus?

   b. Is this a problem? Why or why not?

2. How will you address this person's naturalistic worldview?

Key Terms

a priori: An innate knowledge of something unseen, such as a behavior or understanding right from wrong.

circular reasoning: The attempt to prove that the Bible is true by using the Bible to validate its own claims.

historiography: A critical examination of how we study the validity of a historical claim to a past event.

moral argument: Defending the reality of absolute Truth based on the fact that if one does not have a basis for the idea of "good," then one can have no sound basis for evil. Evil is the absence of good.

ontological argument: A metaphysical assertion that attempts to prove the existence of God. The basic premise from which it draws is that if one can conceive a perfect being, then that perfect being must exist.

Literature Cited or Recommended

Aquinas, Saint Thomas. *An Introduction to the Metaphysics of St. Thomas Aquinas.* Edited and translated by James F. Anderson. Washington, DC: Regnery, 1997.

Augustine of Hippo. *The City of God.* Translated by Marcus Dods. Peabody, MA: Hendrickson, 2009.

Bonhoeffer, Dietrich. *Dietrich Bonhoeffer Works.* Vol. 5, *Life Together: Prayerbook of the Bible.* Edited by Gerhard Ludwig Müller and Albrecht Schönherr. English edition edited by Geffrey B. Kelly. Translated by Daniel W. Bloesch and James Burtness. Minneapolis: Fortress Press, 2005.

Carter, J. Kameron. *Race: A Theological Account.* New York: Oxford University Press, 2008.

Copan, Paul. *That's Just Your Interpretation: Responding to Skeptics Who Challenge Your Faith.* Grand Rapids, MI: Baker Books, 2001.

Corduan, Winfried. *Handmaid to Theology: An Essay in Philosophical Prolegomena.* 1981 Reprint, Eugene, OR: Wipf & Stock, 2009.

Craig, William Lane. *Reasonable Faith: Christian Truth and Apologetics.* 3rd ed. Wheaton, IL: Crossway, 2008.

Feses, Edward. *Aquinas: Beginner's Guides.* 2009. Reprint, London: OneWorld Publications, 2013.

Geisler, Norman L. *Christian Apologetics.* 2nd ed. Grand Rapids, MI: Baker Academic, 2013.

Gilson, Etienne. *God and Philosophy.* 2nd ed. New Haven, CT: Yale University Press, 2002.

Potter, Doug. "Problem of History: Is History Knowable?" Lecture, Southern Evangelical Seminary, Charlotte, NC, September 2013.

Sweis, Khaldoun A., and Chad V. Meister, eds. *Christian Apologetics: An Anthology of Primary Sources.* Grand Rapids, MI: Zondervan, 2012.

Wilhelmsen, Frederick D. *Man's Knowledge of Reality: An Introduction to Thomistic Epistemology.* Englewood Cliffs, NJ: Prentice-Hall, 1956.

Historical Context
Writer's Purpose

Application of Scripture: Philippians and Colossians

Read Philippians and Colossians.

Every writer has a purpose in mind when putting thoughts to paper or in print. When Paul wrote the Epistles (letters) to the Philippians and to the Colossians, he was writing to the churches that he had helped to establish in these communities. He wrote not only to encourage them but also to remind them of the role of the church in the world. Paul's function was often one of a church planter. Paul would often start a church, and then once it was settled, he would move on to another area, always spreading the gospel. The church in Philippi is thought to be the first church established in Europe by Paul,[275] and it still stands today in ancient Greece.

Philippi was a Roman colony, and it is believed that Paul was in a Roman prison, either in

---

[275] Luke Timothy Johnson, *The Writings of the New Testament*, 3rd ed. (Minneapolis: Fortress Press, 2010), 325.

Rome proper or Caesarea (Acts 24:26–27, 28:30), when he wrote this letter to the Philippian community. Although there are scholars who believe that he may have been in the city of Ephesus given its proximity to Philippi, there is no direct or indirect evidence for this theory. There is, however, credence to the idea that Paul was held as prisoner in Caesarea when he wrote this letter (see Acts 24:27). Caesarea was the capital of the Roman province of Judea. From the book of Acts, we learn that the duration of his imprisonment there was at least two years. This time factor would allow for a few communications to go back and forth from Caesarea to Philippi, and also from Rome, which is actually closer to Philippi. Luke, the author of the book of Acts, tells his readers that Felix, the Roman governor in Caesarea at the time, gave orders to allow Paul liberty and to have access to his friends who came to help him (Acts 24:22–23). This fact indicates that he would have clearly been able to communicate with the outside world, making correspondence possible.

As mentioned in previous lessons, it is imperative that the text be fully understood and that the reader give attention to the context in which the document was written. Such is the case here. Notice that in Philippians 1:7 there is the implication that Paul has already been given a hearing, yet he is still imprisoned (Phil. 1:16). These pieces of information are consistent with the events that took place in Caesarea.[276] The book of Acts clearly mentions that Paul defended the Way, the Gospel of Christ, as he stood before Felix and that he remained in prison even after Felix left his position as governor (Acts 24:20–21). It does not truly matter where Paul was when he wrote to the Philippians, because it does not change the purpose of the letter. One thing we know for certain is that Paul was in prison and was expressing his gratitude for the faithfulness of the church in Philippi for supporting him during his imprisonment. What is also beneficial is that the information about the political official Felix mentioned in the book of Acts is also helpful in dating at least one of Paul's imprisonments.

In antiquity, prisoners were not treated as humanely as they are today. The prisoners had to depend on their friends and family to feed and clothe them while in custody. If they had no support from the outside, they would have little to nothing to eat or wear. Paul's letter is structured around the principle of fellowship. The community of believers is admonished to practice true fellowship, unlike the fellowship that the world practices, where everyone seeks after their own personal interests. Even though Paul was not with the Philippians, they continued to treat him as part of their community as they shared what they had with him. They were truly reflecting the meaning of what the Christian community should look like, as God's community knows no geographical boundaries.

When studying scripture, it is also helpful to look into the deeper meaning of keywords or themes in a passage or group of passages. One casualty of translating any text from one language to another, however, is that some of the deeper meanings are lost. Although the overall import and intention of scripture has been preserved for all future generations, the ancient languages of Hebrew and Greek many times were written with a beauty and elegance that the English language fails to capture. Paul's letter to the Philippians is one such case. This is a letter filled with the "language of friendship." In order to appreciate the force of the intended meaning, one must revert to the letter's original Greek language and contextual significance.

---

[276] Gerald F. Hawthorne, *Word Biblical Commentary*, vol. 43, *Philippians*, ed. David A. Hubbard and Glenn W. Barker (Waco, TX: Word Books, 1983), xl–xli.

Greek moralists were captivated with the topic of friendships. Paul's language, therefore, would naturally be directed toward eliciting a response from his Greek audience.[277] In this society, it was clear that friendship was analogous to fellowship. Living in fellowship meant that the community shared all that was material and spiritual with one another. To be at one spiritually was to see each other as "another self."[278] The language that Paul utilized made much use of the Greek prefix *with* (*syn*) since friendship signified a life of togetherness.

Paul's use of the Greek prefix *with* in this context clearly implied "fellow." When the text is studied in its original Greek form, the prefix is found attached to verbs such as *struggle* (1:27, 4:3), *rejoice* (2:17, 18), *be formed* (3:10), *receive* (4:3), and *share* (4:14).[279] This is a constant theme throughout the letter also found in his choice of many of the nouns used. If the reader correctly translates each occurrence adding *fellow* to the verb or noun, the wording becomes very deliberate and powerful. The full meaning is clear and unmistakable. The intent is to convey a community that is at one spiritually.

To be at one spiritually is to be of the same mind. In other words, to be in spiritual fellowship is to have one mind when it comes to the foundational truths of the Christian faith. Understanding the harsh reality of original sin and our natural inclination to reject the things of God is a fundamental truth that must be understood in any Christian community. When there is no acknowledgment of human depravity, for instance, there cannot be a full comprehension of our desperate need of a Savior. If professing Christians do not accept this fundamental truth, then Christ becomes merely a good example on how to live well, but His death on the cross will mean nothing other than an unfortunate predicament. The danger then would be a dysfunctional community where humanity begins to decide what "good" deeds need to be accomplished to work out one's own salvation, with each new generation setting its own agenda.

As a result, salvation is placed in the hands of *mutable* and *fallible* humanity. This is precisely why God provided a way of redemption that would satisfy His ultimate justice. Paul touches on this theological premise in 2 Corinthians 3. His theology also remains consistent in his letter to the Philippian church as he stresses the reality that salvation does not come through human effort, but through the gift of God in Christ. The community of believers is to thus realize that just as Jesus came to serve all of humanity, a Christian community is to serve each other.

A community in fellowship is a community in which the people sacrificially serve each other. It is a society where there is no self-interest and that puts the priority on the welfare of others, remembering how the Christ humbled Himself for our sake (Phil. 2:6–11). It is a population whose members live with a humble heart, as did Jesus (2:3). This is a way of life that was then (and remains to this day) completely antithetical to the way the rest of the world lives. This is an impossible lifestyle that can only be achieved when one is living and operating within the will of God through Christ (2:5). Paul continually exhorts the church at Philippi that the Christian community should be one where all live to imitate Christ and should exhibit a self-sacrificing love for other believers.

This message would have been very striking for these new Christians as the political leaders of the day were scheming to kill each other to gain control of the coveted seats of power in the

---

[277] Johnson, *The Writings of the New Testament*, 328.

[278] Ibid.

[279] Ibid.

Roman Empire. History records that the emperor Nero even had his own mother murdered in AD 59.[280] Christian living should continue to be lived out in stark contrast to the way the *secular* realm naturally lives. Paul even goes so far as to use himself as an example of one who is willing to cast off all titles and prestige given to him through the recognition of fellow humans. Chapter 3 of Philippians is, for all intents and purposes, Paul's highly impressive résumé. He could easily boast about his accomplishments as a Jewish religious leader, but he has chosen to shed all that is of value in the eyes of humanity and instead clothe himself in the humility of Christ. Paul teaches his audience that the better way is the way of the cross.

Do you seek the approval of humanity before you seek God's approval? If so how? What steps can you take to give that idol over to God?

_____

_____

_____

The way of the cross will be far more rewarding than the fleeting recognitions of this world. As you read the letter to the Colossians, notice that Paul continues to encourage the hearers to grow in their knowledge of God through Christ. Colossae was a city situated in the Roman province of Asia. In Paul's day, the city of Colossae was not as significant to commerce as it had been prior to Roman control. Even so, it was still a vital community, and God chose to look upon the Colossian community with favor and plant a church that would bring the hope of Christ in their midst. There may be more than two millennia between Paul's teachings to the early church and the church of the twenty-first century, but the message remains the same, as do the dangers.

The church at Colossae had never met Paul face-to-face, but he knew all too well the challenges that that community was up against. Colossae was known for its captivated interest in the mystical and magical.

Whom does Paul address as a fellow servant in the first chapter of Colossians?

_____

Tradition tells us that Epaphras is the one who founded the church in Colossae. He was also imprisoned with Paul for his faith in Christ. Just as in all of Paul's correspondence with the churches, he uses language that the hearers will understand. In chapter 2, he writes about the mystery of God found only in Christ. He also encourages them not to be taken captive by the philosophies and traditions that are based on human thinking.

What does he beseech the Colossians to do in chapter 2?

_____

_____

_____

---

[280] Merrill C. Tenney and Steven Barabas, eds., *The Zondervan Pictorial Encyclopedia of the Bible* (Grand Rapids, MI: Zondervan, 1977), 4:410–11.

What would be the danger to these new Gentile Christians if their leader were no longer on-site to guide them?

_____

_____

If your response to the question above was syncretism, which is the blending of the ideologies and philosophies of the world mixed with the purity of Christ, then you are correct. Only the Christian message brings true hope to all people. The philosophies of humankind are always based on works and deeds. The problem is that there is never a standard or a final goal that can realistically ever be achieved. It is known that there were ideologies that indicate that there were *Gnostic* influences in this community. These teachings suggest that Jesus's humanity was an illusion and that He did not truly come in the flesh. This belief would render the crucifixion insufficient for atonement and salvation.

Without the sufficiency of Christ, people will be tempted to create their own benchmarks to spiritual achievements. Once there are new rules and hoops to jump through, the claim to spiritual superiority is sure to follow. This mentality is naturally divisive and will always negate the harmony within a community. The people at Colossae would have been an easy target for false teachings of salvation without proper direction. It is important to remember that these new believers were polytheists before they were introduced to the Hebrew God. Without the direction of their pastor, it would have been very easy for them to be convinced by other Jewish sects that they needed to add to what Christ had already done for them or, for that matter, that they did not need to do anything differently in their lives since Christ had come and mastered it all for them. This is commonly referred to as "cheap grace."

Paul shows his deep concern for the people of the Colossian church by the language that he chooses to use. Throughout chapter 2 Paul makes use of monetary metaphors to get his point across to the recipients of the letter. According to some biblical scholars, the term used for treasures (Col. 2:3) was not a common word used by Paul, nor is the phrase used in the Hebrew scriptures. It is believed that Paul specifically uses this terminology because it is the term that the Gnostics used frequently.[281] By using a term that the opposition used, Paul could redirect the church at Colossae to focus on the treasure of wisdom that can only be found through the knowledge of Christ. Furthermore, his purpose was to point out that God's knowledge is in no way "secret."

Paul's intent was always to draw people's attention to the one true God. True wealth comes directly from the knowledge and wisdom of God. The idea that one could become spiritually mature through human accomplishments was then and remains today an illusion. These ideas were the hollow philosophies designed and brought about by humans, as opposed to seeking after and getting to know the true Source of all wisdom. Paul consistently pointed to the living God as the absolute Source of all wisdom and power in the universe. There is no question that Paul was guided by the Holy Spirit and that these truths have been preserved for all who seek and profess the Christian way of life. We too should point others to the wealth that lies in the knowledge of God through Christ.

It seems that Paul spends more time in prison than out of prison during his ministry. The

---

[281] Peter T. O'Brien, *Word Biblical Commentary*, vol. 44, *Colossians, Philemon*, ed. David A. Hubbard and Glenn W. Barker (Waco, TX: Word Books, 1982), 95–97.

letters to the churches in Philippi and Colossae are certainly good indicators of the consequences for standing for God's Word in a pluralistic society.

Paul could easily complain about his circumstances, but instead what does he do? (Phil. 1:12–18)

_____

_____

What reasons does he give for his attitude?

_____

_____

Paul talks about living a blameless life, but how is this achieved? Not only in these Epistles, but also in other writings of Paul, he frequently tells the readers and hearers the importance of being filled with the Holy Spirit. This is a state that can only be achieved through the work of God and the intentional and unrelenting quest for God's direction (1 Thess. 5:17–22). Scripture tells us that we cannot even come to God unless He calls us to Himself (John 6:44).

Many times in life it is natural for us to feel left out or depressed because we feel that no one loves or cares about us. Rest assured, however, if you are reading this material and taking it seriously, that God is calling you to Himself. Otherwise, you would have absolutely no desire to turn to Him. We should always take this invitation seriously and take the opportunity to seek His face. You will find that by seeking the face of God through the study of His Word, you will begin living a life that desires nothing more than to please Him. The apostle Paul was well aware of the beauty and peace that comes only from a true love and reverence for God. That is why he was able to continue on in ministry, spreading the Gospel regardless of the severe persecution that he received.

Although the tools used for the study of the historical validation of the New Testament documents have been proven to be objective and accurate, it is imperative to keep in mind that the Bible is more than a historical document. The Bible is also a theological book as it claims to be *the* Word of God. The implications of this can be overwhelming. The consequence of this claim is that not only should the text be historically accurate, but also it must be theologically sound. It is possible to have all of the historical facts validated, yet end up with a book that is theologically obscure and ambiguous. Throughout the Bible, however, we find an astounding consistency in the nature of the Creator.

While seeking to validate the veracity and authority of the Bible's New Testament documents, we need to test for the continuity of the entire text and make certain that the way God is represented is consistent and coherent throughout. Part of that test is to study the meaning of the words used in their original Greek, found in the New Testament documents. As mentioned above, Paul is intentional when choosing his written words to the people in Philippi and Colossae (as he is also in his other letters). Furthermore, not one of the authors of the New Testament ever distorts the image of God. They are all describing the same immutable ultimate Being in their writings to the various people groups with whom they are engaging.

Every single author of the New Testament is writing in a unique context in their own style of writing, yet the message remains the same, as does the character of God. It is greatly beneficial (but not necessary) to the reader to know the deeper meaning of the original language in order to grasp the passion with which the writer speaks to his or her audience. These accurate translations are also helpful clues for the modern-day reader as they strive to maintain the intended meaning of the Gospel message. The coherence between the various portions of the New Testament stands as evidence to the theological reliability and soundness of the scriptures.

Review:
Study Questions: Is History Knowable?

For Reflection and Theological Focus

1. Paul was frequently persecuted for spreading the Gospel of absolute truth. Can you share with your group a time when you were persecuted for standing for God's truth? Have you ever had the opportunity to explain to others why Jesus is the only way to heaven? If so what happened?

2. In Philippians 1:21, what does Paul mean by this statement?

3. In Philippians 2:12, Paul tells us to work out our salvation with fear and trembling. What does he mean by this? Reread this verse and pay attention to the entire passage. Why should Christians be fearful, especially since Jesus was always telling His disciples not to fear? Hint: read Luke 6:46–49 and Matthew 7:15–27.

   a. Are you convicted to change any of your ways after reading these passages? If so, record what you will do differently starting today, and date this entry.

4. Read Colossians 3:1–17. What is Paul asking people to do? Why would he ask these things?

5. Read Jerimiah 3. After reading this chapter, focus on the last verses, 11–24. What is God calling His people to do?

a. As Christians we have been grafted into the family of Israel. When God sent His Son to show all of humanity the way to return to Him, this was a call for us to repent. When you read this passage, what do you see as the tone that God uses through the scribe?

b. Can you sense the love God has for those He calls to Himself?

c. What are you doing today that is a response to this call?

Group Discussion

1. When you understand the original meaning of the language used in these scripture passages as described in this lesson, do you believe that the character of God is changed from what you find in other parts of the Bible?

   a. Explain your response, and give an example.

2. Do you see the importance of a theological consistency throughout scripture?

   a. Why is coherence so important when discussing the nature and character of God?

   b. Is it important that the Old Testament depict the same characteristics of God as found in the New Testament? Why?

   c. Have you ever been exposed to a religion where the character of God changes? Please give an example, and discuss this with your group.

3. Explain to your group how the translation of the "fellowship language" that Paul uses to the Philippians helped you better understand the passion with which he conveys the Gospel message to the people of Asia Minor.

     a. Do you see a similarity between his message and those of the other authors of the New Testament? Give some examples.

4.   The next time you have the opportunity to have a conversation with a skeptical friend, how will you use this information to defend the historical and theological reliability of the scriptures?

Key Terms

fallible. Not perfect. Having the tendency to make mistakes.

Gnostic. A word derived from the Greek word *gnosis*, which means "knowledge." Here, it connotes the idea of obtaining a "secret" form of knowledge through certain rituals and asceticisms. The heresy in Gnosticism was that its adherents professed that Jesus was not sufficient for salvation, but that He was a starting point to gaining the secret knowledge needed for true salvation.

mutable. Having the tendency to constantly change. People are constantly changing their minds. They are fickle, unlike God, who is immutable and does not change.

secular. Referring to the world. When referred to in the current context, it is meant to convey the ways and mind-set of the world outside the Christian community and biblical worldview.

God's Attributes

communicable – God is the source of all community. God represents community and has always desired to commune with His creation and for His creation to commune with each other.

gracious – He is a God of grace. He came in the form of a human so that we might begin to understand His desires for our lives. Then He humbled himself at our feet (John 13) so that we would begin to realize the depth of our own depraved nature.

immutable – God does not change. He is consistent in His promises and His requirements.

merciful – God is the source of all mercy. He has shown us mercy in the way that He continues to work out our redemption in His plan for humanity.

Literature Cited or Recommended

Evans, Craig A. *Jesus and His World: The Archeological Evidence.* Louisville, KY: Westminster John Knox Press, 2012.

Goldsworthy, Graeme. *According to Plan: The Unfolding Revelation of God in the Bible—an Introductory Biblical Theology.* Downers Grove, IL: InterVarsity, 1991.

Hawthorne, Gerald F. *Word Biblical Commentary*, vol. 43, *Philippians.* Edited by David A. Hubbard and Glenn W. Barker. Waco, TX: Word Books, 1983.

Johnson, Luke Timothy. *The Writings of the New Testament.* 3rd ed. Minneapolis: Fortress Press, 2010.

Motyer, Alec. *Look to the Rock: An Old Testament Background to Our Understanding of Christ.* Grand Rapids, MI: Kregel, 1996.

O'Brien, Peter T. *Word Biblical Commentary*, vol. 44, *Colossians, Philemon.* Edited by David A. Hubbard and Glenn W. Barker. Waco, TX: Word Books, 1982.

Tenney, Merrill C., and Steven Barabas, eds. *The Zondervan Pictorial Encyclopedia of the Bible.* Grand Rapids, MI: Zondervan, 1977.

Torrance, James B. *Worship, Community, and the Triune God of Grace.* Downers Grove, IL: InterVarsity Press, 1996.

Tozer, A. W. *The Attributes of God.* Vol. 1, *A Journey into the Father's Heart*—with Study Guide. Camp Hill, PA: Wing Spread Publishers, 2003.

CHAPTER 7

Higher Criticism: External Criteria Used to Validate Documents

External Source Validation

We will now continue with our intended purpose of making a defense for the historical reliability of the New Testament. The next two chapters will conclude our study of the higher criticism used to defend the historical reliability of the New Testament. Our focus will now shift from the internal evidence to the external evidence found to support the historicity of the New Testament documents. There are two external evidence categories we will place under investigation. First, we will examine the outside sources available that mention Jesus or the events that surrounded Jesus and His mission. Second, we will discuss a few of the archeological evidences that support the claims made in scripture.

It is very possible that if you are an active disciple for Christ, you may have been told that the Jesus found in the Bible was not a real person. It is difficult to believe that with all of the evidence available to modern human beings someone would actually deny Jesus's existence as a human being. This is a critical chapter for you to understand because it will help you make a clear and rational defense for the person of Jesus with indisputable evidence. The previous six chapters have provided you with a solid toolkit from which to draw when you are explaining to others why the New Testament is a reliable document based on *internal* evidence. As you recall, internal evidences are the factors that substantiate the historical reliability of the manuscripts based on the following data:

1. Integrity of the witnesses (the writers)
2. Dating of the original autographs and manuscripts
3. Accuracy of the witnesses (the writers)
4. Accuracy of the documents

Some skeptics may still want more evidence for the historicity of the man Jesus and His legacy that has been left for us. Fortunately, we are able to provide answers from historical material that resides outside of the New Testament. There is an abundance of secular and antagonistic historical evidence that verifies not only the existence of Jesus but also the turmoil and events that surrounded the last days of His life on earth. There are three main categories in which these substantiations will be explained:

1. Rabbinic writings
2. Roman historical sources
3. Extrabiblical traditions

We will begin by exploring the rabbinic writings that have been discovered, and then we will discuss the other two collections of material.

External Sources

Rabbinical Writings

It is a well-known fact that the rabbis of the first and second centuries did not concede to Jesus's divinity. They did, however, leave evidence in the form of writings that verify the fact that there was a man named Jesus who came from Nazareth. The mere point that they did not believe that Jesus was the long-awaited Messiah caused the religious leaders of the first and second centuries to write prolifically. Their writings were meant to ensure that future generations of Jews would not begin to believe that what they might hear about a man named *Yeshu* (Jesus) and His divinity was true in any way, shape, or form. There are three well-known Jewish sources that stem from the first five centuries where we find the person of Jesus and the events surrounding His life mentioned: the *Mishna*, the *Gemara*, and the *Talmud*.

The Mishna is a compiled code of law, mentioned in the New Testament as "the tradition of the elders"[282] (Mark 7:3). The compilation and organization of the Mishna was finalized around AD 200.[283] It was natural that the Jewish religious leaders would study this law, and eventually a series of commentaries began to be written to explain the laws.[284] These commentaries would eventually be used in rabbinical schools in Babylonia and Palestine.[285] The commentaries are known as the *Gemara*. This is much the same as the commentaries written to help people better understand the Judeo-Christian Bible.

The Gemara and the Mishna together are referred to as the Talmud.[286] There are two Talmuds that arose out of the different rabbinical schools in Palestine and Babylonia. The *Jewish Talmud* is the compilation of the Mishna and the Gemara that were produced in the Palestinian schools. It was finalized around AD 300.[287] The *Babylonian Talmud*, on the other hand, continued to be added to until its finalization in AD 500.[288] It is in these Talmuds where we find affirmation of the existence of a man from Nazareth named Yeshu in Jewish historical records.

---

[282] F. F. Bruce, *The New Testament Documents: Are They Reliable?* 6th ed. (Downers Grove, IL: InterVarsity Press, 1981), 102–3.

[283] Ibid.

[284] Ibid., 103.

[285] Ibid.

[286] Ibid.

[287] Ibid.

[288] Ibid.

Not surprisingly, the mentions of Jesus are negative in nature. Fortunately, it does not matter whether the mention of Jesus is positive or negative, because the very mention of His person affirms His existence. The ways in which Jesus is mentioned are intended to be derogatory for the reasons mentioned previously. The earlier rabbis spoke of Jesus as the following:

1. A transgressor
2. A sorcerer
3. A scorner of wisdom
4. A deceiver
5. A distorter of the Law
6. One who was hanged as a heretic[289]

> On the eve of Passover they hanged Yeshu (of Nazareth) and the herald went before him for forty days saying (Yeshu of Nazareth) is going to be stoned in that he hath practiced sorcery and beguiled and led astray Israel. Let everyone knowing aught in his defense come and plead for him. But they found naught in his defense and hanged him on the eve of Passover. (Sanhedrin 43a, "Eve of Passover")

Although our main focus is on the person of Jesus of Nazareth, it is very helpful that the Talmud's early writers also mention five of the disciples by name. The disciples are credited for healing people in the name of Jesus.[290]

It should be clear from the excerpt in the foregoing text box that there are serious discrepancies in the rabbinic writings and the documentation found in scripture. The historian can, nonetheless, surmise that whatever really did happen, there was a man named Yeshu (Aramaic for Jesus) who caused a great stir. He caused enough of a commotion that the religious leaders accused Him of committing heinous crimes that were strictly forbidden by the *Law of Moses* (the first five books of the Bible). Sorcery, for one, is strictly forbidden by God (Deut. 18:10–14). Nevertheless, the mention of the fact that Jesus was crucified (hanged on a tree) serves as a testament to the event itself.

The fact that we have documented Jewish sources from the turn of the third and fourth centuries that mention the person of Jesus is highly validating of the Christian records. It is a perfect example of how God can and will turn evil attempts at distorting His work into works that end up glorifying His name. Scripture is replete with examples of how God will turn humankind's evil into God's glory (Gen. 50:20). It is a well-known fact from scripture that the religious leaders of the first century did everything in their power to discredit God's redemptive work through the Christ:

1. The religious leaders plotted to kill Jesus because many were beginning to believe in Him (John 11:45–51).
2. During His (illegal) midnight trial, the religious leaders sought out false witnesses against Him (Matt. 26:59–60).

---

[289] Ibid.
[290] Ibid.

3. It was the religious leaders who paid off the Roman guards when Jesus's body had vanished (Matt. 28:11–15).

4. Gamaliel speaks up at the council meeting of religious leaders to warn them of their actions (Acts 5:34–40).

However, all of their attempts at distorting the name and person of the Christ has only served to validate the claims found in scripture: that Jesus was indeed a historical person.

Roman Historical Sources

Jesus is not only mentioned in the Jewish rabbinic writings, but he is also written about in Roman history. What is found in the historical documentation of the man Jesus and His exploits in Roman historical writings is more extensive and earlier than what we have of the rabbinic writings. One such Roman historian was Flavius Josephus, who was born sometime around AD 37 or 38. Josephus was a Jew by birth, the son of a Jewish priest and an aristocratic mother.[291] He began his career as a Pharisee and eventually found himself in Rome on business (AD 63) to have a few fellow Jewish priests released from Roman charge.[292]

The high-handed rule of the Roman government over the Jews in Jerusalem eventually precipitated the Jewish War of AD 66.[293] Josephus was sent to Galilee to defend the stronghold at Jotapata, where he was appointed as a commander of the Jewish army.[294] Perhaps because he knew the power of the Roman forces given his recent journey to Rome, in fear he deserted his post when there seemed to be no other way out.[295] After his escape, he was eventually captured by Vespasian, a Roman general at that time (AD 67).[296] After his capture, Josephus was made to act as interpreter for the Roman army. His job was to try to convince the Jews to surrender their stronghold in Jerusalem.[297]

Needless to say, after Jerusalem was officially captured by the Romans and the war ended, Josephus found himself in a very difficult position. The Romans were suspicious of him, and many of his Jewish countrymen hated him, so where would he go to escape ridicule?[298] He decided to return to Rome with Titus, the emperor Vespasian's son, where he was shown "great favor."[299] He became a Roman citizen and developed into one of the greatest historians in first-century Rome.[300] At the encouragement of Titus, he wrote about the discord and eventual war between the Jews and the Roman Empire that spanned a period of 243 years (170 BC – AD 73).[301]

The leaders of Rome intended this famous seven-volume work, entitled *The Jewish War*,

---

[291] Merrill C. Tenney, ed., *The Zondervan Pictorial Encyclopedia of the Bible in Five Volumes—Vol. 3, H–L* (Grand Rapids, MI: Zondervan, 1977), 696.

[292] Ibid.

[293] Ibid.

[294] Bruce, *The New Testament Documents*, 105.

[295] Ibid.

[296] Tenney, ed., *The Zondervan Pictorial Encyclopedia of the Bible in Five Volumes—Vol. 3, H–L*, 697.

[297] Ibid.

[298] Ibid.

[299] Ibid.

[300] Ibid.

[301] Bruce, *The New Testament Documents: Are They Reliable?*, 105.

as a deterrent to others who might consider rising up against the empire.[302] Josephus's twenty-volume work, *Antiquities of the Jews*, is one of the most valued resources for the history of the Jews between 100 BC and AD 100. It is in this work that Josephus's research and documentation provides invaluable material about the land, Jewish customs, the trials and tribulations of the Jewish people, the politics within the Jewish nation, and the outside forces of Imperial Rome and their effects on the Jews. His works have served as highly valued resources not only for secular historical scholars but also for biblical historical scholars. New Testament students will find many of the individuals mentioned in scripture also mentioned in the historical chronicles of Josephus's work (see table 7.1.1).

TABLE 7.1.1. Historical people mentioned in the works of Josephus

Historical Individual	Antiquities	War	New Testament
Gamaliel	xviii.l	ii.8	Acts 5:37
The famine and Claudius	xx.2.5		Acts 11:28
Death of Herod Agrippa I	xix.8.2		Acts 12:19-23
John the Baptizer	xviii.5.2		Mark 1:4
Annas the Priest/Jesus/James (Jesus' brother)	xx.9.1		Luke 3:2 John 18:12-24 Acts 4:6
Jesus	xviii.33		New Testament

The fact that Josephus was Jewish by birth and then became a Roman citizen and a historian gave him a unique insight into both worlds. His writings help us understand what it was like to live as a Jew under Roman rule in the first century. The information that we can gather from his attention to detail is helpful in understanding not only the tension that existed between the ruling religious parties but also the friction between the Jews and the Roman Empire. Josephus acts as a bridge between the secular, pluralistic mind-set of Rome and the Jewish religious leaders. Moreover, the fact that Josephus recorded the discord happening within the Jewish camp as a result of those who insisted on following a man named Yeshu (who claimed to be the long-awaited Jewish Messiah) serves as an invaluable testament to the historical events and existence of Jesus of Nazareth.

It is very helpful and validating to history that the writings of Josephus are recorded from a vantage point that is vastly different from the New Testament accounts. Josephus records events and mentions Jesus from an outsider's point of view, which is exactly what Josephus had. The mere fact that he mentions the people and the events that coincide with the episodes and individuals found in scripture is affirming. It is very clear from the different perspective that he had to offer that there was no collusion going on. Aside from Josephus, there are several other writers who not only were familiar with the Christian movement but also were very hostile toward it.

The Gentile writers were quite perplexed and irritated by this strange sect of Jews who were causing a stir and unrest in the Jewish communities because they followed a crucified man named

---

[302] Tenney, ed., *The Zondervan Pictorial Encyclopedia of the Bible in Five Volumes—Vol. 3, H–L*, 697.

Jesus who was from Nazareth. What may have also been more of a threat to the peace of the nation was the fact that this *Jewish* movement was beginning to draw large crowds of Gentiles to it. Those drawn into these communities that followed the Way of the Christ would begin to question their allegiance to the Roman emperor and to Rome. The *Way* was the term used to identify the early followers of Jesus, as they were seen as mimicking His ways (Acts 9:2). There is very little, if any, reference to the life of Jesus in the historical records from the Gentile writers. This fact should come as no surprise since the Roman Empire had no interest in the life of the Jews.

The Jews were expected to handle their own religious affairs, therefore, the Gentile world had very little understanding of the God of Israel. Historical records reveal many clues, nonetheless, that the events surrounding Jesus's crucifixion and the movement that ensued were indeed historical in nature. Some references to the Christ and the Way are found in the rebuttals of the early church fathers as they defended the Christian faith and its doctrines. Other sources from Roman historical records document an antagonistic view and hatred toward those involved in this new movement. One of the earliest writings from a Roman historical source was written around AD 52, only twenty years after the Crucifixion.

Thallus is the earliest Gentile historical writer that we notice in connection with the Way. He wrote a history of Greece and its association with Asia around AD 52. There is also a record of the writings of an imprisoned man known only as Mara Bar-Serapion, who wrote to encourage his son sometime after AD 73.[303] His letter now resides in the British Museum.[304] Serapion rhetorically asks his son, "What advantage did the Jews gain from executing their wise King? It was just after that their kingdom was abolished."[305] There was no one else who ever fit that description for the Jews other than Jesus.

> But Saul, still breathing threats and murder against the disciples of the Lord, went to the high priest and asked him for letters to the synagogues at Damascus, so that if he found any belonging to the Way, men or women, he might bring them bound to Jerusalem. (Acts 9:1–2 ESV)

We also have records of a Roman historian by the name of Cornelius Tacitus (born AD 52/54), who is considered to be the "greatest Roman historian in the days of the Empire."[306] He was the son-in-law of the governor of Britain Julius Agricola (80–84).[307] This placed him in the unique position of having access to official historical documents.[308] Tacitus's focus was on the history of Rome under the headship of its emperors.[309] Tacitus verifies the crucifixion of Christ and the existence of Pontius Pilate, as well as Pilate's position within the Roman Empire as a government official (Luke 3:1; John 18:28).

All of the foregoing are very important historical details that distinctly match up with the New Testament manuscripts. Interestingly enough, Tacitus is the only Roman historian from antiquity to mention Pilate in his records. Outside of the records written by Tacitus, the only

---

[303] Bruce, *The New Testament Documents*, 116.

[304] Norman L. Geisler, *Christian Apologetics* (Grand Rapids, MI: Baker Academic, 2013), 360–62.

[305] Ibid.

[306] Bruce, *The New Testament Documents*, 120.

[307] Ibid.

[308] Ibid., 121.

[309] Ibid., 120.

other mentions of Pilate are from either Jewish or Christian sources.[310] Another Roman historian of note is Gaius Suetonius Tranquillus, commonly known simply as Suetonius (AD 69–130 or 140). He, like Tacitus, documents the fires in Rome during the reign of Nero and mentions his torturous treatment of those who followed this man Chrestus.[311] Chrestus is believed by historians to be either a variant spelling or a misspelling of the Latin Christus (Christ).[312] Christus was the Greek translation of the Aramaic or Hebrew term used for the Messiah.[313]

As previously mentioned, Chrestus is once again mentioned by Suetonius, who wrote about five years after Tacitus (AD 120).[314] This is important to note because it testifies to the prevalence of the Christian movement in the first and second centuries. Suetonius mentions that the Jews were expelled from Rome in the days of Claudius (*Claudius* 25.4). His documentation asserts that this Chrestus was the cause of rioting,[315] hence disturbing the peace. This is a very telling piece of information, as Luke mentions a couple known as Aquila and Pricilla who were part of the population expelled by Claudius (Acts 18:1–2). It is highly likely that the rioting was caused by the non-Christian Jews[316] who found this new Jewish movement to be blasphemous and an insult to their beliefs.

Historical records also reveal a letter dated in AD 112 from the governor of Bithynia in Asia Minor, C. Plinius Secundus (Pliny the Younger), that was written to the emperor Trajan that mentions Christians.[317] He was requesting advice on how to contend with this group of people who refused to worship the image of Caesar (*Letters* 10.96.7).[318] The implications of this letter are indeed obvious. The mere fact that the first-century and early second-century church was reluctant to bow down to the Roman emperor even in the face of death reveals the state of understanding and respect that the church had for the God of Israel. What seemed to be pure disrespect from the Christians was the fact that they were worshipping a mere mortal (as the Roman officials understood Jesus to be) in the place of the god-ordained image of Caesar.[319]

Historians also learn much about cultures and civilizations of the past by studying the arts and literature produced in that time period. The Christian movement was making such a stir that it is not surprising to find mention of those who followed Jesus in the writings of Lucian of Samostata. Lucian was a Greek satirist from the second century who was known to ridicule Christ followers for worshipping a mortal who was crucified as a criminal.[320] In his satires of the Christians, he also references Jesus as a "sage" (*Death of Peregrine* 11–15).[321] It is completely understandable that a Greek

---

[310] Ibid.

[311] Ibid., 122.

[312] Craig L. Blomberg, *The Historical Reliability of the Gospels*, 2nd ed. (Downers Grove, IL: InterVarsity Press, 2007), 250.

[313] Bruce, *The New Testament Documents*, 121.

[314] Blomberg, *The Historical Reliability of the Gospels*, 250.

[315] Ibid.

[316] Ibid., 122.

[317] Ibid.

[318] Ibid., 249.

[319] Emperor worship had been a cultural custom long before the first century and was well embedded in the Roman Empire. It was believed that the emperor was chosen and ordained by the Roman gods to protect and lead the people. Those who lived in the provinces that belonged to Rome were expected to pay homage to the emperor as if he were a god because he was in charge of their well-being.

[320] Blomberg, *The Historical Reliability of the Gospels*, 250.

[321] Ibid.

Gentile would have such disrespect for God's Messiah since most Gentiles did not understand the God of Israel. It seemed to the outside world that this group of common people were simply a superstitious lot of uneducated troublemakers.[322] In spite of the scorn Jesus's followers received at the hands of Lucian, Lucian's works have only helped to verify the existence of Jesus and the impact that His teachings had on those who faithfully followed Him.

Extrabiblical Traditions

Testimony of the Church Fathers

The writings of the early church fathers are highly significant and historically valuable to the Christian tradition. These church fathers were men who were either direct disciples of the apostles or students of those who knew the apostles. They did not simply represent the general populace, but they were authorized individuals who were trained to teach the Jesus traditions that were formally passed down from Jesus's direct disciples.[323] Critics of the Christian faith have a tendency to try to discredit the writings from antiquity when the matter pertains to the historical integrity of the documents in existence. The accusations stem from the modern-day ideas of how legends were formed. It would be a grave mistake, however, to compare the modern individualists of today with the early writers of the Christian tradition. As mentioned in chapter 4 of this study, the *chain of succession* was taken very seriously, and those who referenced scripture were very careful not to interject their personal opinions into the facts about the Christ.[324]

Two of the best-known first-century writers were disciples of John (the *Beloved* Disciple). Papias (AD 70–163) was one of these earlier writers in the line of first- and second-century Christ followers who became known as the *church fathers*. Papias's letters to others in the Christian community clearly addressed the importance of gathering information directly from eyewitnesses as opposed to hearsay. He was also a friend of Polycarp (AD 69–155), another disciple of John's.

Scholars believe that Polycarp's notes were taken sometime around the eighties AD[325] and that his more formal writings were written shortly thereafter (AD 98–117). Many of the first Christian disciples were martyred for their faith in Christ. Such was the case with Polycarp, as he was ultimately martyred in Turkey around AD 155. Additionally, in the annals of history, we have the writings of the *Bishop Clement of Rome*, who is believed by some scholars not only to have seen but also to have heard both Peter and the apostle Paul.[326] Clement's writings cite both the Old and the New Testaments and were written sometime between AD 80 and 140. These early citings make it clear that the New Testament manuscripts were already heavily circulated throughout the various Christian communities at a very early date.

Another noted church father was known as Ignatius of Antioch. Ignatius was also a student

---

[322] There is a great similarity between how Christians were viewed then and how they are viewed in the pluralistic cultures of the Westernized world today.

[323] Richard Bauckham, *Jesus and the Eyewitnesses: The Gospels as Eyewitness Testimony* (Grand Rapids, MI: Wm. B. Eerdmans, 2006), 297.

[324] Ibid., 296–97.

[325] Ibid., 14, 293–95.

[326] Welborn, "On the internal evidence for the dating of 1 Clement," *Anchor Bible Dictionary—Vol. 1*, 1060, accessed October 19, 2016, http://www.earlychristianwritings.com/1clement.html.

of John's; he was a well-known writer of Christian literature and was eventually martyred for his devotion to Christ somewhere around AD 98–117. Much like their first-century counterparts, those individuals who began to write during the early part of the second century continued to be persecuted under Roman rule. One such disciple was known as Justin Martyr. He is one of the more well-noted Christian writers of the second century. He stood firm as a Christian apologist and wrote a treatise known as *Against All Heresies* that was addressed to the emperor Antoninus Pius. Martyr's writings reveal that there were numerous heresies circulating about Christianity, and his goal was to make clear to the world what the Christian faith was truly all about.

Martyr directly quoted scripture to give a defense for the faith; he did not depend on hearsay or loose interpretations of the Word. Irenaeus was a contemporary of Martyr's and wrote sometime around AD 180–185. Both Martyr and Irenaeus were faithful to the teachings that had been passed down to them through their mentors and the manuscripts that were written by the early disciples. Irenaeus addressed the seriousness of the succession of *tradition* delivery when he wrote to a man by the name of Florinus. Florinus was interjecting his personal views into the Jesus traditions that had been passed down to him through the disciple Polycarp, who was mentioned earlier (*apud* Eusebius, *Hist. Eccl.* 5.20.4–7).[327]

Other second-century Christian writers were men like Tertullian and Hippolytus, the latter of whom was a disciple of Irenaeus. There was also Eusebius, and then Origen, who was a scholar and a theologian. In AD 177/178, Origen wrote an apologetic response to a Greek Gentile philosopher referred to as Celsus. It is from this work that we gain further insight into how the Greek Gentile population viewed the Christian community (Origen, *Against Celsus* 1.28). From Origen's work one can safely surmise that Jesus was seen as the child of an adulteress who used sorcery to delude His audiences into believing that He could perform miracles.[328] Celsus also charged Jesus with intentionally using His sorcery to draw attention to Himself and claim that He was divine. These accusations leveled against Jesus are the same type of assertions found in the Talmud, which is mentioned above.

Far from discrediting Jesus or the Christian faith, Celsus's writings served to confirm several historical facts about Christianity. For one, he clearly recognized that Jesus was indeed a historical figure and not a fictitious individual, as some were beginning to claim. Secondly, Celsus acknowledged that everyone knew that Mary was expecting her first child prior to her formal marriage to Joseph. Thirdly, he pointed out that Jesus did indeed preform miraculous deeds and did claim divinity. Even though his understanding of the Christ and His mission was distorted, Celsus clearly identified many

> These opinions, Florinus, to say no more, are not of sound judgement; these opinions are not in harmony with the Church, and involve those who adopt them in the greatest impiety; these opinions not even the heretics outside the Church ever dared to espouse openly; these opinions the elders before us, who also were disciples of the apostles, did not hand down to you.
>
> Irenaeus

of the well-known historical facts that surrounded the life and events of the man known as Jesus of Nazareth (His birth, His miracles, and His claim to divinity). This sort of acknowledgment from a hostile source outside the Christian community is priceless for the historicity of the Christian tradition.

---

327 Bauckham, *Jesus and the Eyewitnesses*, 295.
328 Blomberg, *The Historical Reliability of the Gospels*, 250–51.

The writings of the early church fathers have been valuable tools to transmit the basic tenets of the Christian faith and its meaning to generations of individuals. We know from their writings that these men took the duty of transmitting the truth very seriously.[329] It has been stated that even if all of the early Greek manuscripts had somehow been destroyed, we would still have the New Testament intact with all but eleven verses thanks to the prolific writings of the early church fathers (see table 7.1.2 for writings of the early church fathers). The fact that the message of the New Testament has been found intact and historically stable since its inception stands as a great testament to the importance that the Creator has placed on His Living Word. Christians can confidently rely on the Word of God, knowing for certain that it is His testament about Himself and the plight of humanity.

TABLE 7.1.2. Early citations from the New Testament

Author	Gospels	Acts	Paul's Epistles	The general Epistles	The book of Revelation	Total
Justin Martyr 150–155	268	10	43	6	3	330
Irenaeus 130–202	1,038	194	499	23	65	1,819
Clement Alexander 150–215	1,017	44	1,127	207	11	2,406
Tertullian 160–220	3,822	502	2,609	120	205	7,258
Hippolytus 170–235	734	42	387	27	188	1,378
Origen 185–254	9,231	349	7,778	399	165	17,922
Eusebius 325–400?	3,258	211	1,592	88	27	5,176
Grand total	19,368	1,352	14,035	870	664	36,289

Excerpt from *A General Introduction to the Bible* by Norman Geisler and William Nix, copyright © 1983. Used by permission of Moody Press.

Nag Hammadi Library (Mid-Fourth Century)

In addition to the documentation by the early church fathers, we have other external documentation that testifies to the life and events surrounding the Christ. The *Nag Hammadi* writings are generally *Gnostic* literature, but the mere fact that they focus on this man from Nazareth stands as a testimony to His existence. Gnostics tend to believe that all matter is evil, which is certainly not what the scriptures claim (Gen. 1–2). They also suggest that only certain individuals are privileged to receive godly knowledge in secret. These Gnostic teachings eventually had their effects on those Christians who did not have a solid grasp on the truth of the Gospel. Over the ages, Gnostic literature has had a profound effect on the uneducated, which is exhibited in the

[329] Bauckham, *Jesus and the Eyewitnesses*, 292–95.

work of Dan Brown's *The Da Vinci Code*. This is where we can clearly see a work of fiction based on the premise of some sort of secret knowledge (*a code*) that would somehow discredit the divinity of the Christ.

What does scripture say about keeping things "secret" from humanity? Write out Isaiah 45:19.

_____

_____

_____

Christianity has not been the only victim of Gnostic literature. New studies into the source and nature of the Muslim religion are beginning to reveal that those involved in the inception of Islam were heavily influenced by the theological tenets of the Nag Hammadi documents.[330] Although these documents mention Jesus and some of the events that surrounded His ministry, they do not insist that they are based on historical facts.[331] Scholars only recognize four of the Nag Hammadi documents as deliberate attempts to elaborate on the historical record of the Jewish Messiah found in the New Testament.[332]

Four heretical Nag Hammadi documents:

1. Gospel of Thomas
2. Apocryphon of James
3. Gospel of Philip
4. Gospel of Truth

The reason why scholars have taken a serious look at these four specific works is because they resemble some parts of the Gospels and quotations that stem from the writings of some of the early church fathers.

These documents were all originally written in Greek and later translated into other languages. These late second-century works took much of their information directly from the New Testament documents and from citations from the works of the early church fathers[333] who cited the New Testament manuscripts and autographs. Some of these writings take verses directly from the New Testament Gospels (such as the Gospel of Thomas 57, which quotes Matthew 13:24–30) but put their own spin on the material. Although the biblical scholar is clearly aware of the obvious discrepancies, the uneducated individual can easily become swept up by the extra fictitious material and view it as truth. Scripture clearly warns of these things (Mark 4:10–20; Col. 2:8; James 4). Nevertheless, the fact that the writers of these documents were quoting pieces of scripture as well as the writings of the church fathers stands as a testament to the fact that the

---

[330] Islamic theology refuses to acknowledge that Jesus was in actuality divine as well as human. Moreover, the entire Islamic faith system is built on secret knowledge given to Muhammad over the course of several years. Scripture is clear: God does not operate in secret when it comes to matters of the salvation of humanity (Isa. 45:19; Mark 14:46–49).

[331] Blomberg, *The Historical Reliability of the Gospels*, 264.

[332] Ibid.

[333] Ibid.

New Testament documents were not only already complete in form but also circulating all over Asia Minor and Egypt well before the second century.

Other Apocryphal Documents

Apocryphal documents represent a set of fictitious literature designed to fill in the gaps of the New Testament writings. It is a well-known fact that the writers of these works took great liberties in embellishing the historical details based around the life and times of Jesus.[334] The known writings that have been discovered, as of today, were written in the second and third centuries. This collection of works is not used by scholars to find accurate historical data about Jesus and the events surrounding His life and ministry.[335] Historians are aware of these documents because many of the first- through fourth-century "Greek and Latin church fathers" mention several of these writings in their works.[336]

Collections mentioned by church fathers:

1. The Gospel of Peter
2. The Infancy Gospels
3. The Protevangelium of James
4. The Unknown Gospel known simply as "Papyrus Egerton 2"
5. The Secret Gospel of Mark
6. *The Gospel of Judas*

Historical scholars are aware that there are other works that have yet to be discovered since they are mentioned (mostly as heretical works) in the citings of the church fathers. Of the six documents mentioned above, Papyrus Egerton 2 has proved to be a very interesting find for biblical scholars. Papyrus Egerton 2 dates back prior to AD 150 and cites dialogues between Jesus and the Jewish religious leaders that mirror His discussions documented in the Gospel of John.[337] In addition to similar versions of Jesus's dialogue with the Jewish rulers (John 5, 9, 10), there are parallel accounts of Jesus's healings (Mark 1:40–44) and His discussions with His disciples (John 3:2), as well as quotes from the book of Isaiah (29:13). These citations clearly indicate that the author had access to the Gospel manuscripts at an early date.[338] This is further evidence that the Gospels were written early in the life of the church and that the manuscripts were widely distributed very quickly.

The documents known as the Infancy Gospels, which are attributed to Jesus's disciple Thomas, are a bit more fanciful as they attempt to fill in the gap between Jesus's birth and His adulthood. Any student who is in the least bit familiar with the Gospel accounts would readily recognize the embellishments as false narratives of Jesus as a child. The tales in this document pose Jesus as a deceptive and hot-tempered youth who is easily provoked. Unfortunately, as has

---

[334] Ibid., 272.
[335] Ibid.
[336] Ibid.
[337] Ibid., 275.
[338] Ibid.

always been the case, individuals who did not have accurate knowledge of the truth of the Gospels accepted these stories at face value. One example of this misinformation and how it has seeped into other forms of literature can be found in the Islamic tradition. Historians have long believed that Muhammad had most certainly come into contact with various Christian or Christian-like literature and that one of the childhood stories from the Infancy Gospels (2:1–7)[339] made it into the Qur'an as truth (Sura 5.110).

The truth of the Gospel message continues to be occluded by ignorance, just as it has been since the second century. Paul warned of the tendency to remain ignorant of the Word of God and the importance of comprehending its meaning (Acts 17:11–12; Eph. 4:13–15). A modern-day example of this ignorance was witnessed after the discovery of one of the apocryphal gospels, the Gospel of Judas (a portion of the Nag Hammadi documents), which caused a great stir in the West after it was translated and then published in 2006. It so happens that long ago, Irenaeus, one of the early church fathers, testified to this apocryphal work in a document that he wrote around AD 180, where he condemns the Gospel of Judas as a heretical piece of literature.[340]

Irenaeus clearly recognized this Gospel as originating from the Cainite sect of the Gnostics.[341] The Gospel of Judas unashamedly pirated from Christian writings to formulate its own set of theological ideologies.[342] Scholars acknowledge that it is evident that the writer of this Gospel was dependent on Greek philosophy for his claims.[343] It was not difficult for the early church fathers to spot fraudulent material. They knew and respected the line of succession and transmission of the Word, and it was evident to them that the theology of the Gnostic writers was not in line with the character and nature of the God of Israel or His plan of redemption. Read the excerpt below[344] and respond:

> Your god … is within you. Let any one of you who is strong enough among human beings bring out the perfect human and stand before my face. (Gospel of Judas)

Write down why you would be suspicious that this is not the legitimate Word of God:

_____
_____
_____
_____

It is important to remember that none of the early church fathers ever took any of the apocryphal gospels seriously. To the contrary, they saw these documents as heretical literature and called for them to be discarded.[345] It has been said many times over that in order to recognize a fraudulent piece of work, one must familiarize oneself with the original. The apostles knew the

---

[339] Ronald F. Hock, *The Infancy Gospels of James and Thomas*, ed. Robert W. Funk, Ron Cameron, and Karen L. King (United States: Polebridge Press, 1995), 107.
[340] Blomberg, *The Historical Reliability of the Gospels*, 278.
[341] Ibid.
[342] Ibid., 279.
[343] Ibid.
[344] Norman L. Geisler and Ronald M. Brooks, *When Skeptics Ask: A Handbook on Christian Evidences* (Grand Rapids, MI: Baker Books, 2013), 166.
[345] Ibid.

Truth because they walked with Him (Jesus) and learned from Him, and then were later filled with the Holy Spirit as promised (John 14:25–26). The church fathers knew the New Testament because they knew the apostles, and they listened and learned and were also sent the Spirit of Truth. We can trust that the scriptures that we hold today have been tried and tested time and time again and have not come up lacking, even over the ages. If you are searching the scriptures the way that the Bereans did (Acts 17:11), you, too, will be able to spot fraudulent material just as they did. God promises that for all who seek Him in earnest, they will find Him (Deut. 4:29; Matt. 7:7).

Whether the external sources about Jesus that we hold today speak well of Jesus or not, they stand as a testament to the reality that Jesus was indeed an historical figure and that the events surrounding His life did make a great impact on the world. The evidence shows that the inside sources that we have discussed in the previous chapters are most certainly historically accurate.

Based on the numerous known external sources, we can discern the following:

1. The fact that Jesus is recognized as a living human being who walked on the face of the earth.
2. That He did perform miracles
3. That He claimed to be divine

These realities represent highly important evidence when defending the authenticity of God's work through His chosen Messiah. It does not matter that not everyone who wrote about Jesus understood His work of redemption. What matters here is the fact that Jesus is mentioned by many sources very early in the life of the Christian church.

Any individual seeking the historical accuracy of people and events must consider the source of the information to better understand the author's intent. All historical sources will represent some type of motive behind them. The outside sources that we have for the life and events of Jesus of Nazareth represent a variety of motives. The rabbinic writers, for instance, wanted to make sure that their Jewish audiences did not begin to believe that this man named Jesus who came from Nazareth was truly their long-awaited Messiah. The Gentile Roman historical writers reported the facts of that time in history from a political standpoint. As for the extrabiblical material, the historian takes into account not only when the material was written but also who wrote the material. In the case of the early church fathers, for instance, many of these men were disciples of the eyewitness apostles, like John.

Those who were not disciples of the first-century eyewitnesses were the disciples of those who were. Their writings were, for the most part, used in spreading and affirming the Gospel message within local communities. It is a common phenomenon that every movement in each generation will begin to spawn variations of the original as it grows and expands outward from its source. Historians expect this and approach historical documents with this in mind. The fact that the Gnostic documents are based loosely on the Judeo-Christian traditions and Gospels and contain fictitious embellishments should not come as a surprise to anyone.

Although the Gnostic writers attributed their documents to the original disciples, all of their works were written after Jesus's disciples had passed away. This fact alone is one of the many reasons why serious scholars do not take these writings as historical fact. The New Testament

Gospels and writings are comparably far superior to those of the Gnostic authors. When comparing them to the canonical writings, it becomes clear that the Gnostic works are nothing more than second- and third-century fakes.[346] The biblical manuscripts are amazingly cohesive in nature and represent historical accuracy that to this day remains unrivaled for its authority and authenticity, especially when compared to other literary works from antiquity.

The number of non-Christian sources that verify that Jesus truly did exist and the events in His life mentioned in the New Testament proves that these events did indeed occur. Not to mention, they outnumber the sources that verify that the Roman emperor Tiberius Caesar actually existed at the time of Jesus.[347] There are nine known such sources that validate the existence of Caesar. When Christian sources are added, Jesus has the emperor outnumbered "43 to 10."[348] Christians are called to be active in their learning in order to be thoroughly equipped for sharing the good news of Christ in a lost and confused world. The information we have today is so abundant that there is no reason not to be prepared for those difficult questions that demand answers.

Review:

External Sources Used to Validate Scripture

Three categories:

1. Rabbinical writings
   - Talmuds
   - Mishna
2. Roman historical sources (non-Christian)
   - See table 7.1.3. External sources that mention the man Jesus of Nazareth
3. Extrabiblical sources
   - Church fathers
     See below, "Church Fathers"
     Nag Hammadi library
   - Apocryphal writings

Church Fathers

Apostolic Fathers (AD 70–150)
Ante-Nicene Fathers (AD 150–300)
Nicene and Post-Nicene Fathers (AD 300–430)

---

[346] Ibid., 165.
[347] Geisler, *I Don't Have Enough Faith*, 222.
[348] Ibid.

Material Cited

End of first century – 14 books recognized by citation
AD 110 – 19 books recognized by citation
AD 150 – 24 New Testament books recognized by citation
End of second century – 26 New Testament books had been recognized (3 John not included)

TABLE 7.1_3. **External sources that mention the man Jesus of Nazareth**[349]

Source	AD	Existed	Virtuous	Worshipped	Disciples	Teacher	Crucified	Empty tomb	Dis. Resurrection	Spread	Persecution
Thallus	52	X					X*				
Josephus	90–95	X	X	X	X	X	X	X	X	X	
Talmud	70-200	X					X				X
Phlegon	80?	X					X	X	X		
Pliny	112	X		X	X	X		X*		X	X
Trajan	112?	X*		X	X					X	X
Tacitus	115	X			X		X	X*		X	X
Suetonius	117–38	X		X	X			X*		X	X
Hadrian	117–38	X*			X					X	X
Lucian	Second century	X		X	X	X	X				X
Mara Bar-Serapion	First–third century	X	X	X		X	X	X*			
Teledoth Jesu	Fifth century	X						X			

* Implied
Excerpt from Christian Apologetics by Norman L. Geisler, copyright © 1976. Used by permission of Baker Academic, a division of Baker Publishing Group.

Non-Christian sources that were written within one hundred fifty years of the Crucifixion include but are not limited to the following:

- **Thallus** (ca. AD 52), a Samaritan-born historian who attempted to explain away the darkness that occurred as Jesus breathed His last breath from the cross as an eclipse, which would not have been possible because it was a full moon (paschal) when Christ was crucified.[350]

---

[349] Information in table 7.1.3 used by permission. Source: Norman L. Geisler, *Christian Apologetics* (Grand Rapids, MI: Baker Academic, 2013), 263.
[350] Norman L. Geisler, *Christian Apologetics* (Grand Rapids, MI: Baker Academic, 2013), 360–62.

- **Mara Bar-Serapion** (AD 73+), a Gentile who wrote to his son, Serapion, in an effort to encourage him to seek wisdom.[351] He placed Jesus on the same footing as Socrates and Pythagoras, counting them as men who pursued wisdom. Mara Bar-Serapion pointed out to his son that those who killed Socrates, Pythagoras, and the Christ all ended up in highly unfortunate circumstances. He mentions the fact that the Jews ended up losing their land and were dispersed as a people.[352]
- **The Jewish Talmud** (ca. AD 70–200), a collection of Jewish writings and historical references, clearly mentions the Crucifixion or "hanging" of "Yeshu of Nazareth" on the eve of Passover, and there is further reference to Jesus as an illegitimate child and one who was possessed by a demon. The New Testament mentions these very accusations in Mark 3:22 and John 8:41.[353]
- **Cornelius Tacitus** (ca. AD 114), a Roman historian who wrote about the atrocities of Nero and his torture of those who followed the one called Christus.[354] He points out that this Christus was executed by the decree of Pontius Pilate during the reign of Tiberius (*Annals* 15.44).[355]
- **Suetonius** (AD 120), a Roman historian and a contemporary of Tacitus. In his work *The Life of Nero*, he mentions how Nero tortured Christians, who were thought of as superstitious troublemakers (xvi.2).[356] He also recorded the expulsion of the Jews from Rome during the reign of Claudius the emperor between AD 41 and 54 in his work entitled *Life of Claudius* (xxv.4).[357] The expulsion of the Jews is also mentioned in Acts 18:1–2.
- **Pliny the Younger** (ca. AD 112), the governor of Birthynia, wrote about his murderous crusades against those who followed this Christ as King and tortured them to force them to recant their faith in Jesus.[358]

Study Questions: External Criteria Used to Validate Documents

For Review and Reflection

1. Look back at chapter 2 and list the *internal* evidences that historians take into account when validating the truth and reliability of the New Testament manuscripts.

    a. _____

    b. _____

    c. _____

    d. _____

---

[351] Bruce, *The New Testament Documents—Are They Reliable?*, 117.

[352] Ibid.

[353] Geisler, *Christian Apologetics*, 362.

[354] Ibid.

[355] Blomberg, *The Historical Reliability of the Gospels*, 250.

[356] Bruce, *The New Testament Documents—Are They Reliable?*, 122.

[357] Blomberg, *The Historical Reliability of the Gospels*, 250.

[358] Ibid., 105.

2. List the three main categories of outside (external) sources that scholars use to validate the historical authenticity of the New Testament documents.

a. _____

b. _____

c. _____

3. Why are these external sources important to historical scholars?

4. Fill out the following table by documenting where in scripture we find the individuals mentioned in the writings of Josephus:

Historical Individuals Mentioned In Josephus' Works	Scriptural References
The Family of Harrods	
Emperor Augustus	
Emperor Tiberius	
Emperor Claudius	
Emperor Nero	
Governor of Syria: Quirinius	
The Procurators of Judea	
Pilate	
Felix	
Festus	

Group Discussion

1. What are historians looking for when they seek outside sources to validate a historical claim?
2. How does the Talmud distort the events of Jesus's trial? Why do you think this happened?
3. How would you discern the reliability of the Gnostic writings, and why?

Key Terms

apocryphal: A collection of fictitious literature designed to fill in the gaps of the New Testament writings, especially pertaining to the life and events surrounding Jesus.

Babylonian Talmud: The compilation of the Mishna and the Gemara that is larger than the Jewish Talmud and was finally completed in AD 500.

Bishop Clement of Rome: One of the early church fathers who was an officer in the church in Rome. He died sometime around AD 110. Some scholars believe that this is the same Clement who worked alongside Paul as mentioned in Philippians 4:2.

end times: The understanding that after the event of the Christ, human history is in its last days and Christians will increasingly face persecution.

Gemara: A set of commentaries that were written to explain the Mishna.

God-fearers: Those Gentiles who had accepted the God of Israel and had converted to Judaism.

Jewish Talmud: The compilation of the Mishna and the Gemara, which were produced in the Palestinian schools and were completed around AD 300.

Law of Moses: The first five books of the Judeo-Christian Bible, also known as the Pentateuch.

Mishna: The Jewish compiled code of law, mentioned in the New Testament as "the tradition of the elders." The Mishna was finalized sometime around AD 200.

monotheism: The belief that there is only one God.

Talmud: The compilation of the Mishna and the Gemara joined together.

the Way: The name given to the early Christian movement that signified those who had chosen to follow the ways of the Christ.

Yeshu: The name of Jesus in Hebrew/Aramaic.

Literature Cited or Recommended

Bauckham, Richard. *Jesus and the Eyewitnesses: The Gospels as Eyewitness Testimony.* Grand Rapids, MI: Wm. B. Eerdmans, 2006.

Blomberg, Craig L. *The Historical Reliability of the Gospels.* 2nd ed. Downers Grove, IL: InterVarsity Press, 2007.

Bruce, F. F. *The New Testament Documents: Are They Reliable?* 6th ed. Downers Grove, IL: InterVarsity Press, 1981.

Geisler, Norman L. *Christian Apologetics.* Grand Rapids, MI: Baker Academic, 2013.

——— and Ronald M. Brooks. *When Skeptics Ask: A Handbook on Christian Evidences.* Grand Rapids, MI: Baker Books, 2013.

Hock, Ronald F. *The Infancy Gospels of James and Thomas.* Edited by Robert W. Funk, Ron Cameron, and Karen L. King. United States: Polebridge Press, 1995.

Tenney, Merrill C., ed. *The Zondervan Pictorial Encyclopedia of the Bible in Five Volumes—Vol. 3, H–L.* Grand Rapids, MI: Zondervan, 1977.

Welborn. "On the Internal Evidence for the Dating of 1 Clement." *Anchor Bible Dictionary—Vol. 1.* Accessed October 19, 2016. http://www.earlychristianwritings.com/1clement.html.

External Criterion Used to Validate Documents
Is There External Evidence to Validate Information Found in Scripture?

Application of Scripture: 1 and 2 Thessalonians

Read 1 and 2 Thessalonians.

In our quest to affirm the validity of the New Testament, we will now seek to find details within the scriptures and test them against outside historical sources. The goal is to validate places, people, and events with factual evidence from history apart from the New Testament. We want to be able to answer questions like the following:

1. Did Paul really exist?
2. Was there an actual place known as Thessalonica?
3. Were the external threats to the recipients of the letters a reality?
4. What is the trustworthiness of the historical sources from which we are drawing our information?

Validating the Author

The Reality of Paul

Our preliminary question is based on the historical person of our writer, Paul. The book of Acts is so well attested to that, as previously mentioned, men like Sir William M. Ramsay, a noted historian and archeologist, actually came to Christ while using the book of Acts to disprove Christianity. Although the focus of the book of Acts is on the person and works of the Christ, Paul and his eventual missionary journeys are well-documented by Luke. It is evident that Luke knew Paul personally by the language that he uses in the book of Acts. There are so many facts about Paul documented in his own writings as well as in the book of Acts that scholars agree that the works attributed to him had to have been written by him prior to his execution in AD 65. This time frame would place Paul in a first-century historical context, writing and evangelizing less than thirty years after the Crucifixion.

Paul's life was surrounded by people and places that are well-documented in history. For instance, in Acts 9:11 and 21:39 the reader learns that he is a Jew from the city of Tarsus. Historically, Tarsus is a well-documented city within the Roman Empire.[359] Prior to Roman rule, the Seleucid Empire recognized Tarsus as "the nation of the Jews in that city."[360] The Jews

---

[359] William M. Ramsay, *St. Paul the Traveler and Roman Citizen*, ed. Mark Wilson, rev. ed. (Grand Rapids, MI: Kregel, 2001), 36.
[360] Ibid., 37.

lost their "clout," however, in AD 70 when Vespasian revoked the superior status of this "Jewish nation," placing the Jews at the same level as the rest of its inhabitants.[361]

It is important to note that the city of Tarsus carried a form of significance during Paul's lifetime while Paul was evangelizing throughout Macedonia, Europe, and Rome. As a Jewish citizen of Tarsus, he was also considered a citizen of the Roman Empire, a highly coveted status in the first century.[362] These two facts alone about Paul gave him an advantage as a vessel for God's calling on his life. Paul claimed his citizenship when he was arrested and tortured (Acts 16:37–38, 22:22–29, 23:27), and it most likely saved his life at that point. When Paul spoke to his audience in Philippi, he made sure to mention that his heritage was that of a Jew (Phil. 3:15) because it was important that he remind them of his Jewish status. It is evident that Paul needed to use his status as both a born Jew and a Roman citizen to validate his credentials as well as his legal rights.

In the Acts of the Apostles there are several accounts of Paul's trouble with the local authorities. After learning about the benefits of having the status of Roman citizenship, it would be historically accurate that Paul was treated differently than if he had not been a citizen. Read the following passages in scripture and write down where the Bible places Paul during two of his recorded encounters and how he was subsequently treated.

Acts 16:37–38 _____

Acts 22:22–29 _____

Paul was also an educated man in both the ways of Judaism and the works of the Greek thinkers of the day, which implies that he came from a family of affluence. His background qualified him to be trusted by those to whom he ministered. We learn that he was a student of one of the most historically notable Jewish teachers of the first century, Gamaliel (Acts 22:3). Paul also exhibits his intimate knowledge of the first-century Greek schools of philosophy when he approaches and converses with the variety of philosophers with ease on Mars Hill (Acts 17).[363] Gamaliel is mentioned in chapter 5, where we studied the historical accuracy of the documents. Paul's speech to the Greeks at the Areopagus (Acts 17) reveals that he spoke to the philosophers known as the *Stoics* and the *Epicureans*. These are well-documented schools of philosophical thought that were prevalent in the first century, both of which still have vestiges in our Westernized culture today.

Historians recognize the early dates given to Paul's correspondence to the Thessalonians, as well as those given to his other letters, because of their historical accuracy. Paul's language, the situations he finds himself in, and the way that he chooses to defend the claims of this new Way could only come from a first-century point of view.[364] Not only did everything begin to change after AD 70, but also by the second century the chasm between the innocence of the first-century Christians and those in the second century had grown because of the extreme persecution inflicted on the people by emperors such as Nero and Domitian.[365] Thessalonica was the second place in Europe where Paul preached to the Gentiles. His letter is believed to have been composed

---

[361] Ibid.

[362] Ibid., 36–37.

[363] Mars Hill still exists today and can be visited in Athens, Greece.

[364] Ramsay, *St. Paul the Traveler and Roman Citizen*, 28.

[365] Ibid., 28–29.

and sent around AD 51, which was only about twenty years after the Crucifixion. Both of Paul's letters to the Thessalonians were quoted early on by the church fathers as well as Gnostic writers (see table 7.2 for a few of those who cited 1 and 2 Thessalonians).

TABLE **7.2. Early Citations**[366]

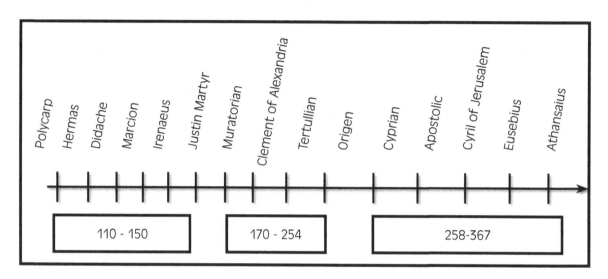

Validating the Location

Thessalonica—a Historically Documented Province

It is highly significant that all of the provinces and villages mentioned in the New Testament can be identified as well documented localities that still exist to this day. Some may be known by a different name, but many can still be identified by the same name as what we find in Scripture. In the case of Thessalonica, it was named after the half-sister of Alexander the Great and is documented as having been founded by her husband the king of Macedonia, Cassander, in 315 BC.[367] Thessalonica is one of the provinces that still exists today under a different name. It is known as Salonica and is located on the Aegean Sea.[368] By the first century, Thessalonica was a well-established and very important port city in Macedonia.[369] Thessalonica had gained a favored status within the Roman Empire for supporting Rome during the Battle of Philippi in 42 BC.[370]

There is ample supporting evidence to show that Thessalonica as a town did indeed exist during Paul's lifetime. Aside from having the favored status of being a *free city*, it is documented that it also accommodated the Roman governor's dwelling.[371] As a free city, the province was

---

[366] Information based on Geisler and Brooks, *When Skeptics Ask*, 153

[367] Charles A. Wanamaker, *The New International Greek Testament Commentary: The Epistles to the Thessalonians*, ed. I. Howard Marshall and W. Ward Gasque (Grand Rapids, MI: Wm. B. Eerdmans, 1990), 3.

[368] Ben Holdsworth, "The Thessalonian Letters: The Greco-Roman Context," *Spectrum* (July 17, 2012), accessed July 6, 2016, http://spectrummagazine.org/article/ben-holdsworth/2012/07/17/thessalonian-letters-greco-roman-context.

[369] Wanamaker, *The New International Greek Testament Commentary*, 3.

[370] Holdsworth, "The Thessalonian Letters: The Greco-Roman Context."

[371] Ibid.

self-governed by elected officials[372] and had the authority to mint its own coins.[373] When Paul came to preach the Gospel of the Christ, this was a bustling and well-respected city. His message would have been heard by a variety of people from all over Macedonia, as Thessalonica was on a main trade route.

Are there street names or places that you know of that have changed names in your or your parents' lifetime? If so, write about those here:

_____

_____

_____

Validating Cultural Climate

Outside Threats and Evidence of Historical Evidence

1 Thessalonians

This letter, like most of Paul's other correspondence, was written to give the people instruction and encouragement as they navigated the nuances of the Christian faith that were entirely foreign to the ways of the culture around them. Paul commends these new converts as they have turned from idols to the living God of the universe (1 Thess. 1:9). He also encourages them to stand firm and avoid sexual immorality (chapters 3 and 4). We will now investigate what Paul was talking about as he taught these new converts. The focus will be on whether or not his warnings are inconsistent with historical reality. The goal is to find out what the real danger here truly was. It is also necessary to affirm any historical evidence that will validate Paul's concern for the people.

Every audience had its own set of internal problems. This is why it is helpful to know whom Paul is speaking to. Historical scholars believe that the majority of Paul's audience in Thessalonica were not the *God-fearers* (Gentiles who had turned to Judaism as a way of life), but the Gentiles who were not as familiar with the God of Israel.[374] The reason given for this observation stems from the way that Paul reminds the people that they have turned from idols (1:9). If the recipients of the letter were those considered as God-fearers, they would not have been worshipping idols (at least not publicly). They would have already been practicing *monotheism* (the belief in one God), just as they were taught by the Jews.

Paul also felt it necessary to remind the people that they were no longer to behave as the rest of the world. He clearly stated that they were to remain sexually pure. He also wrote to give them hope of life everlasting through the Christ in the end times, which would have been a different concept for them. For the purposes of our study we will take a look at the reality of Paul's concern for the people and their moral understanding of purity. It is inevitable, but as time passes the historicity of a culture can become misrepresented. One of the most important things to remember when studying the past is to be very careful not to impose our postmodern ideas of

---

[372] Ibid.

[373] Wanamaker, *The New International Greek Testament Commentary*, 3.

[374] Ibid., 6–7.

life and morality on any culture in antiquity. Fortunately in the West we have access to all sorts of tools that help us gain insight into the first century, most of which we have already discussed in previous chapters.

For the purposes of this study, we will focus on the following questions:

1. What were considered to be idols to the Thessalonians (1:9)?
2. What sexual issues were these people faced with as first-century converts (chapter 4)?
3. How might they have understood the *end times* (4:13–18 and 2 Thess.)?

Idols

What evidence do we have from history that will clarify what sort of idols were these new converts asked to turn away from and how difficult was it for them to hold fast? The way that Paul is using his term for idols tells us that the focus is on the Thessalonian converts' "pre-Christian" religion.[375] Scholars recognize that these idols represented the "totality of their religious experience," which also included their social existence.[376] They believe that Paul's intent is to point out the contrast between the Thessalonians' previous cultural norms and their new way of life.[377] There was a stark contrast in the way Christ followers were to live and the way that their neighbors were still living.

Their neighbors were still worshipping false and dead gods with little change or any real hope in their lives. The Thessalonians would have been worshipping the various array of false gods that were popular in their pluralistic society. There is ample archeological evidence of the many idols that are well-documented and that represent the deities of their world. Aside from archeological findings, it is not unusual for historians to also learn about the history of a society by what they tended to write about. In the first century much of the writings that reveal cultural and societal norms were in the form of carvings in stone as well as notations on papyrus.

Some of these writings were known as *epigrams*. Those who study epigrams are called epigrammatists. One such first-century epigrammatist is known as Philippus of Thessalonica. He not only wrote epigrams but also collected them. It is through his collections that historians know of at least twenty deities who were worshipped and prayed to in first-century Thessalonica.[378] A few of the gods that are represented in these first-century epigrams that these epigrammatists have preserved for us are as follows:

- Artemis
- Apollo
- Aphrodite
- Poseidon
- Sarapis
- Isis

---

[375] Ibid., 86.
[376] Ibid.
[377] Ibid.
[378] Gary M. Burge, Lynn H. Cohick, and Gene L. Green, *The New Testament in Antiquity* (Grand Rapids, MI: Zondervan, 2009), 281.

- Demeter
- Zeus
- Osiris
- Anubis
- Dionysius
- Goddess Roma (Deified Rome)[379]

Other physical evidence of a society's cultural norms can be found in their buildings. The number, type, and purpose of buildings found in any civilization is very telling evidence about the culture in which they are found. Thessalonica, like other parts of Macedonia and Europe, housed temples dedicated to many of these gods.[380] Scholars have unearthed inscriptions that praise the goddess Isis as the eternal creator, forgiver of sins, and savior, among other recognitions.[381]

This would have been disconcerting for Paul given the similarities these beliefs had with the Gospel of Christ. This is a spiritual threat, however, and does not seem to be either a threat to the Christians' moral or ethical way of life, or their livelihood. In a pluralistic culture, no one is seemingly bothered about the convictions of their neighbors, unless it affects their interactions with the community. We are told in the book of Acts that when Paul was preaching and living in Thessalonica for a while, his message caused a great stir in the city (Acts 17:6–7). The commotion was so great that he and Silas were sent away to safety under the cover of darkness. If we can understand what the big deal was, aside from the jealousy of the Jews who did not accept the message of the Messiah, we would gain some insight into why Paul's recipients would rightly be commended for holding fast to their new way of life (1 Thess. 1:9–10).

Why would this be a spiritual threat but not a moral or ethical threat?

_____

_____

_____

Paul's language is meant to point out the superiority of the *one true* God, not only in comparison to all the other religions but also compared to Caesar, who was considered a god. Historical records reveal that there was an interweaving of politics and religion in the first-century Roman territories. Although Thessalonica was considered a free city, it still had ties to the Roman Empire and its religions.[382] A free city was run by the aristocracy, and any threat to their political positions was seen as outright rebellion. The evidence shows that the cults of Cabirus, which was a fertility cult, and Dionysus, also a sexual cult, were the state-sponsored cults in first-century Thessalonica.

---

[379] Holdsworth, "The Thessalonian Letters: The Greco-Roman Context."
[380] Ibid.
[381] Ibid.
[382] Wanamaker, *The New International Greek Testament Commentary*, 3.

What Do Artifacts Tell Us?

One of the most helpful ways that historians and archeologists are able to verify valuable information about any given society is through its monetary system. The study of coins is technically known as *numismatics*. The value of a coin in antiquity was established by its weight. Based on the image on the coin, the trained archeologist is able to determine much about the culture at large. Currency had numerous functions as the coins were used for more than a way to buy and exchange goods.[383] The government or authorities in power would decide what image would be stamped on the coins.

A province's coinage not only served as a political statement but also could be used as a way for the citizens to refuse to do business with a foreign occupier.[384] This was the case in first-century Jerusalem, as we read about Jesus's comment to His disciples in Matthew 22:15–17. For the purposes of this study, our goal is to investigate what was behind Paul's reasoning in his correspondence to the Thessalonians. The tone of Paul's letter suggests that there was a real threat in that the Thessalonians were continuing to cling to their cultural gods. Through the science of numismatics, the evidence can also reveal the dominant cults in any given area. This is one of the ways that we know that the two main cults in Thessalonica while Paul was alive were those of Cabirus and Dionysus.[385]

With this knowledge, we can better understand Paul's concern for the people of Thessalonica, as both of these cults were centered on sexual rituals that were clearly not in line with the behaviors set forth by the God of Israel. Archeologists have found coinage with these two deities stamped on them. Religious rituals were typically used to unify people in the community in an effort to encourage a "common identity."[386] An attack on the state-sponsored cult was seen as an assault on the society.[387] The proclamations that Paul was making would have easily been viewed as a condemnation against the pagan beliefs of the people and, as a result, criticism against the rulers of the society.[388] His assertions would have provoked violence, which was avoided at all costs under Roman rule.[389]

The charges against Paul by the Jews were meant to incite the community to a state of anger (Acts 17:7). His accusers knew that allegiance to the Messiah would mean a rejection of all the religious rituals held in high regard by the political leaders and the community.[390] These new Christians would have to decline participation in the society's religious festivities, which would have been considered also a statement against the political authorities. Paul was clearly proclaiming another king (Jesus). In view of Paul's message, those who were in charge acted quickly to maintain the peace by binding and arresting Jason since they could not find Paul (see

---

[383] Burge, Cohick, and Green, *The New Testament in Antiquity*, 21.

[384] Ibid.

[385] Wanamaker, *The New International Greek Testament Commentary*, 5.

[386] Ibid.

[387] Ibid.

[388] Ibid.

[389] A. N. Sherwin-White, *Roman Society and Roman Law in the New Testament: The Sarum Lectures 1960–1961* (Eugene, OR: Wipf & Stock, 1963), 103.

[390] Ibid.

Acts 17:5–9). This was meant to send a signal to others who might also want to take a stand for this new way of living and worshipping.[391]

List at least two threats to the political leaders in the situation above:

1. _____
2. _____

Charges for disrupting the peace would have been one thing, but it would have been another thing to defy Roman rule. From the archeological evidence of coins found in Thessalonica from the first century BC and AD, there is proof that the Thessalonians recognized Caesar as a god. The people and their leaders were involved in what is known as the *imperial cult*.[392] This connection gave them added security by affiliating themselves with the empire.[393] The coin had not only the head of Caesar on one side as a god, but also had his adopted son Augustus, "with the city's legend," on the other side.[394] The significance of the deified Caesar was the recognition of his power over his subjects, as this power was considered to have been ordained by the gods.[395] Claiming that there was another king that was above all the others became a politically charged assertion.[396]

Although it was not intentional, following the Christ became a political statement and was eventually seen as a threat to Roman rule. The times in which we live in the West are venturing dangerously close to the same sort of threat to those who wish to live in obedience to Christ. In the West, we are not in danger so much for claiming the Messiah as King but because of the lives that we are called to live. If we are to live as God has ordained for humanity, we will find ourselves living in stark contrast to the world around us. One such instance is the issue of sexual diversity that has taken the Westernized world by storm. Those who find themselves standing firm on their conviction of God's boundaries have faced great persecution (publically and politically).

> Finally, then, brothers, we ask and urge you in the Lord Jesus, that as you received from us how you ought to walk and to please God, just as you are doing, that you do so more and more. For you know what instructions we gave you through the Lord Jesus. For this is the will of God, your sanctification: that you abstain from sexual immorality; that each one of you know how to control his own body in holiness and honor, not in the passion of lust like the Gentiles who do not know God; that no one transgress and wrong his brother in this matter, because the Lord is an avenger in all these things, as we told you beforehand and solemnly warned you. For God has not called us for impurity, but in holiness. Therefore whoever disregards this, disregards not man but God, who gives his Holy Spirit to you. (1 Thess. 4:1–8, ESV)

---

[391] Ramsay, *St. Paul the Traveler and Roman Citizen*, 182.

[392] Wanamaker, *The New International Greek Testament Commentary*, 5.

[393] Ibid.

[394] Ibid.

[395] Ibid. Also see S. R. F. Price, *Rituals and Power: The Roman Imperial Cult*, 1985.

[396] This is what eventually led to Paul's imprisonment and execution.

Sexual Immorality

The first-century Christians also faced sexually immoral dilemmas that ended up becoming a threat to the way of life for the elite. The difference was that when Christianity became a higher-profile religion and way of life, the pagans were convicted of their sinful behaviors and chose either to do something about it or not.[397] They did not, however, try to force and persecute those who followed the Christ to recant the Word of God and the instructions for life given to them, as we see today. Paul felt that it was important enough to remind the new converts of their new life in Christ and the importance of sexual purity. Many lives were changed for the better as behaviors that had once brought shame to the individual participants of certain sexual behaviors were now clearly recognized as sinful acts.

Scripture

The significance of this reminder is much more meaningful if we better understand what sort of temptations and lives the people of that day faced on a daily basis. Paul was not making up new rules for the people; he was merely teaching them God's ways as opposed to the ways of humankind (Lev. 18, 20:23, 26). The Gentiles of the first century were much like the people in the West today; they had no idea who the Creator was and His expectations for humanity. The Greek words Paul uses in verse six ("that no one transgress and wrong his brother in this matter, because the Lord is an avenger in all these things, as we told you beforehand and solemnly warned you") clearly connote that "crossing a forbidden boundary" was unacceptable to a just and holy God.[398] Paul was emphatically pointing out to these fledgling Christians that if they disregarded God's boundaries, it was equivalent to disregarding God (1 Thess. 4:8).[399] There is no sound reason to believe that these warnings and instructions are any different for the Christian of today.

What are some of today's most unpopular boundaries that God has set for humanity?

_____

_____

_____

It is important to clarify what Paul is speaking about here since sexual immorality (*fornication* and *pornia*) can have different meanings to modern ears. The Greek word Paul uses pointed out all sexual behavior outside the bounds of marriage.[400] This was a completely foreign concept to first-century pagans.[401] In fact, according to history, it was not until the fifth century that Romans had any concept that sex outside of the bounds of marriage between a man and a woman was wrong

---

[397] See Kyle Harper, *From Shame to Sin: The Christian Transformation of Sexual Morality in Late Antiquity* (Cambridge, MA: Harvard University Press, 2013).

[398] F. F. Bruce, *Word Biblical Commentary*, vol. 45, *1 and 2 Thessalonians*, ed. David A. Hubbard, Glenn W. Barker, and Ralph P. Martin (Waco, TX: Word Books, 1982), 84.

[399] Ibid., 82.

[400] Ibid., 86.

[401] Ibid., 82.

in any way.[402] Our task in this lesson is to verify from historical evidence that what scripture is saying actually has some historical grounding.

One such telling piece of evidence would be the fact that an emperor by the name of Theodosius II enacted a legal reform that called for the ban of any coercion in the sex trade in AD 428.[403] This ban clearly implies that there was an active sex trade in existence at this time in history and that coercion had become a problem. Sexual behavior in the first, second, and third centuries was hindered only by the human imagination. There seemed to be an insatiable appetite for all sorts of erotic behaviors. The evidence of sexual behaviors is personified in literature, art, love poetry, and philosophy. Even satires touched on the drama of life and the sexual experiences practiced as societal norms that represented the Roman Empire in the first five centuries of the Christian era.[404]

If someone were to look back a thousand years from today at some of our government's legislation, what would it tell that individual about our civilization as it pertains to sexual behaviors?

_____

_____

_____

Can you note specific legislation or current legal battles?

_____

_____

What will these legislations tell future generations about our society?

_____

_____

Eros, which is the Greek word for a type of love that is driven by sexual passion, thrived in the Roman Empire, with the aristocracy at the helm. Historical artifacts such as common household lamps reveal a glimpse into the sexual lives of the people. These lamps were adorned with erotic sexual acts painted on them and were used by people as they participated in all sorts of erotic unions by their flickering flames, a practice that did not show any waning until early into the fifth century once Christianity became more prevalent.[405] It is a well-known fact that slave boys were used to satisfy the sexual appetites of their masters.[406] Although there was a sense of shame when continuing a same-sex relationship after the boy began to grow a beard, many felt that it was a matter of fate that they would continue living their lives in what is recognized today as a sexually diverse situation.[407] In other words, it was believed that their situation was destined by the alignment of the stars. Much of the culture's understanding of sexual dominance was explained away by what the cosmos had dealt them for their lives, and free will was not considered to be an

---

[402] Harper, *From Shame to Sin*, 8.

[403] Ibid.

[404] Ibid., 9.

[405] Ibid., 11.

[406] Ibid., 22–25.

[407] Ibid., 24–25.

option.[408] Christianity brought a sense of freedom to the Gentiles in that they did have a choice about their bodies and how they would live.[409]

Part of the reason we know about this behavior is not only archeological evidence, such as the lamps, but also the novels and plays written about the human drama.[410] Historical records have revealed to us a satire written by Lucian (who is mentioned in the first section of this chapter). Not only did Lucian write about his outsider's view of Christianity, but also he wrote from his insider's understanding of his own cultural norms. He wrote a "satirical account of an all-male society on the moon where the boys played the part of wives until the age of twenty-five, at which time they would turn the tables and become the husbands to younger boys."[411] There are numerous accounts of Roman rulers and their abuse of power in their encounters of *pederasty* (pedophilia of a man with a boy): Tiberius, Nero, Domitian, and later Commodus, Trajan, and the well-known relationship between Emperor Hadrian and his lover, Antinous, are but a few examples of this type of sexual behavior.[412]

What is the difference between free will and fate?

____

____

Does being sexually uninhibited bring true freedom? Why or why not?

____

____

____

The public's reaction to the death of Antinous is a telling sign of the times in the second century and is undoubtedly an extension of the previous century's understanding of humanity. When this young man died, there was "empire-wide mourning."[413] He was so loved by the people that he eventually became venerated as a god, as many believed that upon his death a new star appeared in the sky.[414] The number of images in his likeness, which are still in existence, are surpassed only by the images of Augustus and Hadrian.[415] This was clearly a way of life for the pagans in this time of history. There is no question that this new way of living and viewing life and sex was foreign to the Gentile world. Paul was calling these people out of a *deterministic* (the belief that behaviors are determined by outside forces of the will) way of looking at their lives and into a freedom that answered to the "deep logic of a moral order" based on the conviction of sin and the promise of salvation.[416]

The Greco-Roman system had joined their public law and sexual customs to reflect their

[408] Ibid., 14, 20, 21, 24.
[409] Ibid., 13.
[410] Ibid., 19–79.
[411] Ibid., 25.
[412] Ibid., 27.
[413] Ibid., 28.
[414] Ibid.
[415] Ibid.
[416] Ibid., 86.

beliefs in the predetermined call of the cosmos.[417] If you think about it, there is not much difference between the way they believed intimate relationships were predetermined by the individual's station in life and believing that sexual orientations are determined by the sexual impulses one has. This was the world into which God called Paul. He knew God's intended boundaries for humanity and had to somehow get the message of true freedom to the pagan world. If you are a Christian, you, too, are called into this world to bring God's message to a culture that has long ago lost its way to the true freedom offered only by the Creator.

Theological Understanding

Understanding End Times

The word used to define the study of the end times is *eschatology*. Take a moment and write out what you understand of the end times:

_____

_____

The New Testament is a gift that God has given to those who truly seek His face and His favor. It is through the New Testament that we, as Christians, gain our understanding of the end times. The Gospel of Matthew records Jesus's words and warnings to people about the last days (Matt. 24). The book of Revelation is also where we have been given a glimpse of the coming judgment. It is very important to try to understand the mind-set of Paul's audience. Scholars believe that Paul's letter to the Thessalonians was penned prior to the apostle John's vision and his documentation of the insight he was given (the book of Revelation). Therefore, they did not have the luxury of having John's prophetic writing as a reference as we have today.

Many theologians have gleaned their understanding of a rapture before the coming tribulation from this first letter to the Thessalonians (1 Thess. 4:17). This belief in a pretribulation rapture is technically termed *premillennialism*. Paul was fully aware of the daily issues and temptations that his audience faced, so he wrote to encourage them in their walk with Christ.

What are some of the issues that you face daily that affect your life and relationship with God?

_____

_____

_____

_____

Second Thessalonians

End Times

There was seemingly a great deal of confusion about the end times in this first-century community. Paul wrote to encourage this church to hold fast to the promises of God while maintaining the

---

[417] Ibid.

purity of their faith. God cannot be rushed, and the message is the same for us in our day. We are to live out our lives as if Jesus were to return any minute. In Matthew, we have Jesus's warning that no one will know when the Lord will decide to call His elect home (Matt. 24:36). Jesus's disciples were well aware of the fact that we must always be ready for the judgment (2 Pet. 3:10). John recorded Jesus's warning to the world in the book of Revelation (Rev. 3:3, 16:15).

To a Jew like Paul, this preparation for the end was not unfamiliar territory. He would have been well versed from the Hebrew scriptures (Eccles. 9:12) of the serious nature of fending off earthly temptations and evil until the day we die. Every generation seems to have those individuals who desire to take the end of times into their own hands, and they end up making all sorts of false predictions. There have even been some groups in the not so distant past that have quit their jobs and intentionally run up their debt believing that they knew the day of Christ's return, just as those who lived in the first century did (2 Thess. 3:10–12). There have been far too many predictions of the end of the world to begin to mention here, but they can be found easily on the internet.

> For even when we were with you, we would give you this command: If anyone is not willing to work, let him not eat. For we hear that some among you walk in idleness, not busy at work, but busybodies. Now such persons we command and encourage in the Lord Jesus Christ to do their work quietly and to earn their own living. (2 Thess. 3:10–12, ESV)

Imagine how easy it would be to be deceived if you had just learned about this new way of life and the promises it held. Your naivete would have been compounded by the fact that you did not even fully understand the background and foundation of the Jewish faith. To make matters worse, you live in an atmosphere of increasing persecution directed at those who try to live according to God's guidelines for humanity. Then there are people who begin to put their own spin on the teachings of the Christ. The reality is that we all long for a place where we will find peace and an escape from the hardships of this world. These were new converts who had new hope for their lives and the future, but like the apostles, they fully expected Christ's return to be at least within their lifetime.

This hope would have energized them, but at the same time, it made them easy prey for the *Gnostic* influences that were prevalent in the area. The message for us in our day is to live faithfully to God and to trust in the words recorded for us in scripture with the expectancy of Christ's imminent return. We are all expected to live honestly and obediently until God's Messiah returns or until we reach the end of our lives, whichever comes first.

> Blessed are those who wash their robes, so that they may have the right to the tree of life and that they may enter the city by the gates. Outside are the dogs and sorcerers and the sexually immoral and murderers and idolaters, and everyone who loves and practices falsehood. "I, Jesus, have sent my angel to testify to you about these things for the churches. I am the root and the descendant of David, the bright morning star." The Spirit and the Bride say, "Come." And let the one who hears say, "Come." And let the one who is thirsty come; let the one who desires take the water of life without price. … He who testifies to these things says, "Surely I am coming soon." Amen. Come, Lord Jesus! (Rev. 22:14–17, 20 ESV)

Review: Assessing the External Criteria Used to Validate the Historicity of the Documents
Study Questions

For Review and Theological Reflection

External Criterion for Historical Accuracy

1. Is there enough evidence to verify that Paul was a real person in the first century? List at least three things about Paul that can be verified in history about his existence.

   a. _____
   b. _____
   c. _____

2. What was the history behind Thessalonica?

   _____
   _____

3. Name five of the many gods found on epigrams in Thessalonica.

   a. _____
   b. _____
   c. _____
   d. _____
   e. _____

   • Why are these epigrams important to the historical relevance of Paul's letters to the Thessalonians?

4. How did the Roman Empire weave together religion and politics?

   • What effect did this have on the message of the Gospel as delivered by Paul?

5. What is one of the methods used by historians that enables them to learn about the religious practices in any given region in the first century or prior to the first century AD?

Group Discussion

Theological Reflection

1. What is Paul talking about when he warns the people of Thessalonica to abstain from certain behaviors? Why should it matter if the Christ died for all sin?

2. Why is it so important that people understand that God created humanity to have free will?

   - Knowing what you know about evil and depraved humanity, why do you think that throughout human history people have tried to convince others that they are bound by some predetermined precondition to live out their lives in some particular way?

   - How can this hinder a person's growth as an individual? Give some examples, and discuss.

3. How does your view of God affect your view of ethics? of morality? Would you say that your spiritual walk reveals itself in your daily life?

   - What passages do we find in the New Testament that call Christians to live by a different standard than the secular realm around us?

4. How does standing for Christ make a political statement in your culture?

5. Where do people get the idea that there will be a rapture of the true church? Who is the true church?

6. Does the idea of a rapture of the true church appeal to you? Does it frighten you? If so why? If not, why not?

Key Terms

deterministic: The view that all of life is predetermined by some force outside of oneself.

end times: The events of the last days of human history when Israel will rule the kingdoms of the world.

epigrams: Writings carved in stone (like the headstones found in a cemetery), or sayings found in writings on other mediums.

Epicurean: A school of philosophical thought whose adherents' goal was to enjoy all of the sensual pleasures of this world in moderation. The teachings were based on the philosophy of the Greek philosopher Epicurus (founded in 307 BC). This philosophical belief system did not believe that the gods took any notice of humanity and found the belief that people would be punished for wrongdoing to be absurd. They believed that one must enjoy life to the fullest since there was no afterlife and nothing to fear in the way of judgment.

Eros: A type of love associated with sex. It can also mean erotic sexual acts between two individuals.

eschatology: The study of the end times.

fornication: Any sexual act performed outside the bounds of marriage between a man and a woman.

Gnostic: An individual with the philosophical understanding that the creator god is not the same as the god of redemption. The Gnostics did not believe that Jesus was God incarnate; however, they believed that Jesus was spirit and only appeared to be human. The Gnostic believed in a secret knowledge that was only given to a few. The Gnostic believed that matter was evil, and knowledge was thought of as superior.

God-fearers: Gentiles who had turned to Judaism as a way of life.

imperial cult: Worshipping the emperor of the Roman Empire. The worship included paying tribute to the emperor and paying taxes. The larger cities would have temples erected as places of worship to honor the emperor and the Roman Empire.

monotheism: The belief that there is one God.

pederasty: The act of sex between an adult and a minor.

pornia: Sexual acts between two individuals that is outside the bounds of marriage between a man and a woman.

premillennialism: The belief, based on scripture, that Jesus will return to gather the true church before the hardships of the last days begins. It is believed that after seven years of turmoil (based on Daniel and the book of Revelation) is over, Christ will return with His church to rule and reign for one thousand years.

Stoicism: A school of philosophical thought whose adherents believed that wisdom was virtuous and brought happiness and that judgment would be based on one's behavior. Stoicism was founded by the Greek philosopher Zeno of Citium in the early third century BC. The belief was (is) that humans must rely on their own responses to situations and not on external events. Stoics recognized that the world is unpredictable and that life is short, and therefore one should be strong and in control of one's own faculties. They believed that life did not always make sense, so one should make the best of each situation and exercise control over the use of logic.

God's Attributes

providential – The fact that God can see ahead in time: He knew that His Word would serve as a moral guideline not only for the nation of Israel but also for all of humanity throughout history.

sovereignty – God knows how His created order functions at its best to allow humanity to experience true freedom.

Literature Cited or Recommended

Barrett, C. K., ed. *The New Testament Background: Writings from Ancient Greece and the Roman Empire That Illuminate Christian Origins*. Rev. ed. San Francisco: Harper Collins, 1989.

Bruce, F. F. *Word Biblical Commentary*. Vol. 45, *1 and 2 Thessalonians*. Edited by David A. Hubbard, Glenn W. Barker, and Ralph P. Martin. Waco, TX: Word Books, 1982.

Burge, Gary M., Lynn H. Cohick, and Gene L. Green. *The New Testament in Antiquity*. Grand Rapids, MI: Zondervan, 2009.

Geisler, Norman L., and Ronald M. Brooks, *When Skeptics Ask: A Handbook on Christian Evidence*. Grand Rapids, MI: Baker Books, 2013.

Harper, Kyle. *From Shame to Sin: The Christian Transformation of Sexual Morality in Late Antiquity*. Cambridge, MA: Harvard University Press, 2013.

Holdsworth, Ben. "The Thessalonian Letters: The Greco-Roman Context." *Spectrum* (July 17, 2012). Accessed July 6, 2016. http://spectrummagazine.org/article/ben-holdsworth/2012/07/17/thessalonian-letters-greco-roman-context.

Horsley, Richard, ed. *Paul and Empire: Religion and Power in Roman Imperial Society*. Harrisburg, PA: Trinity Press, 1997.

Price, S. R. F. *Rituals and Power: The Roman Imperial Cult*. Cambridge, England: Cambridge University Press, 1987.

Niswonger, Richard L. *New Testament History*. Grand Rapids, MI: Zondervan, 1992.

Ramsay, William M. *St. Paul the Traveler and Roman Citizen*. Edited by Mark Wilson. Revised edition. Grand Rapids, MI: Kregel Publications, 2001.

Sherwin-White, A. N. *Roman Society and Roman Law in the New Testament: The Sarum Lectures 1960–1961*. Eugene, OR: Wipf & Stock, 1963.

Wanamaker, Charles A. *The New International Greek Testament Commentary: The Epistles to the Thessalonians*. Edited by. I. Howard Marshall and W. Ward Gasque. Grand Rapids, MI: Wm. B. Eerdmans, 1990.

CHAPTER 8

Higher Criticism: Assessing External Criteria to Validate Historical Accuracy with Archeology

Archeology

The science of archeology is a very exciting field and incredibly fascinating. Numerous discoveries in the mid- to late twentieth century have given us undeniable evidence that validates the scriptures. Many of the finds not only confirm what the Bible mentions as truth but also serve to further support the consistency of God's message to humanity found throughout scripture. Archeological evidence provides tangible proof for the skeptic as well as for the Christian who desires to share the Gospel with others. Physical substantiation helps to clarify many questions about past civilizations. It is important to remember, however, that it will not answer theological or *metaphysical* questions about the nature of God and His plan for humanity.

When looking for archeological clues to assess the trustworthiness of scripture, it is important to keep in mind that we should not expect to find some sort of physical evidence that came directly from the hand of Jesus. Jesus's sayings and the miracles that He performed are recorded in the numerous manuscripts that we hold today, as well as in the extrabiblical material mentioned in chapter 7. Remember, as far as the world was concerned, Jesus was an unimportant Jew from the small town of Galilee. He was not a high-profile religious leader of the day, nor was he from a wealthy family. Why would there be any notice of him at all?

If the Jewish religious leaders of the first century had not found Jesus to be such a threat to their way of life, He would not have garnered so much attention. Even if there were a miraculous discovery of an ancient papyrus written by Jesus Himself, it would only serve to further establish the validity of the manuscripts that we have already discovered (which would be great), but nothing more. There would no doubt be endless rhetoric denying that Jesus did indeed pen the words on the hypothetical papyrus. Just consider all of the critical dialogue surrounding the New Testament writers that has been discussed in the previous chapters. It would be worse if something were found that scholars claimed was penned by Jesus's own hand. There would also be those who would treat the writings as if they were God Himself, and that material object would be somehow venerated, perhaps the way the Qur'an is treated and viewed by many Muslims.

What archeology attempts to demonstrate is that the people, places, and events mentioned in the New Testament give an accurate representation of what life was like in the early part of the first century. Archeological finds reveal the customs of the day, the topography, the tools used, the living conditions, furniture, workplace environments, roads, coins used, and the buildings in existence. An example of a common household item that was previously mentioned are the Roman lamps that give a glimpse of the erotic lifestyles of many who lived in the pre-Christian Roman Empire. When a discovery is made, it is immediately assessed to find if it indeed corresponds to scripture. For instance, the events and sayings of Jesus begin to take on a true-to-life dimension when we learn about the actual topography as it was in first-century Palestine.

Archeological discoveries not only reveal artifacts but also can make known geographical shifts and changes throughout time. The fossil records preserved in the rock strata are examples of how scientists surmise that the earth was indeed covered by water at one point in history, just like the Bible says it was in Genesis 7:17–25. Many are familiar with the way that archeologists study ancient civilizations and their customs through discoveries of everyday objects such as pottery and preserved seeds and food. Inscriptions on items that have been unearthed prove to be invaluable to researching and accurately reconstructing the past. The Rosetta stone[418] is one example of how discoveries help scientists translate and comprehend an ancient language, which in turn unlocks the meaning of other inscriptions found earlier.

There are many times that an archeologist comes across large stones or items with inscriptions that contain words or phrases that shed light on the meaning of the terms used in the New Testament. This chapter will discuss a few of the many archeological discoveries and how they help Christians defend the integrity of the New Testament. There are numerous aspects of archeological discoveries that bring the first century into focus and that will help us to better comprehend the atmosphere in which the disciples were called to follow the Messiah.

The emphasis of our study will spotlight the following:

1. The sayings of Jesus
2. Words used in the New Testament
3. Places mentioned
4. Events that are recorded

These topics do not exhaust all of the information available, but the discussion will give you a good idea of what solid evidence there is to validate what is written in the New Testament. We will also consider how these excavations help scholars interpret God's revelation of Himself to humanity. At times it is all too easy to forget that life is lived on a multidimensional plane, especially when we read about the past on a two-dimensional level. This is a science that brings in several dimensions to life so that we may gain a better picture of reality in the first century.

---

[418] The Rosetta stone discovery in 1799 was tremendously helpful in deciphering the section of the stone that contained Egyptian hieroglyphs. Once the hieroglyphs were decoded in 1822, it gave archeologists and Egyptologists a better insight into ancient Egypt and, in turn, very early biblical history.

Clues from Archeological Excavations

Sayings of Jesus

Some of Jesus's sayings were very unique for his first-century audience. Scripture reveals how there were times when even His disciples did not understand what He was talking about (Matt. 16:5–12; John 4:27–38), so He would clarify His meaning for them. After the resurrection, the gift of the Holy Spirit opened their minds not only to recall what they had learned but also to understand what they had been taught (John 14:26). There are also sayings that Jesus's followers could understand because they were familiar with the *topography*, or the lay of the land. This is why when Christians visit the Holy Land and the surrounding areas, the Bible comes to life for them, and they return home with a deeper and richer faith.

When Jesus spoke to His disciples and told them that they were the "light of the world," He was speaking metaphorically and preparing them for their roles as disciples (Matt. 4:14). He continued painting a verbal picture for them when He explained, "A city set on a hill cannot be hidden."[419] For those who have visited Jerusalem and the surrounding areas, these words bring a whole new understanding when one gazes "across the Sea of Galilee from Tiberias to the ruins of Hippos that tower in the distance on the southern end of the Golan Heights."[420] From that physical vantage point, it is easy to imagine exactly what the disciples saw with their own eyes in the evening when the city lanterns were lighted.

Jesus also taught the disciples that our lives belong to God and that the earthly demands on us, such as taxes, belong to those who have the authority to claim them. Historical scholars have long used the study of coins, or *numismatics*, to learn more about ancient civilizations. Archeologists have unearthed countless Roman coins with the image of Caesar on them. Many of these coins can be viewed in museums like the one at the Vatican. One of the more famous passages in scripture quotes Jesus teaching His disciples to "render to Caesar the things that are Caesar's, and to God the things that are God's" (Mark 12:17). The coin he was speaking about had the image of Caesar on it.

Write down the things in your life that belong to the authorities in your life:

_____

_____

_____

The image of Caesar becomes quite significant when one understands Roman history. In the United States of America, we too have images of the presidents of the past on our currency, just as the Roman Empire had the image of Caesar on theirs. The reason for placing political leaders on United States currency, however, differs vastly from that of the ancient civilization of Rome. Coins and dollar bills in the United States are stamped with the image of presidents who made a significant contribution to the founding of our country out of gratitude for their service.

---

[419] Matthew 5:14 (ESV).

[420] Craig L. Blomberg, *The Historical Reliability of the Gospels*, 2nd ed. (Downers Grove, IL: InterVarsity Press, 2007), 327.

The previous chapter revealed a much more sinister reason for using the image of Caesar on the Roman currency that was used throughout their vast empire, however.

Caesar's image was a constant reminder to everyone that he ruled over the people and was the reason for their peace and security. Emperor Tiberius (AD 14–37), for instance, is documented as stating, "I am lord of my slaves, *imperator* of my troops, and first citizen of everyone else."[421] The coins were also part of the imperial worship system, as the emperor was depicted as a god equivalent to Zeus. Aside from paying taxes to the Roman government, Jews were known to keep within their own communities when it came to commerce. They used their own currency when trading with other Jews. Jesus reminded His disciples of their status as heirs to God's kingdom and encouraged them to remember to whom they truly belonged.

Despite the carefree way Jesus is depicted in postmodernity, the people who followed Him and heard Him speak clearly understood that He spoke with great authority (Matt. 7:28–29). When Jesus taught, He was very direct. His messages used common objects to make His point very clear. One example from scripture was the mention of the enormous millstones used for grinding grain. His listeners knew that Jesus was serious when He sternly warned them that the penalty for misleading children (also new believers, or those individuals who were truly seeking God) was a violent death. He is quoted as stating that "whoever causes one of these little ones who believe in me to sin, it would be better for him to have a great millstone fastened around his neck and to be drowned in the depth of the sea" (Matt. 18:6).

Think of a common household object from the 1950s or 1960s with which a person would have been familiar at that time but is virtually unknown to someone today. Now, describe it below:

_____

_____

_____

_____

A first-century Jew would have clearly understood that this was the massive stone that required help from an animal to turn in order to grind the grain, as opposed to the smaller millstones also used in that day. This is a far cry from the docile Jesus depicted by many churches in the Western world. It is helpful to the historian and to all of us when archeologists discover items like these millstones, so that we better comprehend the seriousness with which Jesus spoke. Another example would be the imagery of the solid foundations provided by stones. Archeological findings from the first century reveal large stone areas used in the crushing of grapes for wine. A good harvest would have caused the area to overflow with the juice from the crushed grapes. Jesus's audiences would have clearly understood what He meant when He spoke about the abundance that will be given to the individual who truly gives from the heart: "Give and it will be given to you. Good measure, pressed down, shaken together, running over, will be put into your lap. For with the measure you use it will be measured back to you" (Luke 6:38).

The New Testament also points to *Jesus* as the "cornerstone" on which the church would be built. "Have you not read this Scripture: 'The stone that the builders rejected has become

---

[421] Dio Cassio, *Historia* 57.8.2; Gary M. Burge, Lynn H. Cohick, and Gene L. Green, *The New Testament in Antiquity: A Survey of the New Testament within Its Cultural Contexts* (Grand Rapids, MI: Zondervan, 2009), 92.

the cornerstone'" (Mark 12:10). The cornerstone is of great significance; this specific stone is purposefully selected to bear the weight of an entire building or wall. Huge stones were used to form the base of the retaining wall that once surrounded the temple in Jerusalem (some of which remain to this day). Archeologists have been able to study ancient structures in the Middle East yielding significant information for modern-day students.

Words Used

Archeological discoveries reveal how specific words or phrases were used in a given culture. Excavated artifacts shed light on certain cultural and societal divisions when certain words are either included or not included. For instance, the word *corban* that is used in the Gospel of Mark (7:10) can be translated as "dedicated to God," which was placed in another context when it appeared on a Jewish sarcophagus.[422] It is believed that the inscription was intended to "ward off" potential grave robbers.[423] Another phrase that can have multiple meanings is found in Matthew 26:50, which is the passage where Jesus addresses Judas in the garden just before He is taken away. The Greek literal translation is "for what you are here" (*eph ho parei*), which has been translated literally as a statement: "Jesus said to him, 'Friend, this is why you are here.'" Other versions have been interpreted as the following:

- "Jesus said to him, 'Friend, do what you came to do'" (ESV). This can easily be read as a command [Do].
- "Jesus said unto him, 'Friend, wherefore art thou come'" (KJV)? This version is interpreted as a question [Why?].

Archeological discoveries of the time period in which Jesus lived have revealed an Israeli drinking tumbler with the same words inscribed onto it, following the word *rejoice*.[424] The meaning of this phrase, placed into context, would propose that the original intent would be "That's why you are here,"[425] which would unquestionably have the same intent as what is written in John 17:12.

Other archeological excavations in the late nineteenth century brought to light objects with certain words and expressions used by the common person. Two significant discoveries happened between 1875 and 1895. Large quantities of papyrus that originated from wastepaper containers and that date to the first century were discovered inside embalmed crocodiles found in the Fayum province and other parts of Egypt.[426] These papyri shed light on expressions used in the New Testament that were believed to have been found only in the Bible.[427] One of the expressions found on these papyri dated to the time period of the New Testament writings is a phrase found in Matthew 25:19: "made a reckoning" (KJV) ("settle accounts," ESV).[428]

---

[422] Blomberg, *The Historical Reliability of the Gospels*, 330.

[423] Ibid.

[424] Ibid.

[425] Ibid.

[426] Clifford Wilson, *Rocks, Relics, and Biblical Reliability* (Grand Rapids, MI: Zondervan, 1977), 115.

[427] Ibid., 118.

[428] Ibid.

There is evidence of this phrase having been used in other writings found in various parts of Egypt that also date from the New Testament time period. Archeologists see these finds as literary proof and further evidence that the biblical manuscripts are authentic documents that were produced in the first century.[429] Another word that was not found outside of the New Testament writings is the word for *daily*, which is found in what we recognize as the "Lord's Prayer" (Matt. 6:4).[430] The word was found on a papyrus written by a housekeeper to account for the household's daily allowance of food.[431] Not only do words and phrases like the ones above help to shed light on how these terms were used in the first century, but also they serve to verify the integrity of the extant biblical manuscripts that we hold today.

Can you think of any words or terms that may have had a certain meaning at one point in your life but that, as time has passed, are no longer used in the same way? Write your experience below:

_____
_____
_____
_____

Discoveries in archeology can also help us better understand the culture of a society. Papyri are also always valuable finds, and when artifacts are found with words and phrases on them, they too serve as invaluable information. Inscriptions help scholars discern and better understand the meaning of what the same phrases found in scripture mean. It is also a fact that the absence of certain words informs researchers about that specific culture, demographic region, and customs unique to those people. Scientific findings may not fully explain the whys or the why-nots, but they will give a deeper understanding of the ancient cultures and the people of the past that could stand to either validate or invalidate the claims made in scripture.

Sites of Significance

Normally when we think about the science of archeology, we think about finding shards of pottery or discovering fossils. Archeological discoveries also include cultural record keeping or geological information that reveals such things as drought or agricultural hardships during a particular time period in history. Archeology is a helpful way to study the particular pressures or hardships that a culture may have been facing, such as the oppression of the Roman Empire on the common person. The burden of participating in the required monetary system of Rome allows us to better understand what Jesus was teaching His disciples. Knowing more about the geography of the land is also helpful to us when discerning how the disciples understood what Jesus was talking about. The New Testament mentions many geographical locations as well as physical sites where various things happened, and finding these sites and locations helps in verifying that scripture is not only historically accurate but also geographically accurate.

---

[429] Ibid.

[430] Ibid.

[431] Ibid., 118–19.

Places Where Rituals Were Performed

The Bible mentions numerous places where rituals were performed. One of the best ways to validate any document from history is to locate those places to which it refers. Fictional writing tends to elaborate on sites in order to make them more interesting and colorful. Someone who is recounting history, however, will tend to be more accurate in their references to places and situations. When explaining the reliability of the New Testament to others, the goal is to make sure that the information is based on reality and not fiction. Therefore, we rely heavily on responsible and legitimate sources for information. Locating where events took place is a wonderful way of bringing the Bible into perspective for others.

When one studies the topography in Palestine, one sees that it is not difficult to imagine how Jesus and John the baptizer performed baptisms. Scripture states that John baptized out in the wilderness of Judea in the Jordan River (Matt. 3:1–6). The Jordan River is a verifiable river right where the scripture says it is. Another example is the area near the temple ruins that is littered with clusters of immersion pools. These are pools that are also mentioned in the New Testament. Some of these pools were used for ritual purification, and others were believed to have had healing powers (John 5:1–4).

The writers of the New Testament were firsthand witnesses living in the first century. They described these pools of water with great accuracy. The Pools of Siloam (John 9:7–11) and Bethesda (John 5:1) remain right where they were described that they were. The Pool of Bethesda near the Sheep's Gate in Jerusalem is described with great accuracy by John (5:2) and can be viewed today with the five porticos around it that are mentioned.[432] The details of the surrounding areas are also recorded with specific and verifiable landmarks. For instance, other sites that confirm locations mentioned in the New Testament that have been located by archeologists include public buildings and private homes.

Synagogues were prevalent places of worship wherever there was a community of Jews in the Diaspora. They are referenced many times throughout the New Testament. One of the more noted examples of these sacred houses of worship are the ruins of a Jewish synagogue discovered in Capernaum that date back to the first century. It is believed that this is the very same synagogue that is mentioned in Mark and Luke (Mark 1:21; Luke 7).[433] Other buildings mentioned in the

> And they went into Capernaum, and immediately on the Sabbath he entered the synagogue and was teaching.
> Mark 1:21 (ESV)

New Testament that are believed to have been located here are the home of Simon Peter (Mark 1:29) and the home of the synagogue ruler Jairus (Mark 5:22, 38).[434]

Most of us are familiar with reading about Jesus and the temple in Jerusalem. It is the center stage for much of the drama that surrounded Jesus's life (Mark 11:11–2). It is where He was taken as an infant to be circumcised (Luke 2:27, 46). It is also where the religious leaders of the day met and where the Jews gathered for the annual festivals and worship. This was the temple where Jesus taught in the courtyard (Matt. 26:55). This Jewish temple was completed by Herod and is known as Herod's Temple. The foundation of Herod's Temple courtyard has survived the

---

[432] See images of the ruins of the Pool of Bethesda surrounded by the five colonnades, https://www.google.com/search?q=pool+of+bethesda&safe=strict&biw=1093&bih=452&tbm=isch&tbo=u&source=univ&sa=X&sqi=2&ved=0ahUKEwiFyPSkw5HOAhVDcz4KHYNNCC4QiR4IjQE.

[433] Blomberg, *The Historical Reliability of the Gospels*, 328.

[434] Ibid.

millennia, along with a wall that surrounded the temple during the first century. Although the rest of the temple lies in ruins,[435] it all serves as visual historical proof of the impressive building that is described in the Bible.

King Herod is historically noted as having been an avid builder. The ability and authority to command this building of impressive structures was a demonstration of power. Many of the buildings that he designed and had erected during his reign still exist and have undergone the process of reconstruction. One recent discovery includes a highly impressive structure that was built to form a mountain.[436] Other buildings are scattered throughout Israel and can be visited, along with the sites previously mentioned. Herod's ruthless and megalomaniacal tendencies are well-documented in historical records as well as in scripture (Matt. 2:7–18). When looking around Israel, it is not difficult to see that Herod's power-hungry tendencies were not exaggerated when you see all of the Herodian structures that still litter the Israeli landscape today.[437]

List the types of prominent buildings that are in your town. Think about what those buildings say about the culture in which you live. Take some time to write about it here:

_____

_____

_____

_____

Landmarks

Archeological discoveries are helpful in verifying historical claims through evidence that points to certain people like Tiberius Caesar. They are also useful in supporting assertions made about certain behaviors of individuals like Herod. There are other types of historical finds that serve as landmarks. These landmarks help identify either where people came from or even where certain events took place. For instance, in antiquity it was a common practice for a person's last name to be determined either by where they were born or where they lived. Some examples of identifying an individual with their home place are Jesus, Mary, and Simon. Jesus was frequently referred to as Jesus of Nazareth (John 1:45, 19:19; Mark 1:24; Luke 18:37, 24:19; Matt. 26:71). The discovery of a "first century tiled mosaic of a fishing boat with the inscription of 'Magdala' has helped to identify the location of Mary Magdalene's home town mentioned in Luke 8:2."[438] One other noted individual, Simon of Cyrene, can also be verified by the history of what is known about a location identified as Cyrenaica (Mark 15:21; Acts 2:10, 11:20). Other archeological landmarks have been invaluable to the study of and verification of first-century historical Palestine and the surrounding areas. For instance, there is an ancient Byzantine church near the cliffs of the Sea of Galilee. This site is believed to be the same location where Jesus commanded the legion of demons to leave a demon-possessed man and allowed them to inhabit a heard of pigs, which proceeded to throw themselves over the cliff (Mark 5:13).

---

[435] The Jewish temple in Jerusalem was eventually destroyed in AD 70 by the Roman Empire under the command of Titus, the son of the Roman emperor Vespasian.

[436] Barbara Kreiger, "Finding King Herod's Tomb," *Smithsonian Magazine* (August 2009), accessed May 2, 2017, http://www.smithsonianmag.com/history/finding-king-herods-tomb-34296862.

[437] Blomberg, *The Historical Reliability of the Gospels*, 328.

[438] Ibid.

Another well-known landmark is Jacob's well, where Jesus ministered to a Samaritan woman (John 4:5–6). This particular well has been clearly documented for years.[439] There are many others

examples that are too numerous to mention here but that can be easily accessed through various books and websites on the topic. One such text is *The Architecture of Herod the Great Builder* by Ehud Netzer, which talks about Herod's building exploits. The evidence for the claims made in the New Testament are so well-documented that to entertain any

> And they compelled a passerby, Simon of Cyrene, who was coming in from the country, the father of Alexander and Rufus, to carry his cross.
>
> Mark 15:21 (ESV)

skeptic's assertions that there is insufficient evidence would clearly reveal ignorance on the topic.

Noted and well-known archeologists Sir William Ramsay and William F. Albright both concur that there have not been any archeological discoveries made that have ever contradicted any events, any claims made, or any people or places written about in the New Testament. In fact, these two archeologists were previously critical scholars who became aware of the accuracy of the scriptures' mention of people and places to the degree that they could no longer hold to their skeptical or critical views. In his book *St. Paul the Traveler and the Roman Citizen*, Sir William Ramsay records that he first began to approach the book of Acts with great suspicion. He claims that it was not long before he found himself frequently consulting the book of Acts as an authoritative source of information for the society, topography, and antiquities of Asia Minor.[440]

More recently, respected and noted Roman historian Dr. Colin J. Hemer notes in *The Book of Acts in the Setting of Hellenistic History* that the works of Luke (the Gospel of Luke and the book of Acts) were undoubtedly written by an individual who had firsthand knowledge of even the most "minute geographical details known to the readers" of the first century.[441] Moreover, Luke documented specific customs that were unique to the first third of the first century, obscure routes and certain idioms known mainly to specific groups of people, period details, and names of people that would have been familiar to the contemporary society and not necessarily to the vast majority of civilization.[442] Hemer records that in all of his research he has not found that Luke made any errors in his documentation of the life, events, and times that surrounded the birth, life, and death of Jesus of Nazareth. The only groups that continue to reject the Gospels and writings of the New Testament are those from the critical scholarship end who refuse to recognize any supernatural events as reality.

People and Events

People

There are over one hundred references to people, places, and events in Luke's book of Acts that are all verifiable today with the aid of archeological discoveries. In the first verse of the third chapter

---

[439] Ibid.

[440] William M. Ramsay, *St. Paul the Traveler and Roman Citizen*, rev. ed., ed. Mark Wilson (London: Angus Hudson Ltd., 2001), 19.

[441] Norman L. Geisler and Ronald M. Brooks, *When Skeptics Ask: A Handbook on Christian Evidences* (Grand Rapids, MI: Baker Books, 2013), 217.

[442] Colin J. Hemer, *The Book of Acts in the Setting of Hellenistic History*, ed. Conrad H. Gempf (1990; repr., Winona, Lake, IN: Eisenbrauns, 2008), 101–220.

of Luke's Gospel alone, there are sixteen historical references that are astoundingly accurate. Historical scholars note that the accuracy with which Dr. Luke wrote the Gospel of Luke and the book of Acts is incredible. It was precisely because of the details he incorporated into his investigative writings that many critics challenged the historical accuracy and integrity of Luke's works. He was accused of making up obscure names and titles that could not have possibly been legitimate.

> In the fifteenth year of the reign of Tiberius Caesar, Pontius Pilate being governor of Judea, and Herod being tetrarch of Galilee, and his brother Philip tetrarch of the region of Ituraea and Trachonitis, and Lysanias tetrarch of Abilene. (Luke 3:1 ESV)

One such account is found in Acts 18:12–17. Luke mentions a man named Gallio as the *proconsul* of Achaia. Post-Enlightenment critics claimed that this man and his position were a farce. Archeological excavations, however, discovered an inscription at Delphi that mentions the same gentleman along with his official title dating back to the time that Paul was in the city of Corinth (AD 51).[443] In a similar instance, an inscription recording a temple dedication was also found that mentions the title and name of Lysanias as the *tetrarch* of Abilene, whom critics had long believed was another fictitious person with a fictitious title.[444] Even more interesting is the fact that it was dated from between AD 14 and AD 29, which would have been the exact time of the commencement of John the Baptist's ministry as mentioned in Luke 3:1.[445] One other individual believed by critical scholars as an embellishment was known by the name of Erastus. The book of Acts, the letter to the Romans, and 2 Timothy note that Erastus was a treasurer and a citizen of Corinth, which can be verified by an archeological discovery during an excavation of Corinth. An inscription dedicated to Erastus for his service and financing of the paved area near the theater in Corinth[446] is just another of the many examples found in the various excavation sites that serve to further verify the integrity of the New Testament.

Other excavations in 1941 revealed an ossuary containing a group of small coffins belonging to the family of Simon of Cyrene (Mark 15:21),[447] verifying the life of this person and his family. Inscriptional evidence was also discovered in 1961 during an excavation of an ancient theater in Caesarea by the Sea verifying that Pontius Pilate was indeed the prefect of Judea during the reign of Tiberius Caesar, who is mentioned in both the Gospel of Matthew and that of Luke (Matt. 27:2; Luke 3:1). More recently, in 1990, it is believed that the coffin belonging to Caiaphas the high priest was discovered.[448] Any serious historical and archeological scholar must recognize the reality and reliability of the people, places, and events recorded in the New Testament as valid evidence that the people, places, and events are truly historically sound. Once again, it appears that those critics of the Bible who maintain that the Bible is filled with myths cannot sustain their position and should be gently challenged to prove the reason for their skepticism.

---

[443] Ramsay, *St. Paul the Traveler and Roman Citizen*, 199.

[444] Hemer, *The Book of Acts in the Setting of Hellenistic History*, 159–60.

[445] Geisler, *When Skeptics Ask*, 218.

[446] Ibid.

[447] Blomberg, *The Historical Reliability of the Gospels*, 329.

[448] Craig A. Evans, *Jesus and His World: The Archaeological Evidence* (Louisville, KY: Westminster John Knox Press, 2012), 94–103, 147.

Events and Artifacts (What Was Really Going On?)

The New Testament is filled with events that may be quite foreign to modern people and have been questioned by historical scholars since the period of the Enlightenment. One such custom in question was the way that people were crucified. Some critics suggested that those individuals who were crucified did not actually have their feet nailed to the post. In 1968, however, archeologists discovered the remains of a man who died by crucifixion, and the nail used to secure his feet to the wood was still embedded in the bones of his feet.[449] There were also wooden fragments of the post to which he was affixed found on the nail. Another event that took place at the foot of the cross can also be verified by the discovery of an engraving found in a stone in the area of what is believed to be Gabbatha (John 19:13), a place where crucifixions took place. The engravings note the practice of gambling for the garments of those who were being crucified. This custom was known as the "king's game" and is noted in John 19:23–24.[450]

Modern people are familiar with the procedure of the embalmment of a corpse. It might seem quite odd, however, that a person would be doused in all types of spices and ointments, such as was the ritual in first-century Palestine (Luke 24:55–56). Although the custom was to wrap the body in linen and anoint it with oils and spices, it was a ritual that took place after the body was to be buried, not before. For whatever reason, however, the Bible records that one of Jesus's followers was compelled to anoint Him while He was still alive, notably confusing all of the disciples (John 12:1–8). When archeologists unearthed several long narrow-necked perfume jars, it was not difficult to imagine how the woman noted in scripture might have been able to carefully anoint the feet of Jesus using a similar container.[451]

In Conclusion

Archeology has been an important tool in the study of the historical nuances of the New Testament. The excavations have only served to demonstrate the accuracy and care with which the Word of God was recorded for all future generations. As you defend the reliability of the New Testament, the archeological evidence will undoubtedly be helpful to you, especially when discussing the Bible with scientifically minded individuals who need physical proof for everything. Archeology, although a great tool, will not answer fully questions about miracles, evil, or the moral dilemmas of our day. For those issues, one needs to be ready with the more philosophically based understanding of metaphysics and the reality of a transcendent Creator.

Regardless of where one stands on his or her belief in Christianity, the evidence for the validity of the Bible continues to grow daily. The data mounting up not only through the science of archeology but also in the cosmological and biological sciences. The confirmation of the historical veracity of the book of Acts alone is overwhelming, and that of the Gospels far exceeds any other historical writing from antiquity. The Christian Bible is scientifically so well attested to that "any attempt to reject its basic historicity even in matters of detail must now seem absurd."[452]

---

[449] Ibid., 122–26.

[450] Blomberg, *The Historical Reliability of the Gospels*, 328.

[451] Ibid., 327.

[452] A. N. Sherwin-White, *Roman Society and Roman Law in the New Testament: The Sarum Lectures 1960–1961* (1963; repr., Eugene, OR: Wipf & Stock, 2004), 189.

Any report of invalidity of the New Testament manuscripts stems from inaccurate information that has long since been dispelled.

Even Roman historians have taken the historical accuracy of the information found in the New Testament for granted for many years.[453] There is no question that in the twenty-first century, any rejection of the Bible stems from misinformed liberal critics and is seen as purely volitional on the part of the individual who rejects its veracity. The last two chapters of our attention will be focused on the internal criteria that are used to validate the manuscripts from which the New Testament has been formed. Before we begin our study of the internal criteria, we will take a moment in the second half of this chapter to see how the pastoral Epistles can be tested using archeological validation.

Review:

Important Archeological Finds That Validate the New Testament

1. The sayings of Jesus
2. Specific words and phrases used in the New Testament
3. Verified locations that are mentioned
4. Verification of people who are mentioned
5. Evidence that clarifies certain events

Study Questions: Assessing External Criteria

For Review and Reflection

1. What is the goal of the archeologist when conducting research in the field?

2. Why is it unreasonable to expect that scientists would actually find any tangible evidence that the man Jesus of Nazareth actually lived in the first century?

3. If a papyrus dating to the first century was to be discovered and was actually claimed to be written by Jesus's own hand, what would most likely be the outcome?

---

[453] Ibid.

4. How is numismatics helpful to history? What significance does it have to the New Testament?

5. Name two of the many sayings of Jesus that archeological finds have clarified or brought a deeper meaning to:

   a. _____

   b. _____

6. Name two of the most significant archeologists who have contributed to the historical validation of the Bible because of their discoveries:

   a. _____

   b. _____

Group Discussion

1. Many of the archeological discoveries of the late eighteenth century and the early nineteenth century have clearly verified the events and people mentioned in the New Testament. With all of the evidence in favor of the historical accuracy of the New Testament, why do you believe that critical scholars continue to invalidate the Bible?

2. What do you see as some of the more important finds over the past 175 years that have served in validating the New Testament, and why do you find them important for the historical integrity of the Bible?

Key Terms

metaphysical: The reality of the unseen world that includes the existence of a spiritual realm that is not seen with the naked eye but is acknowledged by the effects that are evident in the physical realm.

numismatics: The study of coins for the purpose of learning about history.

proconsul: The title given to the governor of a Roman province.

tetrarch: A term that originally meant the ruler of one fourth of a particular region. By the first century, the title was given to an individual who was appointed as a "petty prince." This political position was lower than a king and was dependent on the Roman Empire.

topography: The physical way that the land is laid out.

Literature Cited or Recommended

Blomberg, Craig L. *The Historical Reliability of the Gospels*. 2nd ed. Downers Grove, IL: InterVarsity Press, 2007.

Dio Cassio. *Historia 57.8*. In *The New Testament in Antiquity: A Survey of the New Testament within Its Cultural Contexts*, edited by Gary M. Burge, Lynn H. Cohick, and Gene L. Green. Grand Rapids, MI: Zondervan, 2009.

Evans, Craig A. *Jesus and His World: The Archaeological Evidence*. Louisville, KY: Westminster John Knox Press, 2012.

Geisler, Norman L., and Ronald M. Brooks. *When Skeptics Ask: A Handbook on Christian Evidences*. Grand Rapids, MI: Baker Books, 2013.

Hemer, Colin J. *The Book of Acts in the Setting of Hellenistic History*. Edited by Conrad H. Gempf. 1990. Reprint. Winona Lake, IN: Eisenbrauns, 2008.

Netzer, Ehud. *The Architecture of Herod the Great Builder*. Grand Rapids, MI: Baker Academic, 2008.

Ramsay, William M. *St. Paul the Traveler and Roman Citizen*. Rev. ed. Edited by Mark Wilson. London: Angus Hudson Ltd., 2001.

Wilson, Clifford A. *Rocks, Relics, and Biblical Reliability*. Grand Rapids, MI: Zondervan, 1977.

Sherwin-White, A. N. *Roman Society and Roman Law in the New Testament: The Sarum Lectures 1960–1961*. 1963. Reprint, Eugene, OR: Wipf & Stock, 2004.

Electronic Sources

Images of the ruins of the Pool of Bethesda surrounded by the five colonnades, https://www.google.com/search?q=pool+of+bethesda&safe=strict&biw=1093&bih=452&tbm=isch&tbo=u&source=univ&sa=X&sqi=2&ved=0ahUKEwiFyPSkw5HOAhVDcz4KHYNNCC4QiR4IjQE.

Kreiger, Barbara. "Finding King Herod's Tomb." *Smithsonian Magazine* (August 2009). Accessed May 2, 2017. http://www.smithsonianmag.com/history/finding-king-herods-tomb-34296862.

Historical Archeological Evidence
Understanding the Context

Application of Scripture: The Pastoral Epistles

Read 1 and 2 Timothy and Titus.

The three letters are known as the "pastoral Epistles." Due to their contextual themes and distinct literary style, there has been much critical debate as to whether or not Paul is indeed the author of these pieces of scripture. Much of the debate is based on the idea that these writings are not accounted for in the book of Acts. All three letters are directed toward the individual leaders of their respective churches. Timothy was appointed the leader at the church at Ephesus, and Titus was based in Crete. They are personal letters, as opposed to Paul's other Epistles, which are written to the various churches. The problem that the critics note is that the context of the letters seems to identify a period in time that represents events that would have occurred after Paul's imprisonment in Rome.[454]

There are historical scholars who also debate the fact that there is no reason not to believe that Paul could very well have been released from prison for a short time and then incarcerated once again by Nero when he returned to Rome. The reason for the debate is based on the abrupt ending of Acts 28, where Paul remains imprisoned in Rome. Scholars know that Paul wrote several letters from prison, and they have been termed the "prison Epistles." Ephesians, Philippians, Colossians, and Philemon are all included in this set of Paul's writings. The pastoral Epistles, on the other hand, are not accounted for, and this is where scholars debate the authenticity of Paul's authorship. According to Eusebius (260–340), who came to be known as the "father of church history," Paul was able to defend himself just before the great fire in Rome (AD 64) and was released.[455] If Paul was indeed released for a short period, it is not unreasonable to believe that he would communicate with Timothy and Titus at this time.

Paul was clearly accepted as the author of these letters from the earliest of church writings, from the late first century and into more modern times. Some scholars believe that there are overtones of 1 Timothy in the writings of 1 Clement (AD 95 or 96) and in those of Ignatius (AD 35–107).[456] Polycarp (AD 69–155), a disciple of the apostle John, is also known to have quoted both 1 and 2 Timothy in his writings.[457] Other early church fathers, such as Irenaeus (AD 130–202), Clement of Alexandria (AD 150–215), and those who followed, referenced the Epistles. All of those who quoted the letters attributed the writings to Paul.[458]

Marcion (85–160), a late first-century leader of the Christian movement, was one who rejected the Epistles as scripture. Scholars, however, recognize the fact that he also rejected most of the New Testament, so it is not surprising to find that he disregarded the pastorals. Marcion could not accept the God of Israel as the Almighty God, but he did accept Jesus as Savior. The

---

[454] Gary M. Burge, Lynn H. Cohick, and Gene L. Green, *The New Testament in Antiquity: A Survey of the New Testament within Its Cultural Contexts* (Grand Rapids, MI: Zondervan, 2009), 364.

[455] Eusebius, *Ecclesiastical History* 2.22.2.

[456] D. A. Carson and Douglas J. Moo, *An Introduction to the New Testament* (Grand Rapids, MI: Zondervan, 2005), 579.

[457] Ibid., 574, 579.

[458] Ibid., 579.

mere fact that he rejected the pastorals suggests that he was familiar with them; that in and of itself tells researchers that Paul's writings were indeed in existence at that time.[459] His work also reveals that he rejected the Hebrew scriptures and any writings that gave credence to them.[460] On a positive note, all three Epistles are found in the Muratorian Canon that dates from about AD 170 and was clearly accepted by the early church.

Since we agree with the earliest church fathers and the care they took to ensure that the writings that have been accepted as part of the canon were authentically written, we approach our study of the pastorals by seeing them as trustworthy and authoritative. It is known from Roman history that Nero died in AD 68. Therefore, the pastorals were most likely written at some point between AD 65 and 68. Historians believe that 1Timothy and Titus were written between 65 and 66 and that 2 Timothy was written around 67 or 68, which would have been Paul's last correspondence before he was martyred. The authorship of the letters has been debated for the past one hundred years because of the rise of liberal criticism. There is another point of contention, however, when it comes to Paul's pastorals, and that is the nature of their content.

The controversy that has ensued over the interpretation of the meaning of 1 Timothy has been nothing less than cacophonous in the twentieth and twenty-first centuries. The problem resides in the interpretation of the role of women in the church, which will be discussed later in this section of the chapter. Noted in the first part of this chapter, we learned that certain types of archeological discoveries are invaluable for the interpretation of literature from antiquity. It is also paramount to pay attention to the geographical location of the recipients of these letters in order to responsibly interpret their intended meaning. The letters addressed to Timothy indicate that he was a leader of the church in Ephesus (1 Tim. 1:3), while the correspondence to Titus reveals that he was in Crete (Titus 1:5).

> As I urged you when I was going to Macedonia, remain at Ephesus so that you may charge certain persons not to teach any different doctrine.
> 1 Tim. 1:3 (ESV)

Each of these locations had its own nuances and cultural dilemmas. In an earlier chapter, we discussed Ephesus and its excessive ties to pagan religious rituals. Ephesus was one of the great cities of the known world in antiquity, situated in the Lycus valley.[461] The Lycus valley was a major roadway for merchants, and as a result, Ephesus was fast growing and had a cosmopolitan atmosphere.[462] Due to its location, its citizens were influenced by the world at large. This is a very important factor to keep in mind when understanding what Paul was instructing Timothy to do. In any growing culture that is exposed to outside influences, it is inevitable that eventually there will be changes in societal morals and mind-sets. Historian sleuths must consider this cultural factor when interpreting historical documents from antiquity.

In the case of the correspondence to Timothy, it would be reasonable to consider that there may have been a *paradigm shift* in the works. Change in a society is often unsettling for some and taken to extremes by others. Somewhere in the middle of the two extremes, a paradigm shift will occur, and the morals of an entire culture will have also shifted. It appears that this may be the

---

[459] F. F. Bruce, *The New Testament Documents: Are They Reliable?* 6th ed. (Grand Rapids, MI: William B. Eerdmans, 1981), 17.

[460] Carson and Moo, *An Introduction to the New Testament*, 580.

[461] William M. Ramsay, *St. Paul the Traveler and Roman Citizen*, rev. ed., ed. Mark Wilson (London: Angus Hudson Ltd., 2001), 282.

[462] Ibid.

case when it comes to the controversy over the roles of women in the church. It is clear that the note to Titus found him in Crete (Titus 1:5), where Paul had left him. Crete was well-known to be a very difficult and hedonistic culture (Titus 1:12).

Have you detected any paradigm shifts in the cultural mind-set from 1959 to our present time? Write about it here:

_____

List at least three shifts that have changed the face of the West:

    1. _____
    2. _____
    3. _____

We will begin by digging into the main theological issues that prompted Paul's correspondence to both Timothy and Titus. The focus of the letters is more about how to manage the church than to admonish and warn the congregation. There is a great deal of emphasis on the behaviors of the leaders and the participants in the body of Christ. As we discuss the theology behind Paul's assertions, we will take the context of these first-century churches into consideration and apply it to our postmodern world. We will then compare the more critical aspects of the letters with historical evidences based on archeological finds.

Theological Theme

The Overarching Purpose

The first and second letters to Timothy are complimentary to one another in that 1 Timothy concerns itself with the ministry of the church and that 2 Timothy points to an Almighty God who is deserving of our proper worship and praise. First Timothy has drawn an unprecedented amount of criticism in the late twentieth and twenty-first centuries. It has become controversial because it has more to say about ministers than any other writing in the New Testament. Paul points out the importance of character throughout this Epistle and says little about the activities of ministers.[463] The author's intent is to set the boundaries as to who is suitable for ministry and who is not.[464]

First Timothy is also the first glimpse of any type of "creedal" formation that we have in the New Testament.[465] Perhaps it is because of Paul's ministry to the Gentiles that he found it necessary to establish a statement of belief that these Gentiles could remember and use as a foundation. It is important to remember that the scriptures from which the first disciples drew were the Hebrew scriptures, as there was no formal New Testament canon as of yet. The formation of creeds and statements of faith often comes about out of necessity.[466] Creeds are normally formed to protect a

---

[463] Carson and Moo, *An Introduction to the New Testament*, 574–75.

[464] Ibid., 575.

[465] Richard L. Niswonger, *New Testament History* (Grand Rapids, MI: Zondervan, 1992), 187.

[466] Ibid.

faith from heretical teachings.[467] The Council at Jerusalem would have been the first sign of any formal type of structure for this new movement, and it seems to have been structured much the same way that the Jewish leaders had been accustomed to, where everyone has a say (Acts 15:1–29).

The boundaries for ministers are very admirable and should unquestionably be taken seriously. Paul lays down the parameters for a character that mirrors the expectations of righteousness found in the Hebrew scriptures (Leviticus). The leaders of the nation of Israel were to show unrelenting devotion to and trust in the God of Israel. There is evidence of this as far back as when Moses led the people out of Egypt. When Moses disobeyed and lost his temper with God and the people right in front of the whole assembly, his punishment was a failure to enter the Promised Land (Num. 20:1–13; Deut. 3:48–52).

It is not that God expects perfection from those who are called into ministry, but He does expect obedience that yields righteous living. Paul's familiarity with the scriptures gave him insight into the character and nature of God that others did not possess. It was important that these new Christians, especially those who were Gentiles, understand that as the image-bearers of the Creator, they as followers of Christ would be the ones through whom the world would find its understanding of God. If the leaders of the church live licentiously, then that is the picture that the rest of the world will have of the God of Israel. In the Hebrew scriptures, we read how those who were appointed as Israel's religious leaders failed miserably as they allowed themselves to be carried away with the ways of the world and eventually misled the nation of Israel.

Give examples of modern-day ministers who are misleading the people. If you take their actions to their logical conclusion, what happens to the congregations that follow these ministers?

_____

_____

_____

_____

Jesus was the symbol of another chance for Israel. He was the perfect picture of God in the flesh. He exemplified obedience as the Teacher of all teachers. Paul's commission to Timothy serves as a reminder that those who minister are serving a God who demands His leaders guide people to Him and to Him alone. Jesus continually pointed people back to the Lord God and away from self and worldly ways. He warned that it was a great offense to mislead young Christians into sin and thus away from God (Matt. 18:6–7).

The disciples were all too aware of the seriousness of living righteously and the call not to mislead those who may be seeking salvation. Jesus's half-brother James warned the people that teachers of the faith would be judged more severely than others (James 3:1). This is perfectly in line with the character and nature of God. To mislead others in the ways of God is to lie and distort Truth. Those who are appointed into ministry are to be ready at all times to give an answer to those who ask, and that the answer would rightly point them directly back to God (2 Tim. 4:2).

Many of the new believers in Ephesus would have been Gentiles by birth, and therefore they would not have been familiar with God's character or nature. They needed to learn about the long heritage into which they were being grafted (2 Tim. 1:14), the significance of which was

---

[467] Ibid.

rich with historical significance and mercy.[468] In 2 Timothy, Paul's focus is not only on charging Timothy with the passing of the torch to qualified future teachers (2 Tim. 2:2), but also on making sure that people understood that God has done everything for them (2 Tim. 1:8–10).[469] These verses are filled with a deep sense of the grandeur of God and His unfathomable grace and mercy.

It was imperative that people grasp a glimpse of the nature and character of the God of Israel. They needed to understand that nothing they could do on their own could match the redemption that He offered through the Christ. Unlike other religions that the Ephesian people may have been familiar with, there were no religious rituals, nor were there endless lists of rules and regulations to follow. In Christ, their salvation was secure. The foundation for eternal life had been laid out for them, and out of gratitude their obedience should reflect their sincere worship of the Lord.

Paul impresses upon Timothy that whatever the latter teaches and passes down to others to teach, the *essence* of Christianity is nonnegotiable,[470] that essence being that the Christ is the center focus of the Christian life. There are no substitutes or other ways to salvation except through the work done on the cross (John 14:6). Paul exhorts that God has given every true believer the power of the Holy Spirit to become "self-disciplined"[471] and to live righteously (2 Tim. 1:7) without the need for religious rituals. He says that while the gift of eternal life is free, it will demand from us a life that, more often than not, will go against the grain of society (1:8, 12; 2:9, 12; 3:11–12).

> Jesus said to him, "I am the way, and the truth, and the life. No one comes to the Father except through me."
> John 14:6 (ESV)

Ever since Jesus brought the message of redemption and salvation to the world, there has been fierce opposition to the absoluteness of God's plan. Many who have followed Christ in truth have faced persecution. Yet, it is of utmost importance to remember that Jesus was the first to be martyred for God's message to the world. Why should we expect any less persecution for bringing the message? When we shrink back from speaking Truth, we reveal our lack of faith in the work of the Lord that leads to life. Paul impressed upon Timothy, and now to us through our reading, that there will be false teachers who will mislead many (3:1–5, 4:3).

If we are not prepared, through our diligent study of scripture, to learn about the face of God, we will, like blind sheep, be headed for destruction. It is only through the study of the Word of God that the Christian will not be fooled by the heretical teachings that have flourished since the second century. Paul was only reiterating what Jesus had taught directly to His disciples (Matt. 24:24) when he spoke of the last days in which we are living. There is no denying that heretical teachings of the Christian faith are rampant, especially in the Westernized world. Unfortunately, the vast majority of the population does not even notice, because they do not take the time to know God. As a result, they will be led down the path to destruction in the end (Matt. 7:13–14).

Give an example of a heretical teaching in the church today that is leading people down the path to destruction:

_____

_____

---

[468] Carson and Moo, *An Introduction to the New Testament*, 580.

[469] Ibid., 580–81.

[470] Ibid., 581.

[471] Ibid.

The letter to Titus reveals a newer and less established church than the churches in Ephesus. Titus was assigned to the church in Crete where Paul had evidently left him (Titus 1:5). He continues with his instructions as to what is expected from those who would act as leaders of the church (Titus 1:6, 7). There were also instructions aimed at the behavior of wives (2:3), men (2:6–8), slaves (2:10), and the congregation as a whole (3:1–2). The people of Crete had a reputation for being a rough bunch (1:11–13), yet Paul placed his faith in the work of Christ in that even those who were raised in a godless atmosphere could be redeemed.

Titus was to stress among the congregation that although the lifestyle they were to lead may have been foreign to them, it was by the grace of God alone that they would be saved for eternity (2:12) and not of their own efforts. It was because of the work on the cross (3:3–7) that they were given the opportunity to raise the bar to a higher righteousness and consciousness than the cultural norms to which they were accustomed. Titus was to charge any appointed leaders with the courage to press on in their teaching, in spite of any opposition (1:10, 3:9). Paul reminded Titus that there was a higher purpose to living rightly, and that was to live in anticipation of the return of the Christ (2:13).

> If anyone is above reproach, the husband of one wife, and his children are believers and not open to the charge of debauchery or insubordination
>
> Titus 1:6 (ESV)

This is a message that those of us living in postmodernity desperately need to hear. Our purpose for higher living is not for our own edification or to set ourselves as superior to those who live without God in their lives. The purpose for living out a higher calling is to acknowledge the imminent return of the Son of God as He comes to usher in the kingdom of God. Our lives should exhibit a joyful anticipation of Christ's return as we are fully expecting to be at one with the Creator of the universe (Rev. 5:9–11, 21:3–5). Out of our gratitude, we are called to proclaim the kingdom of God to all who cross our paths regardless of the opposition that we face in our own day, because the consequences for ignorance are far greater than any persecution we would have to endure here on earth (Luke 13:27).

Character Trumps Activity

As humans, our natural inclination is to take the shortest route to achieving the goal of winning over someone's affections. Normally our efforts would take the form of giving gifts and speaking kind words to the individual. Historical evidence reveals that humanity has forever been performing all sorts of rituals and gift bearing in the form of sacrifices to the gods to find favor in their eyes. Paul, however, is reminding future ministry leaders that when it comes to the Creator of the universe, character trumps works. As mentioned in the preceding section, God has done all the work for us. It is a person's heart and mind that He seeks.

Those who represent the kingdom of heaven are held to a different standard than the rest of the world, and this is what Paul is stressing in these letters. He is pointing out that although church organization is very important, it is the character of the leaders (1 Tim. 3:8–10; 2 Tim. 2:14–26) and of the parishioners (1 Tim. 2:9–15, 3:14–15) that should be the main focus. These letters stress that accepting the salvation offered through Christ (1 Tim. 2:5–7; 2 Tim. 2:8–13) is far more important than concerns about trivial ideologies (1 Tim. 1:4, 4:3, 6:4). Paul emphasizes that *sound doctrine* is the key to leading people to God's perfect plan of redemption (1 Tim. 1:10–11;

2 Tim. 3:14–17). There is no question that inevitably the character of a church's leaders will have a trickle-down effect on the congregation.

The world watches Christians to see if they are actually capable of living at a higher standard. Even amid a society that staunchly touts relativism, deep down people truly want to see someone who exhibits ethical behaviors and standards that are ultimately based on the absoluteness of the God of the Bible. Any other standard will eventually reveal selfish gain or contradictions in its foundational purpose. When the local Christian church compromises the absolute standards of God's Word, the people will also compromise the standards set forth in scripture (even if they read the Word to know better) as they live out their lives. If Christians are to be the light in the darkness, then leaders are to set the example. Paul has stressed this point clearly in these Epistles.

Where do you see the local church compromising God's Word?

_____

_____

How do you think this will affect those who are watching what the church does?

_____

_____

Paul continually called Christians to purity. There has been much talk and speculation about his focus on women's braided hair (1 Tim. 2:9). When we are interpreting scripture, it is important to stay within the context of what the author is saying as well as to regard the historical significance. Paul's admonishment of women's hair is very similar to what is seen in 1 Peter 3:3. It seems obvious that both authors are making a point, that Christian women should place more emphasis on their countenance and disposition than on outdoing one another on the fashion front. This is one of those areas where it helps to better understand what the author is truly addressing by digging a little deeper.

According to historical records, elaborate hairstyles and ways of dressing were time-consuming and expensive.[472] Everyone would have clearly known that the more elaborate the hair or clothing, the more time and expense that was put into it. The point is that Christians as a whole should be focused on living righteously in the presence of God, and that meant a focus on family life and community. Secular historical documents also reveal that the women who had the money and the time to dress elaborately and to spend an inordinate amount of time on their hair were high-priced prostitutes.[473] This information gives us a much better understanding of what Paul and Peter were warning against.

> Likewise also that women should adorn themselves in respectable apparel, with modesty and self-control, not with braided hair and gold or pearls or costly attire. (1 Tim. 2:9 ESV)

---

[472] George W. Knight III, *The New International Greek Testament Commentary: The Pastoral Epistles*, ed. I. Howard Marshall and W. Ward Gasque (Grand Rapids, MI: Wm. Eerdmans, 1992), 135.
[473] Ibid., 136–37.

When studying the historical references found in secular literature, it becomes clear that the mention of costly clothing and braided hair is not the direct focus.[474] It is the connotation that the apparel and the elaborate hairstyles have for the individual sporting them. Literature from historical sources speaks of the sensual appeal that the clothing and hair have on the men who lust after this type of woman.[475] It is the impurity of thought that these ways of dressing provoke and not the hair or clothing alone that Paul becomes emphatic about. Throughout Paul's letters, we witness how quickly the behavior of these new Christian communities begins to change once he departs. Paul finds it necessary to remind those left in charge of the newly converted Christians that it is imperative to focus on the personal purity that reflects one's character.

Perfect Law

Purity of character is nothing more than what God originally asked of His chosen people since the beginning of His known interaction with humanity (Deut. 26:18–19; Exod. 34:9–11). The way to purity is to live within the boundaries set forth in God's perfect law (1 Tim. 1:8). The language he uses in this verse indicates that Paul is claiming that the Mosaic moral law is good because it was given by God.[476] The focus here is on how the Mosaic moral law convicts people of their sin and draws the unsaved to God for redemption. There are some who claim that Paul's statement in verse 9 exempts those who have come to believe in Christ and that this law is for those who are unsaved.[477]

> Now we know that the law is good, if one uses it lawfully. (1 Tim. 1:8 ESV)

This would be an incorrect assumption, as Paul clearly includes himself when he claims that "we know" (1 Tim. 1:8). Paul is asserting by his use of "we know" something that is of common knowledge and has been accepted as such (Rom. 3:19, 8:28; 2 Cor. 5:1; 1 John 5:18).[478] The law includes everyone, but it is the way that the law is interpreted and handled that will justify a person. It seems clear here that there were those who mishandled the law. The grammar used indicates an indefinite use of the law not only in how teachers teach it but also in how it is used by individuals.[479] In other words, although the ceremonial law had been abolished with the advent of the Christ, the moral law was to serve as a natural outflow of the work of the Holy Spirit in the life of a believer.

It is helpful to recognize that each time the Mosaic *moral* law is referenced merely as the law, it is mentioned in conjunction with ethical behaviors and not with religious or ceremonial rituals (Rom. 13:9). Romans 13:8–9 is discussed in connection with moral behaviors. The list of ethical behaviors parallels the *Decalogue*, as well as the way in which the law is applied in Exodus

---

[474] Ibid., 135. (Philo writes of the sensuality of a courtesan [*De Sacrificiis* 21]: "Her hair is dressed in curious and elaborate plaits," she wears "costly raiment," and "bracelets and necklaces[,] and every other feminine ornament wrought of gold and jewels hang round her.")

[475] Ibid., 137.

[476] Knight III, *The New International Greek Testament Commentary: The Pastoral Epistles*, 81.

[477] Ibid., 80.

[478] Ibid.

[479] Ibid., 81.

21.[480] When interpreting what law Paul is writing about (1 Tim. 1:8), it is safe to claim that Paul's mention of the "gospel" in 1 Timothy 1:11 is also pointing to the Mosaic moral law. This is consistent with the author's pattern, as it follows a list of unacceptable moral behaviors (1 Tim. 1:8–9). Paul is consistent in his terminology when he uses the terms *law* and *Gospel*, which are used frequently in conjunction with each other in other letters (Rom. 7–8; Gal. 3–4; Phil. 3:7).[481]

Understanding the purpose of Paul's exhortation is a key to discerning whom he is talking about. Who were these individuals who set themselves up as teachers? It does not seem as though Paul is condemning Judaizers like the ones he called out in the letter to the Galatians in chapter 2, as they were expecting these new Christians to be circumcised. It would not be unusual, however, for there to be individuals in Ephesus who were integrating other belief systems into the purity of the Christian faith. The message to Timothy was to emphasize that God's moral code was not to be understood as some sort of mystery, but its purpose was to redirect sinful lifestyles.[482]

This was not a new teaching for either Timothy or Titus. Nor was it new to any of those who clearly understood the Gospel of grace and that the Mosaic law was intended for healthy living (2 Tim. 4:2, 3; Titus 1:9, 2:1).[483] Ephesus and Crete, however, were far removed from Jerusalem, where the God of Israel had been preached for hundreds of years. This geographical distance made them vulnerable to false teachings and the tendency to *syncretize* local and regional beliefs systems with the message of the Gospel. Paul is reminding these ministers that they had to not only educate the new converts on the Truth but also raise their awareness of false teachings. It was these false teachers whom Paul was pointing out and whose distortion of Truth he was attacking.[484]

What character trait of God's does this perfect law reveal? How does it reveal that trait?

_____

_____

What other passages in scripture reveal how God feels about those who set themselves up as teachers but do so by misrepresenting His laws?

_____

_____

Roles of Women

There are many reasons that 1 Timothy is one of the most controversial Epistles in the New Testament. Aside from pointing out sinful lifestyles that are clearly not acceptable ways to live according to the moral laws set forth in scripture, this letter to Timothy appears to alienate

---

[480] Ibid.

[481] Ibid.

[482] Ibid., 83.

[483] Ibid., 90. The use of the term *sound,* as in "sound doctrine," was understood as *healthy* or *health giving.* This is where many scholars consider that perhaps either the physician Luke wrote this letter for Paul or it may have influenced Paul as he used this medical terminology to explain the benefits of living rightly before the face of the Creator.

[484] John Calvin, *1 and 2 Timothy and Titus: The Crossway Classic Commentaries,* ed. Alister McGrath and J. I. Packer (Wheaton, IL: Crossway, 1998), 23.

women from certain roles in the church (1 Tim. 2:12–13). These topics have given rise to innumerable amounts of ammunition for critics to denigrate the Bible as outdated in its precepts and its integrity. These verses have also given liberal theologians and the militant human rights organizations cause to further their agendas by aligning sinful behaviors with the claim of discriminatory practices against women. I might add here that this is a logical fallacy that does not follow a line of sound reasoning.[485]

> I do not permit a woman to teach or to exercise authority over a man; rather, she is to remain quiet. For Adam was formed first, then Eve. (1 Tim. 2:12 ESV)

Paul's call for women to be kept from leadership roles in the church has also fueled the atheistic view of Christianity as a false religion that promotes outdated male dominance over women. Our goal in interpreting difficult passages in scripture should always be to understand the true meaning of what the author is trying to convey to his or her readers. It is imperative to remember that a responsible interpretation should never go against the nature of God. We should also approach interpreting scripture as objectively as humanly possible. Objectivity is very important, as it is far too easy to become emotional and end up misinterpreting God's message to humanity.

What is Paul stating in these controversial passages? Biblical scholars have painstakingly searched every word and their original Greek meaning or meanings to understand what the author is instructing in these verses. Even with all of the careful word studies done, however, there is still room for debate as to whether Paul's admonishment of women in leadership roles was a contextual dilemma or not. Many scholars recognize that the Greek grammar that Paul uses when he points to the fact that the woman was created after the man (Gen. 2:18, 23) does suggest that the woman was made to *help* the man.[486] Paul understood that God's intent for this *helper* was not to be subservient to man, but to support and strengthen him.

It would follow that He expected women to support the men in the church, yet not in leadership roles. Of course it is natural for those living in a postmodern world to find this very difficult to understand or accept. How do we come to terms with something that is difficult to understand, especially when the desire is to live obediently? This is where it is necessary to dig deeper into the original grammar and the spirit behind the words. The language Paul uses in 1Timothy 2:11 is an imperative call for women to actually learn.[487]

> Let a woman learn quietly with all submissiveness. (1 Tim. 2:11 ESV)

> There is neither Jew nor Greek, there is neither slave nor free, there is no male and female, for you are all one in Christ Jesus. Gal. 3:28 (ESV)

Jewish literature reveals that the call for women to learn would have been a departure from Jewish tradition where men were to be instructed and women were to listen (Babylonian Talmud Hagiga 3a).[488] When he is emphatic about women to learn in submissiveness, this is meant to convey a submissive (respectful)

---

[485] See appendix A for a discussion on the argument for sexual diversity and how all attempts to tie the biological reality of being a woman to diverse lifestyles fail.

[486] Knight III, *The New International Greek Testament Commentary: The Pastoral Epistles*, 143.

[487] Ibid., 139.

[488] Ibid.

attitude toward the teacher, just as we submit to the Lord.[489] There is recognition here as well as in Titus 2:5 that although women were created as man's equal, there should be an acknowledgment that God placed the authority of a household in the hands of the male figure.[490] Careful word studies of 1 Timothy 2:12 do convey that Paul does not condone women to teach men in public (meaning the church).[491] For all intents and purposes, this appears to be very restrictive in the scheme of God's plan for humanity, if not perhaps even contradictory.

Why would God hold women to silence, especially when it comes to spreading and teaching the Gospel of Christ (Matt. 28:19–20)? The appearance of a contradiction forms when passages such as 1 Timothy 2:12 are contrasted to Paul's letter to the Galatians (Gal. 3:28). Paul is adamant about the equality that Christ has afforded to all of humanity. The God of Israel had provided for a redemptive movement that would require that the free Jewish male would now have to share his "privileges of religion, class and caste" with not only Gentiles and slaves but also with women.[492] It is well-known that in the first century, women, children, and slaves were all considered as a lower caste of society.

Christianity offered all people new freedoms, and this is what made it so radically different from the belief system of the day. How do we reconcile this apparent discrepancy (1 Tim. 2:12) without compromising either the message of the Gospel or the character and nature of God? This is a literary struggle and has caused much controversy in many evangelical Christian churches and organizations in the Western world. What has happened here, it seems, is that scholars who read the passages of scripture that restrict women from teaching or holding leadership roles in the church must take the passage out of its historical context in order to maintain that these passages were meant for all women throughout history.

This entire study is based on the importance of context, not only for defending the historical value of the Bible but also for the proper interpretation of God's message to humanity. What makes these passages any different from other passages that reveal God's intent for men and women to be equal? Second Timothy 3:16 clearly states that all scripture is God-breathed, and in light of this it is imperative to interpret the scriptures rightly so as not to distort or confuse either the character or the nature of the main Author. It is clear from Genesis to Revelation that God is at work with His intricate plan for the redemption of humanity.

The pastoral Epistles are not an exception to this plan. There is a continuous redemptive movement throughout scripture, even in the pagan cultures of Ephesus and Crete where Timothy and Titus were ministering. When Paul addresses the various cultures and communities in which he ministered, he always spoke into the unique context of each societal norm. Since the modern reader is privileged to assess this for himself or herself by reading through Paul's letters, it makes sense to understand the message that Paul is conveying to Timothy and Titus in their respective contexts.

The man said, "The woman whom you gave to be with me, she gave me fruit of the tree, and I ate." Then the Lord God said to the woman, "What is this that you have done?" The woman said, "The serpent deceived me, and I ate." Gen. 3:12 (ESV)

Throughout scripture, God is consistent in His redemptive

---

489 Ibid.

490 Ibid., 143.

491 Ibid., 141, 142.

492 Elisabeth Schüssler Fiorenza, "The Praxis of Coequal Discipleship," in *Paul and Empire: Religion and Power in Roman Imperial Society*, ed. Richard A. Horsley (Harrisburg, PA: Trinity Press International, 1997), 230.

message and movement. Genesis 3 represents not only humanity's alienation from God, but also an alienation from self, each other, and creation. There is a distortion of the harmony found in the created order that the Bible depicts in the days prior to the Fall. Immediately after Adam's disobedience, there is a clear tendency to reject accountability and to blame others for our own improprieties (Gen. 3:12–13). The consequence for disobedience for the woman's misdeed would be that she now suffer during childbearing, and that instead of an equal relationship with her husband, there would be a hierarchy where the husband would rule over her (Gen. 3:16).[493]

God's plan of redemption unfolds as the history of humanity progresses. In the Hebrew scriptures, the Creator begins to pull together a nation that is intended to bring balance back to the created order. The purpose of this newly formed nation was that all of humanity would be drawn to a just and holy God (Deut. 4:5–7; Isa. 61:8–9). The inescapable desire for peace and harmony between human beings would be finally realized in the God of Israel as the imbalance of humanity would be brought back onto an equal footing. The Bible clearly shows *Yahweh* setting boundaries that are meant to protect foreigners (Exod. 22:21), women (Lev. 18; Matt. 19:1–9), and slaves (Eph. 6:9; Col. 4:1). It would be uncharacteristic of the God depicted in scripture to redeem all of creation yet leave the imbalance between men and women as static.[494]

The redemptive nature of the Christ is a movement toward "a more just, more equitable, and more loving form" of life toward the way things were originally meant to be.[495] The authors of scripture were writing within the context of the culture being addressed. It does not seem to fit with God's redemptive intent that the words used by Paul be taken in isolation, hence hindering the Creator's initiation of a forward-moving "more fully realized ethic."[496] If this were so, it would be difficult to associate a slave and master relationship with an employer and employee dynamic in the postmodern world.[497]

If indeed it were intended for women to remain in silence or in subservient roles, this would seem opposed to the depictions that scripture reveals of Jesus's treatment of women in the New Testament. One would have to ignore Jesus's encouragement to Mary as she sat at His feet and listened to His every word (Luke 10:38–42). It should also be noted that there is never a mention in the New Testament where Jesus tells the women disciples around Him to keep the message of the Gospel to themselves or only to share it with children. The historical setting and context will help when interpreting God's redemptive movements. The following section will attempt to reveal a historically accurate picture of not only when these Epistles were written but also the cultural atmosphere in which they were penned.

Historical Relevancy

In order to better understand the context into which the author was speaking, it is helpful to remember that Paul's ministry was to the Gentiles (Acts 9:15). Historical records, however, reveal that there were Jews living all over Gentile territory: Asia, Macedonia, and the surrounding areas

---

[493] Genesis 3:16 (TNK).

[494] William J. Webb, *Slaves, Women, and Homosexuals: Exploring the Hermeneutics of Cultural Analysis* (Downers Grove, IL: InterVarsity Press, 2001), 36–37.

[495] Ibid., 36.

[496] Ibid.

[497] Ibid., 37.

where Paul is recorded to have traveled. Although he was called to reach the Gentiles for Christ, scripture reveals that he would begin his ministry in the various cities by first visiting the local synagogue (Acts 9:20, 13:5,14, 14:1). It was because of this practice that he would attract the attention of the Jews, which would invariably cause adversity. One way or another, there were always curious Gentiles who would eventually hear the message of the Way.

Can you think of a time when Paul was in a very difficult situation in Ephesus? Write about what was going on.

_____

_____

_____

One of the ways that scholars discern to whom Paul is directing his message is by studying what he actually says to the hearers. Jews were, and still are, notorious for keeping to themselves (for the most part), and they generally exhibited lifestyles that were different from those of the Gentile population. The pastoral Epistles were specifically directed at two men, Timothy and Titus, who were called to minister to the Gentiles in two areas known for their licentious living and depravity (Titus 1:12). Scholars believe that the pastorals were written between AD 62 and 68, prior to Paul's execution. There was a mix of Jews and Gentiles in the churches in both Ephesus and Crete.

Cultural Characteristics

The focus here will be on the cultural issues in Ephesus since that is where Timothy was being instructed on how to keep order in the church. When these letters were written is just as important as the cultural mind-set of that time. When Paul forbade the leadership of women in the church, was he talking about the Jewish women, the Gentile women, or both? To begin, it is beneficial to take a look at what it would have been like to be a woman in first-century Ephesus. Fortunately, this is one of the areas for which there are ample historical artifacts and writings that reveal how women were viewed in this context.

Historical inscription evidence shows that Ephesian women enjoyed new liberties beginning in the first century BC, when Augustus began to elevate some women to positions of authority.[498] There is also archeological evidence, in the form of coins and epigraphs, that reveals high-profile women were venerated in cultic-type worship rituals.[499] These women would have been the aristocratic women of the day.[500] The influence of Rome on the colonies in Asia was one of patriarchal dominance over women. It was seen as a great privilege to be elevated to the status of veneration as a *vestal virgin*. One great benefit of being chosen as a vestal virgin was that these women were not required to marry. A celibate and unmarried status meant that the women were free and not seen as the property of any man.[501]

---

[498] R. A. Kearsley, "Women and Public Life in Imperial Asia Minor: Hellenistic Tradition and Augustan Ideology," *Ancient West and East* 4, no. 1 (2005): 98.

[499] Ibid., 103.

[500] Fiorenza, "The Praxis of Coequal Discipleship," 232.

[501] Ibid.

Archeological studies reveal that during this particular time period, there was an increase in aristocratic women rising to a higher status in public life, which would afford them new freedoms.[502] This movement was especially notable in the city of Ephesus, where there are temples to honor these women and where numerous coins depicting vestal virgins have been unearthed.[503] This new status of women in society represents the beginning of a *paradigm shift* in the Greco-Roman culture that was present in Ephesus in the first century. The first-century Jewish woman, on the other hand, would not have been involved in this elevated-status system for women of the Ephesian culture. Their lives would have more or less mirrored that of the common woman in the first century.

Biblical scholars frequently point to Paul's letter to the Galatians (3:28) where he emphatically exhorts that all are equal in Christ. This passage does lend itself to criticism when contrasted with Paul's adamant restraint of women as leaders in any capacity in the church (1 Tim. 2:11–15). Whereas in this culture where the elite Ephesian women were being venerated and relieved of any requirements to marry and have children as mandated by the marriage legislation instituted by the Roman emperor Augustus,[504] Jewish women were not included. The Jews of the first century had their own set of rules and expectations for men and women.

A Jew in the first century was held to a certain legal system known as *halakha*, as well as to a system of religious commandments.[505] The legal system governed every aspect of life for the Jew.[506] The halakha reflected custom and the punishments that one would incur for breaking a law. Women were held to the standards set forth in these laws pertaining to custom.[507] When it came to the system of religious commandments, however, women were "assumed to be excluded from any divine service unless otherwise noted."[508] Jewish law, in some instances, forbade women from studying the Torah[509] and, in other instances, suggested that somehow women had learned the Torah.[510]

Halacha did, however, forbid women from teaching men even the simple task of learning how to write.[511] This prohibition was due to the fear that the male students would be sexually attracted to the woman.[512] Jewish scholars note that the exclusion of women studying the Torah was in part instituted to make sure that she did not neglect her household chores.[513] There was an exception for being allowed to study, and that was when a woman could help her husband understand a female's sexual maturity.[514] Amid conflicting accounts, there are stories in rabbinic literature that recount how many women had quoted from the Torah in specific instances.[515] This

---

[502] Kearsley, "Women and Public Life in Imperial Asia Minor," 109.

[503] Ibid.

[504] Fiorenza, "The Praxis of Coequal Discipleship," 232.

[505] Tal Ilan, *Jewish Women in Greco-Roman Palestine* (Peabody, MA: Hendrickson, 1996), 176.

[506] Tracey R. Rich, "What Is Halakhah?" Judaism 101, 1995–2011, accessed January 25, 2018, http://www.jewfaq.org/halakhah.htm#What.

[507] Ilan, *Jewish Women in Greco-Roman Palestine*, 176.

[508] Ibid.

[509] Ibid., 191.

[510] Ibid., 193.

[511] Ibid., 193.

[512] Ibid., 193.

[513] Ibid., 194.

[514] Ibid.

[515] Ibid., 196.

would insinuate that girls and women did indeed know the Hebrew Bible even if was a limited knowledge.

It appears that the first-century Jewish woman had at least come to have a few privileges that her ancestors did not enjoy. The earliest writings of the Hebrew Bible reveal that women were treated as something to be owned, much like slaves and cattle (Exod. 20:17; Judg. 5:30).[516] In addition to lower societal status of women in antiquity, there is no word for "to marry" in the Hebrew language;[517] men "take wives" as one would take or chose a slave.[518] This illuminating historical information clearly reveals the imbalance caused by the fall in Genesis chapter 3, an imbalance that God's redemptive plan would set out to restore to its intended state. Even though some evidence of progress for women as human beings, and not as subjects, does exist, anytime there is a paradigm shift in a culture, there will be an overlapping of the old ways and the new ways.

Although the aristocratic, privileged Gentile women of the first century began to enjoy some freedoms, the common woman was still recognized as a second-class citizen in many instances. History reveals that most Gentile girls were not even named unless they took on the name of their father.[519] Noted archeological scholar of the twentieth century A. N. Sherwin-White notes that if a Roman father's name is Julius, his daughters would be known as "Julia Prima," "Julia Secunda," and so on.

How does this differ from what scripture reveals about women's names as found in Old Testament times?

_____

_____

Paul was aware of the demographic makeup of both the Ephesian and Cretan churches. Therefore, in light of his message to Timothy and to Titus, how is his restriction to Timothy to be taken to restrict women from authoritative positions in the church? Paul's message to the Galatian church (Gal. 3:28) was clearly a call to recognize that the God of Israel was redeeming the world through the Christ. It would stand as a clear contradiction to then turn around and restrict women from teaching or holding positions of leadership in the church. The Ephesian church was clearly a merging of two vastly different cultures. Throughout scripture, there is a consistency in the way that Paul appeals to and teaches the various people groups to whom he ministers. Scripture and archeological records reveal that every culture had a unique set of circumstances, and Paul consistently spoke into that cultural demographic and societal norm. His letter to the Ephesians is no different. It represents a picture of the culture into which Timothy was now appointed to lay down a foundation for the church. Paul's letter to Timothy was indeed "relevant to the Ephesian church because they suffered from all types of unorthodox teachings and pagan rituals."[520]

---

[516] Webb, *Slaves, Women, and Homosexuals*, 165.

[517] Ibid.

[518] Ibid.

[519] A. N. Sherwin-White, *Roman Society and Roman Law in the New Testament: The Sarum Lectures 1960–61* (1963; repr., Eugene, OR: Wipf & Stock, 2004), 162.

[520] Aída Dina Besançon Spencer, "Eve at Ephesus (Should Women Be Ordained as Pastors according to the First Letter to Timothy 2:11–15?)" *Journal of the Evangelical Theological Society*: 216.

Paul references the concern for deception and wrong teaching when he calls the women who believe the unorthodox doctrines "weak women" (2 Tim. 3:5–7). This shows a concern for the gullibility of the women who are in this Ephesian culture (1 Tim. 2:11–15). What is interesting is the language that Paul actually uses in this passage.[521] Paul uses generic terms for those who have deceived these gullible women.[522] The deceivers could very well have been other women who began teaching wrong doctrine out of their ignorance.[523]

> This is good, and it is pleasing in the sight of God our Savior, who desires all people to be saved and to come to the knowledge of the truth.
> 1 Tim. 2:3 (ESV)

In light of this possibility, it would make sense that Paul prohibits these women from teaching since he writes that God desires that all people be saved (1 Tim. 2:3–4).[524] If women would be prohibited from teaching others, even far into the future, this would contradict God's call for everyone to be a disciple for the kingdom (Matt. 28:19). In the book of Romans, Paul makes a strong case for all to become disciples and share the message of the Gospel (Rom. 10:14–15). If women are not included, then it would deny the fact that women are also prompted by the Holy Spirit to speak and teach, not to mention the mere fact that women are now called to learn and are prompted to share the Gospel of the Christ as a direct fulfillment of prophecy (Acts 2:16–21).

As mentioned earlier in this chapter, Jewish law did not include women in the process of active learning of the Torah. Paul, on the other hand, calls for women to committed learning (1 Tim. 2:11). This call would have been a radical departure from the Halakha.[525] Men and women would now be called to learn right doctrine side by side. When Paul writes to the Galatians, he stresses the equality that God's redemptive plan has brought about (Gal. 3:28).

Jesus stressed the freedom that would come with obedience to His Word (John 8:31), and likewise, Paul taught the Galatians that true freedom comes to those who give their lives to Christ (Gal. 1:4). Before God, all are equal in Christ. These freedoms undoubtedly stood in stark contrast to the patriarchal societies amidst which these new Christian communities existed.[526] The redemptive movement brought to the ordinary citizen a new way of life that included everyone to participate as equals.

Those who began to follow Christ were unknowingly creating a subculture within the greater context of the Greco-Romanized societal norms. Undoubtedly, this new subculture brought about unexpected situations that had to be dealt with accordingly. It appears that the only place where this restrictive mandate for women is found is in Paul's instruction to Timothy. There must be a reason for this. It would not be surprising or unusual to find that there would have been a mixture of not only common women in the Ephesian church but also aristocratic women. This demographic reality would have presented a clash of cultures but also an exciting new form of freedom never before offered to women. It would not be unreasonable to imagine how a relatively uneducated woman might become so excited about sharing the message of Christ that she inadvertently taught the Gospel incorrectly to others.

---

[521] Ibid., 217.

[522] Ibid.

[523] Ibid.

[524] Ibid.

[525] Ibid., 218.

[526] Fiorenza, "The Praxis of Coequal Discipleship," 229–30.

Write about an incident that you know of where either you or someone you observed shared the Gospel incorrectly:

_____

_____

_____

We know from outside historical evidence that there were indeed women as leaders in the early development of the church. One of the letters from Pliny to the emperor Trajan serves as evidence that there were women in leadership roles in the Christian church (in Bithynia) in the beginning of the second century (Pliny, *Epistles* 10.96)[527] and most probably even earlier. Careful contextual studies are imperative in the aid of interpreting the author's intent, especially when there is apparent conflicting information in the Word. Paul writes to the other churches with an emphasis that all are equal before God, and Jesus commends Mary for choosing to learn. Further study on how this divine redemptive movement began to change the lives of the people is warranted to better grasp this controversial piece of scripture.

What Does It All Mean?

What is known from contextual historical evidence is that Paul's restrictive statements about women clearly reflect the cultural norms.[528] The status of women in a first-century Jewish community is revealed through a well-known prayer found in rabbinic texts: "Blessed be He who did not make me a Gentile: blessed be He who did not make me a boor (ignoramus, peasant, or slave): blessed be He who did not make me a woman."[529] According to Jewish literature, women were not obligated, as were men, to attend the temple rituals.[530] An examination of the historical knowledge that we have of the temple that Herod built clearly reveals that when women did chose to attend the temple, there was a section set aside just for them. This women's court was designed so that men and women would not intermingle.[531] These are evidences that reveal to the modern-day reader of scripture the atmosphere and context for the Jews into which Paul writes his letters to Timothy and Titus.

In light of the rabbinic prayer mentioned above, how do you think that the religious leaders felt about the equality that Jesus brought?

_____

_____

---

[527] Ibid., 225.
[528] Webb, *Slaves, Women, and Homosexuals*, 160.
[529] Ibid.
[530] Ilan, *Jewish Women in Greco-Roman Palestine*, 178.
[531] Ibid., 180.

Can you think of a place in the Bible that reveals the attitude of the religious leaders toward the common man? Write about it below:

_____

_____

_____

Even though the Jewish women were kept at arm's length, there is Old Testament evidence of women having knowledge of the God of Israel and His promises of salvation to the people of Israel. The Gentile women from Ephesus, on the other hand, would have been completely new to this whole concept of sin, salvation, and the redemption of the soul. It should not surprise anyone that in their enthusiasm to spread the good news to others, they had many misunderstandings of this God of Israel. It is highly plausible that they also very likely inadvertently passed along misinformation to others. It would, however, be remiss and unfair to women not to think that the men were also guilty of doing the same. Historical records reveal that whether a woman was Jewish or Gentile, she had no access to the education and societal freedoms that men of the first century had.

Scientific Relevancy

Biblical Interpretation

In light of what has been presented in this chapter, it is important to keep in mind that the number one goal is to rightly interpret the Bible. When studying difficult passages like1 Timothy 2, it is helpful to study the cultural norms using archeological and literary data to responsibly interpret what the original intent of the author was. Historical data, however, will not always tell us exactly what the writer had in mind. In his letters to Timothy, Paul insinuates that women are more easily deceived than men (1 Tim. 2:14) and that there are gullible women who are loaded down with sin (2 Tim. 3:6). Observation of life shows us that neither history nor the reasons why people do what they do arise in a vacuum.

When sharing the Gospel with a postmodern skeptic, how do we reconcile Paul's injunction to silence women in the church? This can be a major stumbling block for men and women alike in the world today. This is true especially because there have been many women around the world who have made significant contributions and had numerous accomplishments that have greatly benefited humanity. How can the modern individual actually believe that all women are more easily deceived than men, especially in light of the fact that there is a direct correlation between knowledge and gullibility?[532] This is where it helps to know the historical backdrop against which the passage was written.

A person is less inclined to be deceived or thought of as gullible with regard to a certain subject when that individual is educated in the particular topic being discussed. Paul is dealing with new Jewish Christians (*Messianic Jews*) as well as new Christians who were previously pagan Gentiles. Neither group was truly familiar with the doctrine of redemption, but the Gentiles were less familiar with it. Judging by what is known of the Ephesian culture and the customs of

---

[532] Webb, *Slaves, Women, and Homosexuals*, 113.

the women, a careful reading of 1 Timothy 2 seems to indicate that Paul is referring more to the Gentiles than he is to the Jewish women. Historical evidence reveals that it was the aristocratic pagan women who would adorn themselves with fine clothing and braided hair, not the Jews.

The newly converted Gentile women would have had very little education on the nuances of either the Jewish or the Christian faith and the magnitude of its implications. This is not to say that the Jewish women would have comprehended everything about the Christ, but they would have at least had a background knowledge of who the Messiah was and would have been familiar with the wonder and glory of the God of Israel. Any proper interpretation of the Bible must be sought in its context to best be understood. The character of God can be seen and should be sought after, especially in a difficult text such as this.

Questions from Postmodern Ears

Throughout scripture the Creator is revealed as His plan for humanity unfolds. The reader is privileged to come to know God as His character is made known through His interactions with people. His plan of redemption is always forward-moving and is hindered only because of the reluctance of humankind. Nevertheless, if we keep this in mind, we are better able to understand the tenor of and the fervency with which the authors write. It is a fact that the modern world today relies heavily on scientific studies to validate many assertions.

It is very important, however, to discern what scripture actually records when we appeal to or explain passages that are difficult to comprehend. There are instances in scripture that modern readers reject simply because modern culture claims that scientific evidence reveals that certain people are born with genetic flaws or that times have changed. No matter how we interpret scripture, the explanation should always be measured up against the character and nature of the Creator. If at any point an attempt to qualify the meaning of scripture that is countercultural distorts the character or nature of God, it cannot be validated as truth.

A Better Understanding Based on Science

Paul is claiming that women are more gullible than men and that because of this flaw, they are easier to deceive. Is this assertion actual, or is this perceived? This idea has been proven scientifically false.[533] The factors that contribute to deception of both men and women alike are as follows:

1. Crossing cultural or economic boundaries
2. Age (younger people are more easily deceived)
3. Experience
4. Socialization of the individual
5. Intelligence
6. Knowledge and formal education
7. Personality (believed to be associated with a nature vs. nurture factor).

---

[533] Ibid.

It is clear that Paul is speaking into the Ephesian culture and more specifically to the Gentile women of that time. There are passages in the New Testament that mention women as leaders in ministry. Paul and the other writers are respectful of them, acknowledge them in their respective roles, and do not question their authority (see table 8.2).

TABLE 8.2. Women leaders in the New Testament[534]

\VOMEN LEADERS	SCRIPTURAL REFERENCE	OUTSIDE SOURCES
The Daughters of Philip *Prophets*	Acts 21:9	Eusebius: *Church History III, 37*
Junia - *Apostle*	Romans 16:7	
Euodia & Syntyche - *Evangelists*	Philippians 4:2-3	
Phoebe - *Evangelist*	Romans 16:1-2	Theodoret of Cyrrhus (393 - 460 AD)
Nympha - *Led House Church*	Colossians 4:15	
Priscilla - *Teacher*	Acts 18:24-26	
Apphia - *Led House Church*	Philemon 2	
"Chosen Lady" - *House Church Leader/Pastor*	2 John 1	
"Chosen Sister"	2 John 13	
Lydia - Led House Church	Acts 16:40	

The important thing to ask here is that if we interpret this passage as meant for a specified time and audience and not meant for all women for all time, would this distort the character of God? No, it would not. God works within every cultural context known to humanity, and in His redemptive movement He is seen as continually leveling the playing field of human existence. Therefore, an interpretation that appeals to the comprehension of God would not stand to distort the character of God as He moves to redeem humanity.

> But whoever causes one of these little ones who believe in me to sin, it would be better for him to have a great millstone fastened around his neck and to be drowned in the depth of the sea. (Matt. 18:6 ESV)

This does not make Paul wrong in making this assertion, as it was undoubtedly his observation of the reality of this culture and others like it. Jesus soberly warns all of those who follow Him that they should be very careful not to mislead others about God (Matt. 18:6). The penalty will be severe for those who distort the character of God, which would then cause a young[535] believer

---

[534] Marg Mowczko, "Women Church Leaders in the New Testament," Marg Mowczko: Exploring the Biblical Theology of Christian Egalitarianism, July 28, 2010, accessed February 3, 2018, http://margmowczko.com/new-testament-women-church-leaders/.

[535] Although the passage involves a little child, new believers of any age are considered as children before God.

to sin. Paul was right to want to prevent this from happening, and we should be just as cautious today. Although women are the focus in this passage, the guidelines for men are also very strict (1 Tim. 3:1–13; Titus 1:5–9).

Give an example of men or women in church leadership who are distorting the character of God through their unorthodox teachings:

_____

_____

_____

Archeological Finds

Learning about cultures in antiquity is undoubtedly benefited by the science of archeology as we have learned in this chapter. To conclude this chapter and this study of higher criticism of the New Testament, we will look at some archeological evidence that has helped scholars better understand the people of first-century Asia Minor. Evidence that has helped to better explain the role of women in Ephesus has not only included material found in literature but also has been discovered in the form of epigraphs and coins. In light of the evidence, the women of Asia Minor were experiencing a slightly less oppressive lifestyle than their counterparts in Rome. The epigraphic evidence of women holding public titles continues to mount.[536] The evidence reveals that public offices were held by the royal and elite women of society.[537] Their public roles included political decision makers (*Pythodoris*)[538] as well as those who held the elevated status of vestal virgins in the imperial cult worship system.[539]

Several of Paul's letters refer to sexual immorality (1 Tim. 1:10; Rom. 1:27). Although Paul frequently attracts all of the attention, his are not the only references to sexually immoral behaviors (Mark 7:21; Jude 1:4, 7; Rev. 21:8). The Jew was very familiar with what was meant by sexual immorality because of the boundaries set forth by the God of Israel (Lev. 18). The Gentiles, on the other hand, had to have these behaviors spelled out for them. In the New Testament, the act of sexual diverse relationships was frequently associated with perverse behavior (1 Tim. 10:1; Jude 1:7). Many today point to Jesus and claim that He was silent on this issue. That is a false assumption. Contextually, Jesus is speaking to Jews who knew the sexual boundaries set forth in the moral law. His audiences were very familiar with the punishment received by the populations of Sodom and Gomorrah.

The Westernized postmodern cultures around the world have worked diligently to erase the stigma of same-sex relationships, brought about by the Christian ethic. All of their efforts, however, neither will erase history nor expunge the fact that this sexual behavior is not acceptable to a holy God. Historical records and archeological discoveries reveal that even in the Roman Empire into which Paul frequently spoke, this sort of activity was recognized as erotic and fatalistic.[540] This

---

[536] Kearsley, "Women and Public Life in Imperial Asia Minor," 100.

[537] Ibid., 103.

[538] Ibid., 101–2.

[539] Fiorenza, "The Praxis of Coequal Discipleship," 232.

[540] Kyle Harper, *From Shame to Sin: The Christian Transformation of Sexual Morality in Late Antiquity* (Cambridge, MA: Harvard University Press, 2013), 6–7, 23–25.

behavior was associated with *pederasty* and dominance over slaves.[541] An archeological find of silver goblets (known as the Warren Cup) engraved with descriptive illustrations of men having relations with boys serves as a clear indicator of the moral conscience of the day.[542]

Conclusion

Archeological artifacts are invaluable to discerning the cultural and political climate into which the writers of the New Testament were speaking. Archeological discoveries also aid in affirming the geographical locations mentioned in scripture. One thing that is consistent throughout scripture is the fact that God is forever meeting people where they are. In the Gospels, Jesus treats His audiences much differently than he does the religious leaders who stand in opposition to Him. Due to the fact that Jesus was focusing on the Jews (Mark 7:27–28), He did not have to explain the law and guidelines to them in detail the way that Paul had to explain them to his Gentile audiences.

In the first century AD, Paul was used as God's vessel to address situations and individuals in the cultures in which they lived in order to meet them where they were. God is always consistent in His character and continues to meet humanity in the twenty-first century wherever they may find themselves. Understanding that the Lord is always forward-moving in redeeming humanity, while at the same time never compromising or contradicting His own Word, will aid the reader with a better comprehension of God's Word and His intent. To better comprehend scripture is to better understand the Creator. Using the tools found within higher criticism will aid in validating scripture and its historicity, but it will not automatically serve to know the heart of God. Higher criticism will, however, shed light on how the Creator has operated throughout time. Knowing God requires a heart that truly seeks His face while reading His Word (Hosea 4:5–7).

Review: Assessing External Criteria
Study Questions: Archeology

For Review and Theological Reflection, and for Assessing Historical Accuracy and Interpretation

1. Why is it important to understand why Marcion rejected the pastoral Epistles? What else did he reject?

_____

_____

_____

2. What other factors need to be considered when interpreting scripture?

_____

_____

_____

---

[541] Ibid., 26.

[542] Ibid.

3. Why is it important that Timothy and Titus emphasize to their congregations that Christ not only has done all of the work for their salvation but also is the essence of Christianity? Give three main reasons:

   a. _____

   b. _____

   c. _____

4. Is personal purity really that important to a Christian? Why or why not, and what scripture do you find to back up your assertion?

   _____

   _____

5. Why is it necessary to interpret scripture as objectively as possible? What are the dangers when subjectivity and interpretive liberality is in effect?

   _____

   _____

   _____

6. Why would the Jewish women most certainly not have been vestal virgins?

   _____

   _____

   _____

Group Discussion

1. Discuss with your group why it is important to pay attention to the geographical location of the recipients of the letters written.

2. What parallels do you see between the cultures of Ephesus and Crete and your own culture? Is there hope for your country? What will it take for the world around you to change?

3. What were some of the differences between the Ephesian cultural norms with regard to women and the Jewish cultural customs? How does this help interpret Paul's intent?

4. Discuss how Paul's injunction that prohibits women from leadership positions would be a stumbling block for modern-day skeptics as well as for Christians.

Key Terms

Decalogue: A term used to signify the Ten Commandments.

essence: The fundamental nature of the faith.

halakha: The Hebrew word for "to walk" or "the way." The name given to the legal system that governed every aspect of life of the Jew. It reflected custom and the punishments that one would incur for breaking the law.

Messianic Jews: Jewish people who came to realize and recognize that Jesus of Nazareth was the long-awaited Messiah sent by the God of Israel.

paradigm shift: A change in an entire culture of beliefs, morals, and the way things are done.

pederasty: The act of molesting a child.

Pythodoris: A Roman queen who held the highest political office in Pontus (in Asia Minor) during the first century. Augustus promoted men and women to political power during his reign. She is an example of an aristocratic woman who held public office in the first century, which indicated a break with Roman tradition and the roles women were allowed to have.

sound doctrine: A teaching that is not distorted and that represents truth.

syncretize: The merging of two or more belief systems into one convoluted understanding.

vestal virgin: Females from aristocratic families who were elevated to the status of worship as part of the Roman cultic worship system. They were chosen between the ages of six and ten to serve the Roman goddess Vesta. They were vowed to chastity for thirty years, after which time they were allowed to marry.

Yahweh: The Hebrew term for the God of the covenant. It is the divine name for the God of Israel. It is used over six thousand times in the Old Testament.

God's Attributes

immutability – Throughout scripture we are privileged to witness a God who is consistent in His plan of redemption. He continues to move to a more equitable world as He works with humanity and the imbalance that was generated by the Fall.

<u>justness</u> – The Lord is just. This becomes evident in the way that the Father continues to include those who have been mistreated by society because of their age, gender, or societal status.

<u>sovereignty</u> – God made sure that future generations would be able to discern His message by leaving just enough evidence from various societies and cultures in the first century. These clues give scholars a better glimpse of the past in order to properly interpret the Bible.

Appendix A

The argument given by contemporary advocates for sexually diverse lifestyles is one that follows a line of reasoning that is fallacious at its core. There is a deliberate attempt by progressive scholarship and others to downplay the apostle Paul's integrity by making his remarks about women in leadership roles as limited to a certain time in history and then comparing that to his call for purity in lifestyles. While it may be true that Paul was speaking on a contextual level about certain women in a specific culture, there is not a connection to the lifestyle that one chooses to live and the fact that one is a female. The attempt to bind these two forbidden areas is a deliberate appeal to modern minds. The thought is that those living in the twenty-first century know that educated women are adept at holding leadership positions and are capable of imparting accurate information to others, so that to discriminate against a woman and keep a woman from leadership in the church stems from an antiquated ignorance. Therefore, the lure is an attempt to associate Paul's mandate for women to be banned from leadership with his call for purity and the rejection of a sexually diverse lifestyle.

The next stage to their argument is to equate being a woman with being a homosexual. Unfortunately, the modern Westernized mentality has become lax in testing for truth, as the vast majority are like sheep, blindly following the masses. The mass media holds a vexing sway over the minds of an unsuspecting and lazy public. The attempt to equate women to a group of individuals who practice sexually diverse lifestyles does not follow any sort of logical reasoning. A woman is born with a set of chromosomes that indicate clearly that she is biologically a female. There are no chromosomes or genes that indicate that one is biologically a homosexual. The fallacious argument being made is flawed at its very core. Sexual diversity is a choice of lifestyle, whereas being a female is decided at conception through the joining of two sets of chromosomes. That is a well-known scientific fact. Frankly, it should be angering to women everywhere that they are being used as pawns in a sham that was designed to silence anyone, especially Bible-believing Christians, who does not approve of sexually diverse behaviors. It is nothing short of insulting.

God has given human beings free will to behave and live any way that they deem fit. He has also gifted each individual with a uniqueness that cannot be matched by anyone else in the universe. A big part of that uniqueness is embedded in our DNA and the chromosomes that each human has been given. There is a line of distinction that should be recognized between one's chosen behaviors and one's genetic makeup. Everyone makes a choice in how they will live out their lives, but to equate a lifestyle choice with the color of one's skin, ethnicity, or gender is slanderous and logically flawed. It is dehumanizing, and in cases where the behaviors are contrary to God's will, it is further marring of the One in whose image we were all created.

Literature Cited or Recommended

Burge, Gary M., Lynn H. Cohick, and Gene L. Green, *The New Testament in Antiquity: A Survey of the New Testament within Its Cultural Contexts.* Grand Rapids, MI: Zondervan, 2009.

Calvin, John. *1 and 2 Timothy and Titus: The Crossway Classic Commentaries.* Edited by Alister McGrath and J. I. Packer. Wheaton, IL: Crossway, 1998.

Carson, D. A., and Douglas J. Moo. *An Introduction to the New Testament.* Grand Rapids, MI: Zondervan, 2005.

Eusebius. *Ecclesiastical History 2.22.2.*

Fiorenza, Elisabeth Schüssler. "The Praxis of Coequal Discipleship." In *Paul and Empire: Religion and Power in Roman Imperial Society,* edited by Richard A. Horsley, 224–41. Harrisburg, PA: Trinity Press International, 1997.

Harper, Kyle. *From Shame to Sin: The Christian Transformation of Sexual Morality in Late Antiquity.* Cambridge, MA: Harvard University Press, 2013.

Ilan, Tal. *Jewish Women in Greco-Roman Palestine.* Peabody, MA: Hendrickson, 1996.

Knight, George W. III. *The New International Greek Testament Commentary: The Pastoral Epistles.* Edited by. I. Howard Marshall and W. Ward Gasque. Grand Rapids, MI: Wm. Eerdmans, 1992.

Mowczko, Marg. "Women Church Leaders in the New Testament." Marg Mowczko: Exploring the Biblical Theology of Christian Egalitarianism. July 28, 2010. Accessed February 3, 2018. http://margmowczko.com/new-testament-women-church-leaders/.

Netzer, Ehud. *The Architecture of Herod the Great Builder.* Grand Rapids, MI: Baker Academic, 2008.

Niswonger, Richard L. *New Testament History.* Grand Rapids, MI: Zondervan, 1992.

R. A. Kearsley. "Women and Public Life in Imperial Asia Minor: Hellenistic Tradition and Augustan Ideology." *Ancient West and East* 4, no. 1 (2005): 98.

Ramsay, William M. *St. Paul the Traveler and Roman Citizen.* Rev. ed. Edited by Mark Wilson. London: Angus Hudson Ltd., 2001.

Rich, Tracey R. "What Is Halakhah?" Judaism 101. 1995–2011. Accessed January 25, 2018. http://www.jewfaq.org/halakhah.htm#What.

Sherwin-White, A. N. *Roman Society and Roman Law in the New Testament: The Sarum Lectures 1960–61.* 1963. Reprint, Eugene, OR: Wipf & Stock, 2004.

Spencer, Aída Dina Besançon. "Eve at Ephesus (Should Women Be Ordained as Pastors according to the First Letter to Timothy 2:11–15?)." *Journal of the Evangelical Theological Society* 17, no. 4 (Fall 2004): 216.

Webb, William J. *Slaves, Women, and Homosexuals: Exploring the Hermeneutics of Cultural Analysis.* Downers Grove, IL: InterVarsity Press, 2001.

"Behold, the days are coming," declares the Lord God, "when I will send a famine on the land— not a famine of bread, nor a thirst for water, but of hearing the words of the Lord." (Amos 8:11 ESV)

CHAPTER 9

Lower Textual Criticism

What Is It?

The Bible is like no other document in human existence, merely because of the fact that it claims to be *the* Word of God. The Bible, more than any other document in the world, should indeed be scrutinized for its serious claims. If a person is asked to live within the guidelines set forth in scripture or else face the penalty of an eternity in utter misery, then this ancient book must somehow be validated as truth. It is a well-known fact that the care with which the Old Testament scriptures were copied from one generation to the next has been studied in detail by Hebrew scholars.[543] The New Testament has also been taken apart word by word in an effort to validate every detail found within its pages. Lower textual criticism's main concern is textual reliability of the documents that form the foundation of what Christianity claims as God's written Word.

Lower textual criticism is the analytical work of assessing the reconstruction of both the Old and New Testaments. Scholars aim at making certain that the language used is as close as possible to the original wording. The focus is also on validating that the historical claims made do indeed match up with the evidence found in the Hellenistic and Jewish cultures of that time period in history. One of the main reasons why people have difficulty accepting the Bible as the inerrant Word of God is the sharp and misleading criticism that it has faced since the nineteenth century. The New Testament has been bombarded with numerous denunciations including, but not limited to, the accusation that it was written for political purposes.[544] The claim is that the New Testament was created as a way to control the people living under Roman rule in the fourth century by the emperor Constantine (306–337).[545]

As a result of many unfounded criticisms, there is now a pervasive belief that the Bible is unduly corrupt with little hope of recapturing any of its original meaning or contextual accuracy. After studying the last eight chapters of *Under Investigation*, however, you should be able to say with confidence that nothing could be further from the truth. You would not be alone in

---

[543] See Emanuel Tov, *Textual Criticism of the Hebrew Bible*, 3rd ed. (Minneapolis: Fortress Press, 2012).

[544] Craig L. Blomberg, *Can We Still Believe the Bible? An Evangelical Engagement with Contemporary Questions* (Grand Rapids, MI: Brazos Press, 2014), 43.

[545] Ibid.

your assurance in the Bible as an accurate representation of the original texts and the historical context in which the authors penned the words that we hold today. Well-respected historians of Roman antiquity have long accepted and valued the integrity of the New Testament scriptures.[546] Unfortunately, the main skepticisms that have continued into the twenty-first century stem from liberal theological scholars and not well-noted historical secular scholarship.[547]

Regrettably, far too many skeptics and professing Christians are not willing to question the claims made by liberal scholarship, and they continue to take the Bible lightly. Is this due to the fact that people are so lost in their own self-reliance for salvation that to question outdated skeptical claims seems unimportant? It is as if there is a spell over the vast majority of the Westernized population and they are in a coma, blind to reality. Admittedly, it does take time to research the reliability of the Bible, but your eternal salvation may depend on it. The purpose of this chapter is to help the reader understand how the textual criticisms leveled against the New Testament are assessed and addressed.

What Historians Look For

Assessing lower textual criticism is the process of investigating the actual source documents that are in possession today. The manuscripts that still exist are known as *extant manuscripts* and are the documents that have been used to reconstruct the New Testament as we have it today. *Source investigation* researches both *external evidence* and *internal evidence* to make decisions that are intended to either validate or invalidate the integrity of the New Testament.

Source Investigation

External evidence includes the study of the following:

- The number and type of manuscripts available that are used to compare and contrast the various readings.
- The age of the extant manuscripts available.
- The quality of the manuscripts.
- The geographic location where the manuscripts originated.
- The similarities evident when compared to other reputable manuscripts.

Internal evidence includes the study of the following:

- The types of mistakes that a scribe would have likely made (intentionally or unintentionally).
  1. Confusing syntax
  2. Unusual vocabulary
  3. Theological oddities
  4. Brief comments

---

[546] A. N. Sherwin-White, *Roman Society and Roman Law in the New Testament: The Sarum Lectures 1960–1961* (1963; repr., Eugene, OR: Wipf & Stock, 2004), 189.
[547] Ibid.

5. Accidental misspellings
6. Accidental duplication or omission of letters, words, or lines of text, or odd punctuation

Criticisms Placed on the New Testament

Scripture Passage Anomalies

Granted, there are some passage anomalies that scholars have found puzzling, but in each case there is a clear recognition of the odd passage to make sure that it is not conflicting in its nature.

One of the most glaring anomalies in the New Testament can be found in the Gospel of Mark, 16:18. The passage mentions that true believers will be nearly impervious to venomous snakebites and the ingestion of deadly poisons. This particular verse is part of a passage (Mark 16:9–20) that scholars repeatedly point out as written by someone

> They will pick up serpents with their hands; and if they drink any deadly poison, it will not hurt them; they will lay their hands on the sick, and they will recover.
>
> Mark 16:18 (ESV)

other than Mark.[548] The thought is that Mark's ending was quite abrupt in the way he seems to stop writing his version at verse 8, and it is likely that the scribe copying it added a few verses that seemed appropriate.[549]

The added material would not have been anything that the first and second generation of believers did not already know, especially when it came to the resurrection.[550] Scholars believe that the reference to snake handling was most likely inserted because of the mention of what is found in Acts 28:3–6. Paul was not affected by the snakebite that he endured while on the island of Malta, and this was seen as the protection of God on Paul's life. Due to the fact that some of the earliest manuscripts do not include the added passages to the end of Mark's Gospel, biblical scholars have been prompted to double bracket these verses in the majority of the Bibles that we hold today. It is important to point out, however, that this addition was an early addition made prior to the second century. Any good study Bible will make a special notation of this anomaly.

Why would a scribe feel the need to add anything at all? This is a difficult question to answer since there is no documentation to clarify what actually happened. What biblical historians do know, however, is that more often than not the exposed end of a scroll was very vulnerable to tears. The reason the Gospel of Mark ended as abruptly as it does in some of the extant manuscripts could very likely be due to the fact that it simply tore off over time.[551] It is also possible that Mark simply did not have the opportunity to complete it. In real-life circumstances it is rare that a writer is given the time to write everything that he or she has to say in one sitting. Perhaps the scribe making a copy decided to give it an ending that would encourage believers of the time to hold fast to the reality of the power of the resurrection and faith in the Christ. The most important thing to understand and recognize, however, is that the addition in no way takes away or adds to the events surrounding the resurrection or the nature of the Creator.

Fourth-century church historian Eusebius notes that this section of the Gospel of Mark is

---

[548] Blomberg, *Can We Still Believe the Bible?*, 18–19.
[549] Ibid., 19–20.
[550] Ibid.
[551] Ibid., 20.

found only in a few manuscripts that were at his disposal.[552] Nevertheless, there is evidence that second-century church fathers Irenaeus and Tatian were familiar with this longer ending to Mark.[553] The fact that there were early church fathers who recognized these last verses of the Gospel of Mark serves as evidence that this was an early insertion and a not a later addition with any sort of theological or political agenda tied to it. This is not the case, however, with another scriptural passage that has been the target of a great deal of liberal skepticism, John 7:53–8:11.

Very few of the "oldest, complete, and most reliable manuscripts" include this passage about the woman caught in adultery.[554] Oddly enough, the few manuscripts that do contain this event are found either in the Gospel of Luke just after 21:38, at the end of his Gospel narrative, or after John 7:36.[555] Although there is nothing about this story that is theologically troubling, the ESV Study Bible notes do caution readers about its uncertain origin.[556] It remains in the Bible narrative because it is found in a limited number of early manuscripts, although few and far between, and it does not contradict any sound theological doctrine. Most important to note is that this passage does not take away from an understanding of the grace that Jesus continually extended to humanity during his earthly ministry. Some may ask the question, why would the church leave in a passage that is only found in a limited number of manuscripts? The reason lies in the brevity with which the early church took the words written about our Lord. They respected those recorded events as holy and did not see it as their right to discount any events that depicted the disciples and their accounts of their experiences with the Messiah.

Although the above scripture passages are anomalies, they have been left in the New Testament because they are found in enough of the extant manuscripts to warrant keeping them. Biblical scholars have not discovered any other such glaring anomalies in the twenty-five thousand extant manuscripts that are held today.[557] Scribes were known to be as careful as humanly possible to copy the *autographs* and manuscripts of their time in a painstaking effort to preserve the Word of God as they found it. Aside from the accidental miscopy of individual words, scholars can only guess at why a certain piece of scripture may be a fraction different in one manuscript than in another. Even with anomalies, the variations in no way change the character and nature of Jesus as the Son of God.

Textual Variants

Regardless of what type of variant is found in scripture, good study Bibles will have clear footnotes on the variations that exist. There are "around 200–300 *textual variants* in the New Testament."[558] This is astounding considering that there are roughly twenty-five thousand extant manuscripts in possession today. One such variant can be found in Luke 22:43–44. Some early manuscripts

---

[552] Ibid., 18.

[553] John MacArthur, *The MacArthur Study Bible: New King James Version*, footnotes Mark 16:9–20 (Nashville: Thomas Nelson, 1997), 1502.

[554] Blomberg, *Can We Still Believe the Bible?*, 20.

[555] Ibid.

[556] Ibid.

[557] Ibid., 21.

[558] Ibid.

contain these two verses, and others do not.[559] Even with the existing variants in this case, there is nothing theologically confusing or contradicting about the meaning of the event being recorded. In this particular case, Dr. Luke is making a simile by his use of the word *like*, which describes the duress that Jesus was under in the garden of Gethsemane.[560] The point to take note of in the few instances where there is a variation, like this one, is that the meaning does not change what is historically taking place.

> And Philip said, "If you believe with all your heart, you may." And he answered and said, "I believe that Jesus Christ is the Son of God." (Acts 8:37 NASB)

Biblical scholars decide on the veracity of a variant passage by studying the *external evidence* and the *internal evidence*. The external evidence would be how often the passage shows up in early literature outside of the biblical text. When internal evidence is scrutinized, scholars consider the various known extant manuscripts and compare them with each other to determine how many contain or do not contain the variations of the passage. If the evidence for variant passages or words is weak or insufficient, then the majority of biblical translations will relegate the word or passage to a "marginal reading."[561] If there is a variant reading that has very little consistent evidence, then the vast majority of Bibles will include it only in the footnotes.[562] One such passage that is mentioned only in the footnotes of most Bibles is Acts 8:37.

There are only a handful of textual variants that are considered interesting enough to take note of, and in each case the variant does not in any way change the theological veracity of the text. Most of the time, the variants that consist of only a single word in a passage, which may qualify as anomalies, are not of great significance or interest. In the cases where a word variation has been discovered, scholars research the surrounding script to capture the original intent of the author.[563] It is possible for the Greek language to have words that change meaning if only a single letter in the word is changed. In the case where there is one letter in a word that is in question, it is accepted that the scribe more than likely inadvertently inserted a letter that looks like another letter in their alphabet (Ω = omega and O = omicron). The variant letter in a word, in most cases, will not change the definition of the word, only how the word is interpreted. For instance, a change of letter may either cause the interpretation to suggest a command or might infer a state of being, sometimes noted as a "mood verb."[564] Romans 5:1 is a good example of a word variation that can be translated as either a command or a mood verb. In the above verse, the Greek word used for "have" could either be translated as "let us have peace" (a command) or "we have peace" (a state of being or mood) depending on the insertion of either an omega or an omicron.[565] According to the research done on this word within this verse and surrounding text, the internal evidence appears to have been more conclusive than the external evidence. In this particular case, the use of *have* is accepted as a mood verb by scholars.[566]

---

[559] Ibid., 23.

[560] Ibid.

[561] Ibid.

[562] Ibid.

[563] Ibid., 24.

[564] Ibid.

[565] Ibid.

[566] Ibid.

Amid the numerous early manuscripts, there are a few word variations that exist, but none of them pose any threat to the theological tenor of the passage as it works with the surrounding text. There are several reasons why there are words that pose a slight variation from one manuscript to another. The modern reader should always keep in mind that Christianity had spread very quickly, and although the scribes were very faithful to the manuscript texts from which they copied, the scribes would have been scattered, along with the disciples, in various geographic locations. We learn from Paul's writings that in Gentile territory it was, at times, necessary to explain theology in a way that the people could best understand so that the readers and listeners could better grasp the theological doctrine being conveyed within their own context. The debated verses and passages may contain simple word variations that have a word in the singular in some manuscripts and the same word listed as a plural in others (Jew/Jews; John 3:25). Other variants might include the addition of a pronoun for the purpose of clarification as to whom the author is referring ("his" in John 3:16), and in still other verses, there are variations in the use of the Greek verb tense that is used to match a prior verse ("believe," John 3:12).[567] None of the variations change the meaning of the text and appear to have been added if only for the purpose of grammatically smoothing out a passage within its literary context.

> ESV: Now a discussion arose between some of John's disciples and a *Jew* over purification.
>
> KJV: Then there arose a question between some of John's disciples and the *Jews* about purifying.
>
> John 3:25 (emphasis added)

Rectifying Criticisms

It is not news that the entire New Testament has been scrutinized with what would be equivalent to a magnifying glass many times over. Every single variant has been addressed by highly qualified individuals, many of whom have spent their entire professional careers devoted to the study of the textual variants found in the Bible. One of the leading and most vociferous New Testament critics of the twentieth century is a professor by the name of Bart Ehrman. Aside from pointing out the word variations found in the New Testament, he has postulated that the early autographs and manuscripts were most likely not as conforming to a standard as the copies created after the emperor Constantine in the fourth century.[568] While it is true that the biblical texts became more standardized after Christianity was legalized, Ehrman's implications of a wide variety of textual diversity are unsubstantiated.[569] His suppositions are not based on any type of factual data; they are conjectures based on his own theories.[570]

Fortunately, there is evidence that is contrary to any claims that the earlier extant manuscripts reveal vast amounts of diversity within and between the various texts. Scholars have recovered over 102 copies of books from the New Testament dating to the second and third centuries, and none of them reveal problematic textual variations.[571] Every single early manuscript is found to have been carefully penned by a professional scribe and not to be the product of careless and

---

[567] Ibid., 25.
[568] Ibid., 27.
[569] Ibid.
[570] Ibid.
[571] Ibid.

illiterate scribbling, as is the accusation of liberal critical scholarship.[572] Amid the loud and repeated unfounded criticisms from a select group of critical scholars who continue to ignore the evidence to the contrary, it is imperative to be reminded that the evidence reveals that less than one-tenth of 1 percent of variants are actually considered important enough to be included in the footnotes of most English-translated Bibles.[573] This is such a small percentage that even one of the New Testament's most staunch critics, Ehrman, admits that the theological doctrine of the Christian faith is not affected in the slightest by any of the variants found in the New Testament.[574]

Existing Manuscript Evidence

The New Testament has absolutely no rivals when it pertains to the amount of hard evidence in the form of available early manuscripts that have been discovered over the last few centuries. New Testament documentation far exceeds that of any other work of literature from either secular or other religious texts from antiquity in both quality and quantity. The New Testament finds itself in a class of its own as to its historical accuracy and reliability. The Bible can boast that there are well over fifty-eight hundred early Greek manuscripts known today of the New Testament. This number far exceeds that of any other text from antiquity. It is with these extant manuscripts that scholars have been able to reconstruct the New Testament scriptures.

The process of reconstruction is like any other reconstruction of literature from history. When manuscripts are discovered, they are carefully compared with other accepted and scrutinized documents already in possession. When there are variations, the surrounding text is taken into consideration, and the document is rejected either because its integrity is obviously not acceptable or accepted because it is obvious that it belongs as part of the New Testament. It is helpful to have as many extant manuscripts to compare to each other as possible to gain an accurate representation of how the autographs were meant to be read. As God would have it, there are more manuscripts and higher-quality manuscripts of the New Testament in existence than for any other piece of literature from antiquity.

Existing Extant Manuscripts

The *John Rylands Fragment* is housed in the John Rylands Library in Manchester, England. It is probably the earliest-known extant *papyrus* manuscript in possession as it dates between AD 117 and 138. Some scholars suggest that it could be dated even earlier than AD 117.[575]

The *Chester Beatty Papyri* is a collection of ancient manuscripts dating from 1800 BC to AD 800 that are a part of the library collection of Chester Beatty, a collector of ancient manuscripts and codices. The New Testament documents found in this collection date from AD 200 to 250 and include all four Gospels and the book of Acts all in one complete book. The collection also

---

[572] Ibid.

[573] Ibid.

[574] Cited by Daniel B. Wallace, "Has the New Testament Text Been Hopelessly Corrupted?" in *In Defense of the Bible: A Comprehensive Apologetic for the Authority of Scripture*, ed. Steven B. Cowan and Terry L. Wilder (Nashville: B&H Academic, 2013), 161.

[575] Norman L. Geisler, *Christian Apologetics*, 2nd ed. (Grand Rapids, MI: Baker Academic, 2013), 343.

contains the entire letter to the Hebrews, most of Paul's Epistles, and most likely the earliest copy of Revelation.

The *Bodmer Papyri* is a collection that dates to around AD 200 that includes Jude, 1 and 2 Peter, and most of the Gospels of John (AD 125) and of Luke (AD 225).

The above collections alone represent testimony to the birth, life, crucifixion, and resurrection of Jesus all written within one hundred years of the events that they portray.[576] That these documents are extant manuscripts is an indication that the autographs were penned even earlier and closer to the dates of the actual events. One of the most famous *vellum* collections of manuscripts that represents the completed Bible as we know it today is held by the Vatican in Rome. This collection is known as *Codex Vaticanus* and dates from around AD 325 to 350. It represents the most complete works of the Old Testament and the New Testament books. It lacks only the front and the back books of scripture because they were torn, which was a common fatality in antiquity with written works.[577] There are other well-documented early Greek manuscripts that are too numerous to include here, as they represent well over fifty-eight hundred documents.[578] There are no other works of literature from antiquity that can begin to come close to the number of manuscripts from which to validate the integrity of the writings.

Reliability Comparisons

All significant ancient literature has undergone the reconstruction process to bring it as close as possible to its original form. Reconstruction scholars are able to restore a document by comparing all manuscripts that have survived over the centuries. Reconstruction of the originals is greatly aided by the number of manuscripts still in existence and by the dates that they were written. The closer in date that a manuscript was written after the original, the more accurate the reconstruction will be. Fortunately, the New Testament manuscripts are not only more abundant than other ancient literature but also were written much closer in date to the originals than other writings from antiquity. The manuscripts that we have at our disposal have greater support than ten of the finest examples of classical literature combined.

Part of the historical validation process, is to compare the New Testament manuscript evidence to those documents that have been accepted by scholars as valid representations of events in history. One of the most notable writings from antiquity is that of Homer. The secular writings of Homer come the closest to the earliest-known New Testament manuscripts regarding the time that lapsed between what is believed to be the work's original written date and the date when the earliest-known manuscript was discovered. Historical scholarship reveals fragments of manuscripts of Homer that date to 111 years after their original inception and full copies that date to 346 years after the original. The total number of reliable manuscripts available for validating the work's integrity is 643. Table 9.1 gives a representation of this and other writings from antiquity as they compare to the available manuscript evidence for the New Testament writings.

---

[576] F. F. Bruce, *The New Testament Documents: Are They Reliable?* 6th ed. (Grand Rapids, MI: William B. Eerdmans, 1981), 6–7.

[577] Michel D. Marlow, "Codex Vaticanus (B)," Bible Researcher, 2001–2012, accessed June 5, 2018, http://www.bible-researcher.com/codex-b.html.

[578] Geisler, *Christian Apologetics*, 344.

TABLE **9.1.** Comparison of available manuscripts and time lapse of notable historical documents

Document	Time gap in years	Number of manuscript copies
New Testament	25	5,686
Homer	346	643
Demosthenes	1,400	200
Herodotus	1,400	8
Plato	1,200	7
Tacitus	1,000	20
Caesar	900	10
Pliny	750	7

It is clear that the New Testament extant manuscripts far exceed those of any other works of literature from antiquity in number, but what about the accuracy of these documents? Scholars measure accuracy by careful consideration of the variants found when comparing the individual works of literature to each other. They study the total number of lines of text with the number the number of written lines that are questionable when making comparisons between the available documents. This is how historical scholars determine percentage-wise how reliable the text is to what the original autographs would have represented. The following comparisons have been made with other writings from antiquity:[579]

Reliability of the New Testament as Compared to Other Notable Literature[580]

Literature from Antiquity	Estimated Total Lines of Text	Total Number of Words Believed to be Questionable	Percentage of Text Believed to be Reliable
Homer's *Iliad*	15,600	764	95%
India's National Epic *Mahabharata*	Approximately 260,000	26,000	90%
New Testament (Greek Manuscripts)	20,000	400 40 lines in question	99.90%

There is clearly no comparison when it comes to the number and reliability of the earliest manuscripts of the New Testament and those of other works of literature from antiquity, whether of a religious tenor or secular.

Among the various works written by the Roman historian Tacitus, there are only two surviving manuscripts, known as Tacitus's *Annals of Imperial Rome*. It is from these remaining works of literature that modern man finds historical information about Rome in the first century. The surviving extant manuscripts of the *Annals* that pertain to Rome in AD 1–6 are from 1510,

---

[579] Ibid., 344–45.
[580] Information is based off of Bruce Metzger's *Chapters In The History of New Testament Textual Criticism*, 1962 and Norman Geisler's *General Introduction of the Bible*

and those manuscripts containing information from AD 11 to AD 16 are dated from 1430, both well over one thousand years after the events and noted autographs. Other religious texts from antiquity are also not as well-documented as the New Testament. One of the criticisms placed on the New Testament, has been that it was standardized after the emperor Constantine, and in that standardization the basic doctrines were amended to politically benefit the Roman Empire.

Fortunately, there is so much preexisting material in the form of extant manuscripts, which include early partial and full copies of the New Testament together with the Old Testament, that those types of criticisms are clearly unfounded and inaccurate. The Islamic Qur'an, on the other hand, was subject to a massive reorganization and standardization in AD 653 that is said to have been ordered by the Caliph 'Uthmān.[581] History records that there were numerous efforts to standardize the Qur'an text that led to the suppression and destruction of the variant materials in existence at some point between 632 and 653.[582] The first canonical text form was held and interpreted by 'Uthmān between 653 and 705.[583] It is recognized that there were other variations held by a few Islamic religious leaders who refused to give up their own private versions, which implies that they felt that their version was superior to that of 'Uthmān's.[584] As a result, it is difficult to tell if the copies of the Qur'an in existence today are entirely the same as the various and "loose body" of material that was around when Muhammad was building the Islamic religion (610–632).

Unfortunately for the Qur'an, unlike the New Testament, the sources that are available are inadequate for reconstructing the original text from the time of Muhammad or even immediately after his death (AD 632).[585] Without the ability to reconstruct from any original sources of direct extant manuscripts, critical scholars are not able to affirm what the original text actually said or if there was one at all. New findings also reveal that the Qur'an was more than likely mostly originally written in Syriac, and not Arabic as is customarily claimed.[586] Without any documentation to the contrary, critical scholars suggest that the Qur'an is a conglomeration of rabbinic writings, Syrian legends, and Christian liturgies that were in existence long before either Muhammad or the date that the Islamic religion is claimed to have been formed.[587] In essence, there is absolutely no comparison between the veracity of the Holy Bible and that of the Islamic Qur'an.

A very important indicator for dating literature from antiquity is the existence of external documentation that cites from the original autographs. It should go without having to say that if a piece of work is cited, that is a clear sign that it was written prior to its documentation. God made absolutely certain that His Word would survive even the mass destruction of Christian literature during the reign of the Roman emperor Diocletian (AD 284–305). Even if there were no extant manuscripts from which to draw, the citations of the New Testament found in the writings of the early church fathers are so numerous that all but eleven verses are quoted repeatedly. The entire New Testament could be reconstructed using the writings of these early church fathers.

---

[581] Keith E. Small, *Textual Criticism and Qur'ān Manuscripts* (United Kingdom: Lexington Books, 2012), 177–78.

[582] Ibid., 179.

[583] Ibid., 165.

[584] Ibid.

[585] Ibid., 177.

[586] Daniel J. Janosik, *John of Damascus, First Apologist to the Muslims: The Trinity and Christian Apologetics in the Early Islamic Period* (Eugene, OR: Pickwick Publications, 2016), 46–48. Citing Fred Donner, *Narratives of Islamic Origins*, 20.

[587] Janosik, *John of Damascus, First Apologist to the Muslims*, 47–50.

The early church fathers were as follows:

- The Apostolic Fathers (AD 70–150)
- Ante-Nicene Fathers (AD 150–300)
- Nicene and Post-Nicene Fathers (AD 300–430)

These were men of integrity and some of the first Christian apologists who wrote to defend the Christian faith and way of life in the early years.[588] Their documentation was intended as a way to educate those outside the church and clear up the many misconceptions held by those who did not understand what Christianity was.[589] The Apostolic Fathers are those who were actually disciples of the apostles and were very familiar with their trials and tribulations as well as with their writings. Between all of the citations, there are over thirty-six thousand spread out across all of their works. There are no such writings with which to compare the Qur'an. Unfortunately for Muslims, the printed material available to historians to reconstruct the original intent and historical validity of Islam is based on Islamic tradition in the medieval period and not on factual data that can be gathered from the time of Muhammad. To conclude, the New Testament documents are far superior to any other known piece of literature from antiquity.

Review:

Source Investigation: External Evidence Considerations

- The number and type of manuscripts available that are used to compare and contrast the various readings.
- The age of the extant manuscripts available.
- The quality of the manuscripts.
- The geographic location where the manuscripts originated.
- The similarities evident when compared to other reputable manuscripts.

Internal evidence includes the study of the following:

- The types of mistakes that a scribe would have likely made (intentionally or unintentionally).
  1. Confusing syntax
  2. Unusual vocabulary
  3. Theological oddities
  4. Brief comments
  5. Accidental misspellings
  6. Accidental duplication or omission of letters, words, or lines of text, or odd punctuation

---

[588] Hans Küng, *Christianity: Essence, History, and Future*, trans. John Bowden (New York: Continuum, 1995) 133–34.
[589] Ibid.

Study Questions: Lower Textual Criticism

For Review and Reflection of Lower Textual Criticism

1. What is meant by the external evidence of a passage when looking for textual variants? Give two examples.

2. What is meant by the internal evidence of a passage when considering textual variants? Give two examples.

3. Have there been any word variations that have changed the theological meaning of the text?

    If so, give an example.

    Was this variant found to contradict the character or nature of God? If so, how?

4. Give two reasons why scribes might use a variation of a word or phrase.

Group Discussion

1. What are the benefits of understanding what lower textual criticism is about?

2. Are variants unusual? Why or why not?

3. Why is it good to compare the Bible to other writings?

4. Discuss some ways that you can use your knowledge of lower textual criticism to help others understand the historical integrity of the New Testament documents.

Key Terms

autographs: The original documents.

doctrine: A teaching.

extant manuscripts: The documents that have been used to reconstruct the New Testament.

lower textual criticism: The process of investigating the actual source documents that are in possession today.

papyrus: A type of paper made out of papyrus reeds found in the northern regions of Egypt and the Near East.

source investigation: The research of external and internal evidence with the purpose of validating the historical integrity of the New Testament documents.

- **external:** The focus is on the actual physical element of the manuscripts in possession.
- **internal:** The focus is on the variations that exist between each document in the comparison process.

textual variants: Part of the source investigation that focuses on the content of the manuscripts. Historians seek both external and internal evidence.

- **external evidence:** Evidence found outside of the New Testament documents, such as citations and allusions to scriptural passages and events.
- **internal evidence:** The comparison of all the extant manuscript evidence to each other piece in the process of reconstruction.

vellum: A type of paper made from specially treated leather.

Literature Cited or Recommended

Blomberg, Craig L. *Can We Still Believe The Bible? An Evangelical Engagement with Contemporary Questions.* Grand Rapids, MI: Brazos Press, 2014.

Bruce, F. F. *The New Testament Documents: Are They Reliable?* 6th ed. Grand Rapids, MI: William B. Eerdmans, 1981.

Geisler, Norman L. *Christian Apologetics.* 2nd ed. Grand Rapids, MI: Baker Academic, 2013.

Janosik, Daniel J. *John of Damascus, First Apologist to the Muslims: The Trinity and Christian Apologetics in the Early Islamic Period.* Eugene, OR: Pickwick Publications, 2016. Citing Fred Donner, *Narratives of Islamic Origins,* 20.

Küng, Hans. *Christianity: Essence, History, and Future.* Translated by John Bowden. New York: Continuum, 1995.

MacArthur, John. *The MacArthur Study Bible: New King James Version,* footnotes Mark 16:9–20. Nashville: Thomas Nelson, 1997.

Marlow, Michael D. "Codex Vaticanus (B)." Bible Researcher, 2001–2012. Accessed June 5, 2018. http://www.bible-researcher.com/codex-b.html.

Sherwin-White, A. N. *Roman Society and Roman Law in the New Testament: The Sarum Lectures 1960–1961.* 1963. Reprint. Eugene, OR: Wipf & Stock, 2004.

Small, Keith E. *Textual Criticism and Qur'ān Manuscripts.* United Kingdom: Lexington Books, 2012.

Tov, Emanuel. *Textual Criticism of the Hebrew Bible.* 3rd ed. Minneapolis: Fortress Press, 2012.

Wallace, Daniel B. "Has the New Testament Text Been Hopelessly Corrupted?" In *In Defense of the Bible: A Comprehensive Apologetic for the Authority of Scripture,* edited by Steven B. Cowan and Terry L. Wilder, 161. Nashville: B&H Academic, 2013.

Assessing Lower Textual Criticism Reliability
The Viability of Philemon

Application of Scripture: Philemon

Read Philemon.

Dating the Literature

These last two chapters of our study on how scholars validate the documents that make up the New Testament scriptures will discuss how critical scholarship assesses both Philemon and Hebrews. Philemon is a powerful piece of scripture written around AD 61. It is a picture of forgiveness in the face of discord and personal loss. Paul beseeches Philemon to forgive his slave Onesimus, who steels from him and betrays his trust. He is asked not only to forgive this former runaway slave but also to accept him back under his roof as a brother (vv. 11–16). This sort of extraordinary behavior goes against our human nature, our demands for retribution, and our understanding of justice. In response to allegations that the New Testament was a concerted effort to gain control over an entire population, this letter would not seem to be of any use. How do the critics reconcile their accusations that the New Testament was amended for political gain when considering scripture like Philemon? Forgiving those who are in your service, even in the face of outright theft, would seem more to the benefit of the working class and not that of those in power.

Give a time when God asked you to do something nice for someone who hurt you. What was it like to obey?

_____

_____

_____

_____

_____

_____

_____

_____

Paul's letter to Philemon, like the vast majority of the New Testament, was cited early in the history of the Christian movement, long before Rome took any interest in it. The existing citations, as well as the book's acceptance by the church prior to the rule of Constantine in the fourth century, help to verify the early date that this letter was penned. Early citations of Paul's letter to Philemon can be found in the works of the heretic *Marcion*, which date to AD 140, as well as in the *Muratorian Canon*, which is dated at AD 170. Those are two of the earliest citations for Philemon that are in known existence today (see table 9.2 for a list of early citations of both Philemon and the letter to the Hebrews).

> **The Facts**
>
> - AD 130–202: By the time of Irenaeus, all New Testament books are cited with the exception of 3 John.
> - AD 170: By the time of the Muratorian Canon, all of the New Testament books are cited.
> - AD 393: All the New Testament books as we know them are accepted by the church.

Why are these early citations important to validating the New Testament?

_____

_____

_____

Kathryn V. Camp, D.Min.

The Facts[590]

TABLE 9.2. Early external citations of Philemon and Hebrews

Who Cited Scripture	Philemon	Hebrews
Pseudo Barnabas (70–130)	✓	
Clement of Rome (95–97)	✓	
Hermas (I 15–140)	✓	
Marcion (140)	✓	
Irenaeus (130–202)	✓	
Muratorian Canon (170)	✓	
Clement of Alexandria (c. 150–215)	✓	
Tertullian (c. 150–220)	✓	
Origen (c. 185–254)	✓	
Old Latin (c. 200)	✓	
Cyprian (d. 258)	✓	
Apostolic (c. 300)	✓	✓
Cyril of Jerusalem (c. 315–386)	✓	✓
Eusebius (c.325–340)	✓	✓
Athanasius (367)	✓	✓
Jerome (c. 340–420)	✓	✓
Hippo (393)	✓	✓
Canhage (397)	✓	✓
Augustine (c.400)	✓	✓

✓ = citation or allusion

Excerpt from When Skeptics Ask by Norman L. Geisler and Ronald M. Brooks, copyright © 1990. Used by permission of Baker Academic, a division of Baker Publishing Group.

Literary Style

Philemon is the shortest of all of Paul's correspondence found in the New Testament. In the original Greek, it totals 350 words.[591] This letter proves to be quite different from his other documented works. Paul's writings are usually written to entire congregations in specified regions and are prepared for instructional purposes. Even his pastoral Epistles (1 and 2 Timothy and Titus) are basically instructional in their nature. Paul's letter to Philemon, however, is written more in the literary style of an "ordinary private letter" of the first century.[592] Although it is stylistically unique for the canon of the New Testament, it still represents a missionary type of appeal to the

---

[590] Norman L. Geisler and Ronald M. Brooks, *When Skeptics Ask: A Handbook on Christian Evidences*, rev. ed. (Grand Rapids, MI: Baker Books, 2013), 153.

[591] Peter T. O'Brien, *Word Biblical Commentary*, vol. 44, *Colossians, Philemon*, ed. David A. Hubbard and Glenn W. Barker, New Testament ed. Ralph P. Martin (Waco, TX: Word Books, 1982), 265.

[592] Ibid.

recipient.[593] The entire letter is written in second-person singular, which would be expected in an intimate type of communication.[594] It is believed that although this letter is of a personal nature, it made its way into the New Testament canon as a viable representation of the Christian ethic possibly because of Onesimus. Tradition has it that this runaway, or former, slave eventually became the bishop of the church at Ephesus and may have influenced its inclusion.[595]

Literary scholars link Paul's letter to Philemon with the former's correspondence to the Colossians and to the Ephesians. It is believed that he was imprisoned in the same place when he wrote all three letters (Philem. 1; Eph. 3:1, 6:20; Col. 4:10, 18).[596] There is also a connection between those who are with Paul at the time that this letter and the other two were composed. Mark, Aristarchus, Demas, and Luke (vv. 23–24) are persons mentioned not only in Philemon but also in Colossians, Acts, and 2 Timothy as Paul's companions at various times during his missionary journeys. The letter to the Colossians mentions these same individuals, in addition to a few others (Col. 4:9–14). Although Tychicus (Col. 4:7–9) is not mentioned in Philemon, he provides a link between the letter to the Colossians and the correspondence to the Ephesians (Eph. 6:21–22). Paul sends Tychicus and Onesimus (Col. 4:9) to report to the Christ-following community about his progress and situation. The fact that Onesimus is sent together with Tychicus links Philemon with Paul's letter to the Ephesians. The three letters give the reader a multidimensional picture of how the missionary work of Paul and the other missionaries was interlocked and interdependent in the spread of God's message to the world.

What do all of these connections tell you about the early Christian movement?

_____

_____

_____

_____

How do the connections between God's people above differ from how evangelizing is done today?

_____

_____

_____

How is it the same?

_____

_____

_____

---

[593] Ibid.
[594] Luke Timothy Johnson, *The Writings of the New Testament*, 3rd ed. (Minneapolis: Fortress Press, 2010), 338.
[595] O'Brien, *Word Biblical Commentary*, vol. 44, 265.
[596] Johnson, *The Writings of the New Testament*, 338.

Theological Implications

There are several theological themes in this succinct but powerful piece of literature. The overpowering message is one of forgiveness, but there are two others that should not be overlooked.

> Beloved, never avenge yourselves, but leave it to the wrath of God, for it is written, "Vengeance is mine, I will repay, says the Lord."
> Rom. 12:19 (ESV)

Paul's directive to forgive is coupled with a plea to love and recognize those who are a part of God's family as family (Eph. 2:12–15, 19). These dictates will require a great deal of patience with others. It is one thing to study the scriptures with a scientifically critical eye, as we do in the "lessons," and it is another to capture the meaning as we view it through a theological lens based on the character and nature of God, which can only be realized through the reading of scripture. When Paul spoke to the audiences in Berea (Acts 17:10–15), they were eager to learn. They were, however, cautious and compared everything that they heard with the Hebrew scriptures. In this way they could be certain that it was truly the Word of God and not the word of humankind. When learning and teaching others, it is imperative to make sure not only that what you hear matches with scripture but also that the character and nature of God is revealed in the interpretation.

Forgiveness is a theme seen many times in the Bible. The Old Testament is filled with the people of God continually asking for His forgiveness as a collective group. In the New Testament the Son of God steps it up a notch and calls for the people of God to forgive others and to let God have the final say, even when others are unrepentant and have caused God's people harm (Deut. 32:35; Rom. 12:19). It is only through the propitiation of the Son that people are forgiven as the children of God (Matt. 12:31–32, 26:28; Mark 1:4, 4:12; Acts 2:38, 10:43). As creatures who have been created in the image of the Creator, it is only natural that we recapture His character trait of forgiveness as we become more like the Son. In many cases, this is much easier said than done, but this is why God asks that we hand it over to Him and tells us not to sin in our anger (Eph. 4:25–27). The disciples are reminded that they have been forgiven of much, and they are called to forgive others in the same manner (Matt. 18:21). Paul calls on Philemon to forgive his runaway slave even though the latter may have done him harm financially (Philem. 15–17).

Why is Philemon asked to forgive? Why and when does God forgive?

_____

_____

_____

_____

> We have all become like an unclean thing,
> And all our virtues like a filthy rag.
> We are all withering like leaves,
> And our iniquities, like a wind, carry us off.
> (Isa. 64:5 TNK)

Forgiveness is one thing, but then Paul calls on Philemon to accept this slave as an equal, and even worse, as a brother in the Lord. This is a very tall order meant for all of us who claim to be

Christians. It is a serious reminder of who we are before a just and holy God. We are all sinners (Rom. 3:23) and deserve death for our rebellious and prideful hearts. It is only by the grace of God that we are allowed to take refuge under the blood of the perfect sacrifice given by Jesus the Messiah. It is never by our own works (Is 64:6). If we are honest with ourselves, we will see that our own works are motivated by some sort of self-benefit and do not arise from a convicted or contrite heart and mind. This is also about family and accepting other faithful Christians as equals because they too have been accepted by God to be called children (Matt. 3:9; John 1:2; Gal. 3:26; 1 John 4:10–12). Therefore, just as God brought us into His fold when our hearts and minds began to recognize our selfish and sinful ways, followed by our serious desire to seek solace under His care, we are to accept other Christians as family.

Write about a time when you or someone else was wronged and the difficulty that you had forgiving the offender.

_____
_____
_____
_____
_____

What did you do to forgive the person? Why did you do this?

_____
_____
_____
_____

In Old Testament times, the nation of Israel was seen as one big family with the God of Israel at the helm and Abraham as their father (Luke 3:8). When God came to dwell among us, the invitation to become His children was extended to the rest of the world (Rom. 1:15–17). This is a good place to point out that not everyone is or will be considered as part of God's family (John 8:41; Rom. 8:13–15) and not all will be granted salvation (Matt. 7:22–24). Philemon is asked to be patient with his runaway slave as the latter returns to live under the roof of the former. Exercising patience with someone who has offended or harmed us goes against our natural inclination to get even. It is, however, a character trait of God that the people of God are called to emulate. God was, and continues to be, very patient with each and every person who answered His invitation to accept Jesus as their one and only Savior (Matt. 7:22–24; John 14:6). It is imperative to understand that all professing Christians must exhibit the same patience with others as they work out their salvation with fear and trembling (Phil. 2:11–13).

How is God's justice different from humanity's justice? Use scripture to back up your response.

_____
_____
_____
_____

Onesimus's encounter with Paul changed his life and challenged Philemon's Christian witness. Everyone seeks forgiveness, as it is part of our nature and desire for peace. It is, however, very difficult and challenging to extend forgiveness, especially in the face of adversity. Paul's letter to Philemon is a stark reminder of what is expected of all who profess to be followers of Christ. This powerful correspondence is a lesson in humility and gratitude, humility because we are all equal in the eyes of the Creator and even though our world may have hierarchies, in God's kingdom we are all creatures created in His image who have sinned and have fallen short of His glory (Gen. 6:5–6; Rom. 3:9–10). The realization of our depravity should encourage us to live out our lives with an overwhelming sense of gratitude for God's gracious kindness and forgiveness, allowing for those who repent to become welcomed children in His household (Matt. 3:1–3; John 11:3; Rom. 8:13–15)

How has your encounter with the Word of God changed you?

Who is a God like you, pardoning iniquity and passing over transgression for the remnant of his inheritance? He does not retain his anger forever, because he delights in steadfast love. (Mic. 7:18, ESV)

To equip the saints for the work of ministry, for building up the body of Christ, until we all attain to the unity of the faith and of the knowledge of the Son of God, to mature manhood, to the measure of the stature of the fullness of Christ, so that we may no longer be children, tossed to and fro by the waves and carried about by every wind of doctrine, by human cunning, by craftiness in deceitful schemes. (Eph. 4:12, ESV)

Review:

Key Theological Themes

1. Forgiving others
2. Recognizing other Christ followers as family
3. Extending love to other believers because we are all equal before God
4. Practice patience with each other. God is always patient with you.

Study Questions: Assessing Lower Textual Criticism

For Theological Review and Reflection

1. What are two important documents that validate an early date for Philemon?

   a.

   b.

2. Is it likely that this piece of scripture was inserted for political influence? Why or why not?

3. What makes Philemon a difficult piece of scripture?

4. Even though it is a personal letter, what makes it an important piece of correspondence to the church?

5. Does God call on His people to accept *everyone* as brothers and sisters in Christ? Give scripture as evidence to support your response.

Group Discussion

1. Do you believe that people are capable of doing good works?

2. Do you believe that people are innately good? Give scripture and empirical evidence to validate your answer.

3. Discuss examples of times when people do good works.

a. Scripture talks about how all of our righteous deeds are tainted. In light of this, how are these acts self-serving?

b. Can we escape this truth?

4. Have you encountered anyone who believes that all people are children of God? Discuss ways of tactfully explaining what scripture says and what empirical observation reveals about human behavior.

Key Terms

Marcion: A second-century anti-Semitic heretic who believed that the God of the Old Testament was inferior to the God represented in the New Testament. He rejected the Old Testament as well as the parts of the New Testament that revealed any links to the Jewishness of Jesus.

Muratorian Canon: A fragment of an Italian document that was published in 1740 by Cardinal L. A. Muratori. The fragment is a reproduction of a manuscript that is dated to the seventh century, and it contains one of the earliest lists of books of the New Testament. Historians deduce that the original document was written around 170 given the mention of the role of Pius 1 of Rome as recent (he died in 157).[597] Scholars agree that the original language was Greek, given when and where it was written, which was later translated into Latin.[598]

God's Attributes

forgivingness: The Lord frequently reminds humanity that He desires to forgive their iniquities if they learn and turn from their wicked and rebellious ways.

justness: God is perfectly just. No one is above another, and all are treated equally regardless of race, whether slave or free, rich or poor.

lovingness: God is love. God wants none to perish, but for all to come to everlasting life. He does not give up on anyone.

---

[597] Michael D. Marlow, "The Muratorian Fragment," Bible Researcher, 2001–2012, accessed July 3, 2018, http://www.bible-researcher.com/muratorian.html.
[598] Ibid.

patience: Philemon is called to be patient with Onesimus's situation. God is by His nature patient with humanity because He continues to give each and every individual the opportunity to repent and turn to Him up until their last breath (2 Pet. 3:8–10).

tolerance: God's tolerance is exhibited in the way He allows humanity to continue to exist, even though many commit unspeakable atrocities around the globe and, even more than that, live in rebellion against Him and His Messiah.

Literature Cited or Recommended

Geisler, Norman L., and Ronald M. Brooks. *When Skeptics Ask: A Handbook on Christian Evidences.* Revised edition. Grand Rapids, MI: Baker Books, 2013.

Johnson, Luke Timothy. *The Writings of the New Testament.* 3rd ed. Minneapolis: Fortress Press, 2010.

Marlow, Michael D. "The Muratorian Fragment." Bible Researcher, 2001–2012. Accessed July 3, 2018. http://www.bible-researcher.com/muratorian.html.

O'Brien, Peter T. *Word Biblical Commentary*, vol. 44, *Colossians, Philemon.* Edited by David A. Hubbard and Glenn W. Barker. New Testament editor, Ralph P. Martin. Waco, TX: Word Books, 1982.

Wallace, Daniel. *Revisiting the Corruption of the New Testament: Manuscript, Patristic, and Apocryphal Evidence.* Edited by Philip Miller. Grand Rapids, MI: Kregel Academic, 2011

CHAPTER 10

Lower Textual Criticism and Textual Reliability

Manuscript Reconstruction

This last section of our study covers how the experts went through the process of reconstructing the Bible from all of the extant manuscripts discovered over time. Authenticity is the most important aspect of validating both the Old and the New Testaments, making reconstruction a crucial piece to the integrity of the Christian faith. The purpose of this study has been to show the many criteria that have been required for accepting what is known to us today as the Holy Bible. In this final section we will take a look at two more critical steps that have gone into deciding the integrity of the extant manuscripts that were chosen over hundreds of others to be considered as part of the biblical canon. We will take into consideration the following:

1. How the scholars knew from what time period the manuscript originated.
2. How the results of reconstruction were accepted.

Time Period Verification

Mediums Used

There are numerous ways for modern sleuths to examine and date items from the past, but what about the manuscripts that were used to create the Bible? How did the scholars know from what period in time certain pieces of literature came? When studying any piece of writing, there are several details that a historical scholar will look for that will yield clues as to what time frame the writing originated. Aside from the type of physical material on which the literature is written, the style of writing is also very telling. When researching lower critical substantiations, scholars look for evidence that supports a document's overall quality, the age of the manuscript, the location of its origin, and its similarity to other reputable manuscripts.[599] The current extant manuscript evidence *medium* is, for the most part, either *papyrus* or *vellum*. Historical artifacts reveal that

---

[599] Craig L. Blomberg, *Can We Still Believe The Bible? An Evangelical Engagement with Contemporary Questions* (Grand Rapids, MI: Brazos Press, 2014), 18.

papyrus was used as a medium from around 3200 BC to the eighth century AD, when its use began to wane. There is also another writing material known as *parchment* that was popular between 197 and 159 BC and was used as early as the Ptolemaic era (305–30 BC). Parchment was a specially treated form of leather and became a favored writing surface because of its accessibility. Unlike papyrus, parchment could be produced anywhere.

Every time period reflects the technology used for creating writing surfaces. Papyrus is one of the oldest mediums used for paper apart from the writing surfaces of stone tablets or clay cylinders. Papyrus was made from the papyrus reeds found in the northern regions of Egypt and the Near East. It was stored in rolls and did well in the arid climates of the desert. Papyrus was expensive because of its regional availability and as a result was often recycled and frequently written on both sides to make the most of this precious commodity. As discussed earlier in this study, many early papyrus manuscripts were discovered in the cavities of mummified crocodiles in Tebtunis.[600] The use of papyrus as a writing surface began to be phased out by the third century and was eventually replaced by vellum, which was a much more readily available medium. Vellum was a higher-quality version of parchment. About the time that papyrus rolls were phasing out, a new method of retaining large amounts of written material became popular, the *codex*. A codex was made of either parchment or vellum that was cut into uniform pieces and bound together, creating a book-like collection of information very similar to the books that we hold today. Although not impervious, vellum proved to be a more lasting material on which to store written data.

Methods and Styles of Writing

While it is helpful in dating a literary work to know the medium that is used, historical scholars also study the writing methods and styles used on the manuscripts. The majority of the New Testament manuscripts are written in Greek, which was the universal language of the first century in that part of the world. Although Latin and various Semitic languages were also common, Hellenism was well established during the time that the disciples were writing the New Testament. Much like other languages, the Greek language evolved over time as it became more common. Stemming originally from the Phoenician languages used since 1100 BC, the Greek language was made by tweaking the Phoenician alphabet to best suit the Greeks' own tongue.[601] By the eighth century BC the Greeks had added pitch accents, which would be equivalent to vowels, and had implemented quantity (or a time value) into their written language.[602] It wasn't until the fifth century BC that the Greeks would actually standardize their written form to read from left to right and to orient their letters to be fixed and upright.[603]

The early Greek manuscripts reflect their standardized alphabet dating to the fifth century BC. All of the letters were in uppercase, there had yet to be any type of punctuation developed into the language, there were no paragraphs to break up thoughts, and there were no spaces between words. A written document would appear to be one long string of letters. The *John Rylands Fragment* is one of the earliest extant manuscripts in possession and reflects this style of

---

[600] See chapter 8, the Assessing External Criteria lesson.

[601] Cristian Violatti, *Ancient History Encyclopedia*, s.v. "Greek alphabet," February 5, 2015, https://www.ancient.eu/Greek_Alphabet/, accessed June 6, 2018.

[602] Ibid.

[603] Ibid. The Phoenician written word, similar to Hebrew text, was read from right to left.

writing. This is the oldest fragment known in existence today, dating to AD 117–138. It was discovered in Egypt and was most likely originally written in Asia Minor, signifying the early expansion and transmission of the Gospel message.[604] The early spread of the Christian movement stands as a testament to how far the net was cast as the first- and second-generation disciples were transmitting the Word of Life to the ends of the earth. By this point in history, the Greeks had also created large compound words as part of their written language development. By the first century AD, the Greek alphabet was well imbedded in the vast majority of West Asia, Asia Minor, the Mediterranean, and beyond.[605] Once there was a familiarity with the written Greek language, different styles began to emerge. The straight abrupt markings to create letters began to yield to a curvier and more rounded in shape set of letters referred to as *uncials* in the third century and well into the ninth century.

Uncials were used in more formal works found in Greek and Latin manuscripts.[606] The style of an uncial was of larger, more upright lettering known as a *majuscule* and was a bit more ornate than common forms of writing. What had not changed, however, was that uncials are uppercase letters. The use of uncials did not yet exhibit lowercase lettering or any punctuation markings, and the words were not yet separated by spaces. A smaller cursive script referred to as a *minuscule* was introduced in the seventh century and slowly began to replace the uncial by the mid-ninth century. About the time of the emperor Charlemagne (768–814) in the eighth century, the use of spaces between words became a new writing style. Actual punctuation markers (syntax used to help with understanding) did not become fully developed and integrated into written form until the fifteenth to the eighteenth century.[607] All of these factors help historical scholars determine the era in which a manuscript was written. See table 10.1 for a visual of the gradual changes of writing styles.

TABLE 10.1. Evolution of the Greek writing system

Time period	Greek writing system evolution
Eighth century BC	Pitch accents added, vowels introduced
Fifth century BC	Standardization of writing style: letters fixed and upright; words would be read left to right
First century AD	Large compound words present Greek language spread: West Asia, Asia Minor, Mediterranean, and beyond
Third century	Introduction of uncials
Seventh century	Introduction of minuscule
Eighth century	Spaces introduced
Ninth century	The use of the minuscule replaced the uncial style
Fifteenth to eighteenth century	Punctuation introduced and integrated

* Both Codex Vaticanus (B) [AD 325–350] and Codex Sinaiticus (א Aleph) [fourth century] are in uncial form.

---

[604] Norman L. Geisler and Frank Turek, *I Don't Have Enough Faith to Be an Atheist* (Wheaton, IL: Crossway, 2004), 225.

[605] Violatti, *Ancient History Encyclopedia*, s.v. "Greek alphabet."

[606] Ibid.

[607] Ibid.

How Are the Results of Reconstruction Accepted?

Biblical manuscripts have undergone far more scrutiny and have been the subject of more critical analysis than any other documentation from history. The Bible, unlike other literature, has had to meet not only secular historical scrutiny but also theological critical analysis. We have covered the secular standards of historical authority and integrity in this text, but what about on the theological end of the spectrum? Does the Bible contradict itself? Many people say that it does, and others claim that it does not. Obviously both sides of the argument cannot be right; that would be a contradiction, and theologically that would require that God be *mutable*. A God who changes is not stable and would morph into whatever the individual reads into the text. A mutable God would be no different from the gods represented by all other faiths outside of the Judeo-Christian tradition. This is why it is crucial to understand the standards that the Bible has had to reach in order to maintain the claim that it is indeed the absolute word of an ultimate Authority.

Seeking Divine Authority

A large part of the reconstruction process requires that scholars filter through all of the accepted manuscripts and compare them one to another. This process of filtering and comparing is essential in discovering the original intent and form of each Gospel or Epistle. It is safe to say that the original letters were copied by trusted scribes who knew the disciples and undoubtedly were also devoted disciples themselves of the Christian movement; otherwise, why would they have been entrusted to make copies of the autographs? The answer is simple: they would not have been. There is no question that it is helpful in the reconstruction process to have multiple copies from which to compare what was written. Fortunately, since the New Testament has over fifty-eight hundred early Greek extant manuscripts to compare to each other, not to mention the other twenty thousand manuscripts written in fifteen various languages that represent the rapid spread of the Gospel geographically between the late fourth century and into the fifteenth century, scholars have plenty of documentation from which to restore the original writings.

Scholars agree and accept the fact that certain passages will have varying word orders, but these anomalies represent only the style and perhaps the dialect of the respective scribes' geographical and educational history. The same is true today. The way an author presents his or her material will represent his or her educational and, many times, geographical background. Once the early church began to canonize the Gospels and Epistles that make up the New Testament, they used only what had already been in use and accepted by the churches.[608] It was not their practice or intention to insert random stories or obscure manuscripts for the sake of political gain or to fill in the missing gaps.[609] Although by the time the Bible was fully canonized (by the Councils of Hippo [393] and of Carthage [397]), there was a great deal of Gnostic and additional literature that mimicked the writings of the New Testament. These Gnostic writings were easily detected and discarded by the church.

It is important to point out that even though some passages may have various word orders, it

---

[608] F. F. Bruce, *The New Testament Documents: Are They Reliable?* 6th ed. (Grand Rapids, MI: William B. Eerdmans, 1981), 22.

[609] Craig L. Blomberg, *Can We Still Believe The Bible? An Evangelical Engagement with Contemporary Questions* (Grand Rapids, MI: Brazos Press, 2014), 64–70.

does not present a problem, as there are no instances where the word order changes the theological meaning of the text.[610] John 1:21 is an example of a passage that has at least five different word orders in the various manuscripts when compared to each other. Regardless of these discrepancies, the intended meaning of the passage remains the same.[611] The following is an example of what biblical scholars would look at when comparing manuscripts. Remember that the purpose is to reconstruct as closely as possible the original text:

Matthew 27:59–60

1. And Joseph took the body, wrapped it in a clean linen shroud, and laid it in his new tomb.
2. And Joseph took the body and wrapped it in a clean linen shroud and laid it in his own new tomb.
3. And Joseph took the body and wrapped it in a shroud and laid it in his own tomb.
4. And Joseph wrapped the body in a clean linen and laid it in a new tomb.
   - Original: And Joseph took the body and wrapped it in a clean linen shroud and laid it in his own new tomb.

Regardless of the claims made by a few Bible critics that there are numerous "errors" in the New Testament, in reality there are very few, and the ones that exist are nothing of consequence. This false accusation requires that we begin with clarifying terms. What they are claiming as errors are in actuality more accurately called variants. Variants are not the same as errors. Furthermore, in order to get the attention of the general public, these critics count these variants in an exaggerated fashion. For instance, when there is a misspelled word that has been found in twenty-five hundred copies, they count it as if there are twenty-five hundred "errors" in the manuscripts that are used to reconstruct the New Testament, even though it is the same word in each instance.[612] It is an interesting fact that historians are much more prepared to accept the historicity and the veracity of the New Testament than are theologians.[613] This is the case even though historians use the exact same criteria for validating historical accounts of any other secular writing from antiquity.[614] It is important to stress the fact that the Bible receives no special treatment by historical and literary scholars when validating the historicity of the scriptures.

In Conclusion

It is helpful to remember that when one is working with literary criticism and critical scholarship, it is a form of study that seeks the historical authenticity of a particular claim being made. Critical scholarship is not necessarily about criticizing, but instead it seeks historical truth in order to understand our world in a realistic fashion. Understanding history also helps us to get a glimpse

---

[610] Norman L. Geisler and Ronald M. Brooks, *When Skeptics Ask: A Handbook on Christian Evidences*, rev. ed. (Grand Rapids, MI: Baker Books, 2013), 171.

[611] Ibid.

[612] Ibid., 172.

[613] A. N. Sherwin-White, *Roman Society and Roman Law in the New Testament: The Sarum Lectures 1960–1961* (1963; repr., Eugene, OR: Wipf & Stock, 2004), 186–92.

[614] Bruce, *The New Testament Documents*, 10.

into the human condition and how people tend to repeat the same mistakes throughout time. We see how greed, the quest or desire for political power, and the quest for sexual pleasures all affect human behavior. For the theologian, the glimpse into the behaviors of humanity throughout time is invaluable in understanding why the Creator would set down the moral and ceremonial boundaries that He set. These guidelines in turn reveal the character and nature of a just and holy God.

The New Testament documentation is the most complete and historically validated record of events from antiquity known to humankind. Historical scholars are satisfied that with the existing evidence, the events surrounding Jesus of Nazareth and His disciples were documented early in the life of the Christian church and do reflect historical reality.[615] It is accepted that the majority of the documents were completed before AD 70 and the destruction of the temple in Jerusalem. This means that within forty years of the crucifixion of Jesus, the bulk of the New Testament was complete. Historians agree that even in the secular realm as writers begin to document events, even if it is as far off as one hundred years later, there is a level of integrity and accuracy to the content.[616] The claim is that even with a gap of one hundred years between the event and the documentation, it is too soon for myths and legends to form. Facts and events are still transmitted faithfully. The biblical documents, however, not only were written early in the history of the Christian movement but also have undergone far more analysis than any other document in history. The writings of Herodotus (mid-fifth century BC), "the father of history," have undergone less scrutiny based on form criticism than the documentation centered around first-century Christianity, and Herodotus's documentations are accepted at face value.[617]

There is no question that there is not an ancient text in existence that has the credentials that the Bible we hold today does. Unfortunately, in the twentieth and twenty-first centuries, there has been such disregard for the authoritative Word of God that modern man has chosen to loosely interpret the scriptures as he sees fit. For example, there are versions of scripture that have carefully replaced any gender language with generic terms. The New Revised Standard Version (NRSV) of the Bible has replaced male gender pronoun notations with neutral nouns (i.e., boy to child; men to people). There are also versions such as a recently published Bible called *Good as New*, "rewritten by former Baptist minister John Henson, which takes great progressiveness with the written Word."[618] As an example of his liberality with the text, here is an excerpt from 1 Corinthians 7:1–2, first the ESV version and second the Good as New version:

> Now concerning the matters about which you wrote: "It is good for a man not to have sexual relations with a woman." But because of the temptation to sexual immorality, each man should have his own wife and each woman her own husband. (ESV)

> Some of you think the best way to cope with sex is for men and women to keep right away from each other. That is more likely to lead to sexual offences. My advice is for everyone to have a regular partner. (Good as New Bible)[619]

---

[615] Sherwin-White, *Roman Society and Roman Law in the New Testament*, 188–89.

[616] Ibid., 189–91.

[617] Ibid., 192.

[618] David Kupelian, *The Marketing of Evil* (Nashville: WND Books, 2005), 217.

[619] Ibid., 218.

There are still other versions, such as the Today's New International Version (TNIV—not to be confused with the NIV) and the Queen James Version (QJV), that distort other portions of the Bible in order to accommodate the Westernized postmodern culture in which we live.

Fortunately, there are still plenty of Bibles that honor the Word of God and recognize its authority over humanity and all of creation as the holy inspired Word of God. Some of these include the King James Version (KJV), the New King James Version (NKJV), the New International Version (NIV), the English Standard Version (ESV), and the New American Standard Bible (NASB). The prophet Amos prophesied about times to come and warned that there would come a time when there would be a famine of the Word of God in the midst of abundance (Amos 8:11–12). I believe that we are living on the cusp of that time and that as Christians we have an absolute obligation to speak Truth as it is noted in God's holy and written (not rewritten) Word, recognizing God for who He truly is as we honor His Word with integrity. Regardless of the modern distortions and attempts at changing the Word of God, the amount of historical evidence for the original form and meaning of the scriptures is undeniable by any honest scholar. Christians everywhere should rejoice in the fact that no matter what hurdles the world requires the Word of God to jump over to prove its validity, the Creator saw it all coming long, long ago and made certain that all of humanity would have no valid excuse to claim that He is unknowable.

> For "All flesh is like grass and all its glory like the flower of grass. The grass withers, and the flower falls, but the word of the Lord remains forever." And this word is the good news that was preached to you. (1 Pet. 1:23 ESV)

> Praising the Lord for His sovereignty and His transcendence of time! Only the perfection of You, O Lord, could have known all of the trials and scrutiny Your holy Word to us would be subjected to throughout time. We praise You for preserving the revelation of who You are in order that we might come to love and know You more with each breath that we are given. Help us to become faithful servants that desire nothing more than to know You and bring You glory through our actions and deeds according to Your Word. Amen.

Review:

The Process of Reconstruction

- What time period was the manuscript produced?
- Focus on what mediums were used.
- What was the style of writing used?

Study Questions

For Review and Reflection of Lower Textual Criticism and the Process of Reconstruction

1. What factors do scholars consider in the reconstruction process? List at least three factors, and mention why each is important to the validation process.

   a.

   b.

   c.

2. Why did vellum become a preferred medium over papyrus?

3. How do scholars use writing styles to date written documents from history?

4. Name three factors that would reveal the time frame in which a document was written:

   a.

   b.

   c.

Group Discussion

1. Why would skeptics feel the need to exaggerate textual variants in the Bible?

2. Do you think that it is fair that the Bible is scrutinized far more than any other historical document? Why or why not?

3. How will you use the information that you have just learned? Create a real-life scenario of a skeptic who does not believe in the Bible, and share it with your group.

Key Terms

John Rylands Fragment: Otherwise known as Fragment P[52], this is the earliest piece of a manuscript in possession today. It contains sections of John 18:31–33, 37–38. It was discovered in Egypt and is now housed at the library of the University of Manchester, in Manchester, England.

majuscule: The style of an uncial that was a larger, more upright way of presenting letters of the alphabet.

medium: The surface on which written information was transmitted.

minuscule: A smaller cursive-like script, much like a lowercase letter. It was introduced in the seventh century.

papyrus: A paper made from papyrus reeds found in the northern regions of Egypt and the Near East.

parchment: A writing surface created from a specially treated form of leather.

vellum: A more advanced writing surface created from a treated form of leather.

uncial: Rounded uppercase letters generally used in more formal works of literature.

Literature Cited or Recommended

Blomberg, Craig L. *Can We Still Believe The Bible? An Evangelical Engagement with Contemporary Questions.* Grand Rapids, MI: Brazos Press, 2014.

Bruce, F. F. *The New Testament Documents: Are They Reliable?* 6th ed. Grand Rapids, MI: William B. Eerdmans, 1981.

Geisler, Norman L., and Frank Turek. *I Don't Have Enough Faith to Be an Atheist.* Wheaton, IL: Crossway, 2004.

Geisler, Norman L., and Ronald M. Brooks. *When Skeptics Ask: A Handbook on Christian Evidences.* Revised edition. Grand Rapids, MI: Baker Books, 2013.

Kupelian, David. *The Marketing of Evil*. Nashville: WND Books, 2005.

Sherwin-White, A. N. *Roman Society and Roman Law in the New Testament: The Sarum Lectures 1960–1961*. 1963; Reprint. Eugene, OR: Wipf & Stock, 2004.

University of Manchester Library in London. http://www.library.manchester.ac.uk/search-resources/special-collections/guide-to-special-collections/st-john-fragment/, (CC BY-NC-SA 4.0).

Violatti, Cristian. *Ancient History Encyclopedia*, s.v. "Greek alphabet." February 5, 2015. https://www.ancient.eu/Greek_Alphabet/. Accessed June 6, 2018.

Assessing Lower Textual Criticism Reliability
The Viability of Hebrews

Application of Scripture: Hebrews

Read Hebrews.

The message to the Hebrews, like all other scripture, has undergone thorough scrutiny in the reconstruction and validation process. As we come to a close on how critical scholarship continues to verify the integrity of the New Testament, we will take the letter to the Hebrews into account. The focus will be on a few of the important aspects that have been researched in the validation and reconstruction process, as follows:

- What written documents have survived?
- Who wrote Hebrews, and when was it written?
- What external evidence is there to validate its content?
- Does this letter represent sound doctrine?

Reconstructing the Text

Time Period Verification

Scholars use not only the available manuscripts in the validation process in an effort to date the original time of authorship but also external trusted citations. The letter to the Hebrews seems to have been written quite early in the Christian tradition. When taking note of external citation evidence, we find that Hebrews was clearly quoted and cited by an early church father known as Clement of Rome (see 1 Clement 17:1, 36:2–6).[620] Scholars date 1 Clement between AD 80 and 140. Considering the fact that Clement quoted the message to the Hebrews extensively,[621] and based on the internal content of Hebrews, it is possible to date the Hebrews document as early as AD 60, less than thirty years after the resurrection. Responsible scholarship will also focus on

---

[620] William L. Lane, *Word Biblical Commentary*, vol. 47$_A$, *Hebrews 1–8*, ed. David A. Hubbard and Glenn W. Barker, New Testament ed. Ralph P. Martin (Waco, TX: Word Books, 1991), lxii.

[621] Luke Timothy Johnson, *The Writings of the New Testament*, 3rd ed. (Minneapolis: Fortress Press, 2010), 408–9.

the internal content of the written document and seek out mention of real-time events in order to come as close as possible to dating the material. In the case of the message to the Hebrews, the author commiserates with his readers in that they had all suffered great hardship including the loss of property (Heb. 10:32–34).[622]

Early citations in 1 Clement[623]

Type of Appropriation	Citing Reference	Hebrews Scripture
Allusion To	*1 Clement* 17:1	Use of 11:37
Explicit Dependence On	*1 Clement* 36:2–6	Dependence on 1:3-5,7
Direct Quotation Of (Ps 104:4)	*1 Clement* 36:3	"Precise wording" 1:7

He assures the hearers that they are not alone in their suffering and persecution. According to the letter, these recipients had responded to the Christian message as a result of the preaching of those who had been discipled by Jesus (Heb. 2:3–4).[624] Although these early teachers were prominent figures who were instrumental in the formation of the early church (13:7), they were no longer alive.[625] The preceding information would suggest that perhaps one or two decades had now passed since the resurrection of Jesus, making these recipients the second generation of believers. Therefore an early date is respectably feasible.[626] It is also possible to date this message as having been penned no later than AD 70 because the author mentions nothing of the Jewish temple in Jerusalem having been destroyed. One thing is most certain, that the addressees were in danger of *apostasy* (3:12) amid the present hardships of persecution (12:4, 13:13–14).[627]

> Take care, brothers, lest there be in any of you an evil, unbelieving heart, leading you to fall away from the living God. (Heb. 3:12 ESV)

According to Hebrews, what was the threat of apostasy to the people?

_____

_____

_____

External evidence supports the persecution faced by both Jews and Jewish Christians (10:32–34). It is well-documented by the Roman historian Suetonius (*Lives of the Caesars*, AD 120) that it was in AD 49 that the emperor Claudius expelled the "Jews" from Rome for causing a great disturbance because of one *Chrestus*.[628] It was commonplace for those who were expelled to lose property and also suffer public abuse.[629] This type of expulsion was the beginning of a wave of

---

[622] Lane, *Word Biblical Commentary*, vol. 47$_A$, *Hebrews 1–8*, lxiv.

[623] Ibid., lxii.

[624] Ibid.

[625] Ibid.

[626] Ibid.

[627] Ibid.

[628] Lane, *Word Biblical Commentary*, vol. 47$_A$, *Hebrews 1–8*, lxiv.

[629] Ibid., lxvi.

persecutions for the Jewish-Christian communities in the years that followed. The Christians who were the focus of this correspondence were evidently under a new form of persecution (2:15, 12:3–4). These events appear to correspond with the terrifying and torturous treatment of Christians under *Nero*, who was a notorious emperor of Rome (AD 54–68), as documented in the annals of the Roman historian Tacitus (AD 56–120) (*Annals of Rome* 15.44).[630] The writer encourages his audience to be strong and have faith as they await the promise of the Parousia (10:25, 36–39). The author also mentions Timothy's release from prison (13:23), which has led many scholars to suggest the date of this document to be no later than somewhere between AD 64 and 68.[631]

What were some of the atrocities committed against Christians by the emperor Nero?

_____

_____

Authorship

Although there are many verifiable historical events that help scholars date the original writing of this document, it has proved slightly more challenging to be sure of the author. Hebrews is different from the other Epistles in that it does not mention the name of its author. It was, however, ascribed to Paul at a very early date.[632] The earliest copy of the message to the Hebrews in possession is "exclusively" bound together with Paul's letters.[633] This collection of Paul's letters is better known as the Chester Beatty Papyri ($\mathfrak{P}^{46}$) and is dated to the end of the second century and the beginning of the third century.[634] In this papyrus collection, it is simply listed as "To the Hebrews" in the same way that the other letters are listed "To the Romans" or "To the Corinthians."[635] In the Chester Beatty manuscript, the letter to the Hebrews is positioned in between Paul's Epistle to the Romans and his letter to the Corinthians, but it is placed in various locations in the other uncial codices.[636]

It is not surprising that early theologians began to place this work with Paul's other correspondence given the similar wording and understanding (see table 10.2 for similarities). Making sure that the author was either a firsthand witness to Jesus and His life events or an individual who personally knew and worked with the firsthand witnesses has always been of key importance and priority when validating works that claim to be scripture, and this message to the Hebrews is no exception. The internal evidence for authorship does seem to point to the apostle Paul for many reasons. The author's deep concern for his hearers is very Pauline in nature (2:3, 3:12–4:1, 6:4–8, 12:12, 16–17), as are his words of encouragement to them (3:7–14,

---

[630] Ibid.

[631] Ibid. The great fire in Rome occurred in AD 64, and the date of death of Nero is noted as AD June 68.

[632] F. F. Bruce, *The New Testament Documents: Are They Reliable?* 6th ed. (Grand Rapids, MI: William B. Eerdmans, 1981), 5.

[633] Lane, *Word Biblical Commentary*, vol. 47_A, *Hebrews 1–8*, lxix.

[634] Ibid.

[635] Ibid.

[636] Ibid.

4:1–13, 6:13–20). Even with all of the internal similarities, however, there was question as to who authored this message to the Hebrew Christians early on in the formation of the church.

TABLE **10.2.** Scriptural similarities of Hebrews to Paul's correspondence[637]

Theological Understanding	Hebrews	Pauline Similarity
"Access" to God is given by Christ"	4:16 and 10:19-22	Rom.5:1 Eph. 2:18
"God's Promise to Abraham"	6:13-18	Gal. 3:16-18
"Abraham's Response to Faith"	11:8-12 Rom.	4:1-25
"The Faith of Jesus as Understood as Obedience"	5:1-10 and 12:1-3	Rom. 5:12-21

Early church father Tertullian (AD 150–220) thought that Barnabas might possibly be the author because of the mention of Timothy and his knowledge of him.[638] It is well-known that Paul worked closely with both Barnabas and Timothy. Origen (AD 185–254), on the other hand, thought that Luke was a likely candidate as the author, or transcriber of Paul's thought process, which could have been possible considering the time that they spent together.[639] Sixteenth-century Martin Luther proposed the possibility of Apollos, whom we meet in Acts 18:24–28 and who is mentioned as an associate of Paul's in 1 Corinthians (1 Cor. 1:12, 3:4–22, 16:12), as well as in Titus (3:13).[640] What scholars do know is that the literary style in which this discourse is written reveals that the author had a command of the Greek written language not rivaled in the whole of the New Testament.[641] They recognize that the author was very knowledgeable in the Hebrew scriptures, was well educated in rhetoric, had thoughts that were greatly influenced by "the symbolic world of *Alexandrian Judaism*," had a passion for exhortation, had sound understandings of morality, and was a clear thinker and communicator.[642] Some scholars take into consideration that these skills fit not only Apollos but also Paul, and perhaps even Priscilla.[643] One thing is certain, and that is that whoever wrote this incredible piece of literature knew what they were saying and knew well the face of the living God.

Name three reasons from scripture why we know that this author is truly in tune with the character and nature of God:

1.
2.
3.

---

[637] Johnson, *The Writings of the New Testament*, 408.
[638] Ibid.
[639] Ibid.
[640] Ibid.
[641] Ibid.
[642] Ibid.
[643] Ibid.

The Message and Theological Implications

Although the identity of the author remains somewhat of a mystery to us, internal evidence reveals that the hearers were very well acquainted with him or her (13:19).[644] The relationship with the audience was one of familiarity and ministerial leadership (13:22). Those being addressed are also familiar with Timothy (13:23), as they are given an update on his prison status. Timothy, as we know from scripture, was a close associate of Paul's. The literary form in which this message is written is that of an exhortation or *homily* and not as a letter.[645] This is further internal observation that the hearers were familiar with the author, especially given the first-person plural use of language.[646] This was a message to a congregation and is written in a form that suggests it should be read out loud.[647]

> I urge you the more earnestly to do this in order that I may be restored to you the sooner. (Heb. 13:19 ESV)

Why would a homily reflect familiarity?

The author was intimately familiar with the Jewish sacrificial system and the ceremonial laws set forth in the *Torah*. He was well versed in the trials and tribulations of the prophets and was familiar with Israel's tumultuous past with *Yahweh* and the promise of the Messiah to come. He was also clearly a redeemed soul, filled with the Holy Spirit, and like all of the other authors of scripture was living out his faith and sharing the heart of God as he was led by the Spirit (Heb. 1:1). He recognized that the promised day had come and that a new age had begun in the very life and death of the *Promised One*. He recognized that "the power of *the living* God has entered into human life" and the "new age" has begun in the life of Jesus (Heb. 6:5, emphasis added).[648]

There was in the beginning a wonder at the miracles and signs that followed the Christ as He healed and fed the masses. Even so, Jesus recognized the tendency of the human heart to fluctuate its allegiance based on selfish gain and therefore continually beseeched His hearers to focus on the One from whom these gifts came (John 2:22–24, 10:25, 38, 14:11). In that age, there was a desire to hear and seek truth. It is truly unfortunate for those in the West today that the vast majority no longer seek ultimate truth. The Westernized individual lives in a state of suspicion and arrogant indignation to the things of God. Miracles are explained away as happenstance or flukes. The affluence of those in this culture has blinded the masses and created a false sense of security to the reality of their true identity and ultimate eternal state.

---

[644] Lane, *Word Biblical Commentary*, vol. 47$_A$, *Hebrews 1–8*, xlix.

[645] Johnson, *The Writings of the New Testament*, 406.

[646] Ibid.

[647] Ibid.

[648] Bruce, *The New Testament Documents*, 69.

Give an example of how people fluctuate in their allegiance to God in scripture:

_____

_____

_____

How do people fluctuate in their allegiance to God in our day?

_____

_____

Fortunately, God continues to work in the lives of those who are truly seeking Him (Deut. 4:29; Isa. 55:6–7; John 14–15) and remain open to the things of God. The human heart has not changed as everyone continues to seek to fill the void that only a relationship with God can fill (Eccles. 3:11). The effects of vast affluence, however, have clouded the mind of the average individual. The author of Hebrews encourages the hearers not to lose heart and to stay the course, even in the face of severe persecution that will most assuredly escalate in the near future (12:1–2). God's message remains the same even for those living in the twenty-first-century Westernized parts of the world where the persecution is that of intimidation and a militant-like force that threatens the livelihood of true believers who desire nothing more than to live in obedience to God.

In the first three centuries of Christian growth, the persecution came as a result of refusal to give allegiance to the emperor of Rome as lord. In the postmodern world of the twenty-first century, Christians are persecuted for refusing to accept the laxity of the day's morality as they do their best to remain true to the Word of God (John 14:15–16). Times may have changed, but the persecution remains the same. Christians continue to be persecuted for their allegiance to a holy God and not to the world (1 John 3:1–2). Before, it seemed that Christians were simply rebellious, but now the accusations are much darker in nature as Christians are accused of hating others because they are unable to approve of the lifestyles that are opposed to the will of God (Luke 8:21; Rom. 1:31–32; Rev. 22:15). True believers recognize that the ways of God are clearly countercultural and that no matter how hard we try to keep peace, we cannot do so at the expense of compromising the Word. To compromise the Word of God is to distort the very nature and character of the living God, not to mention that it is a form of denying Jesus and everything that He is.

Give three examples of how compromising God's Word either is denying Jesus or not denying Jesus. Make sure to back up your response with scripture and not personal opinion.

1. _____

   _____

2. _____

   _____

3. _____

   _____

Distorting God's nature is to deny His power and the intent and purpose of His plan of redemption (1 John 2:18–20). It is to create a god after our own image. Hebrews should stand as a word of encouragement that the power of the living God has entered into the lives of humanity and that this power has been passed on through His Son Jesus to all true believers (12). His faithfulness remains as He is as immutable today as He has ever been (Heb. 13:8). Most of us have yet to shed our own blood for our faith, yet some of us have sustained staunch criticisms in the face of those who hate the living God and live opposed to His Word, even posing as Christians (1 John 2:3–11). There will always be a few who have truly been redeemed and will enter into His presence because they chose obedience (Matt. 7:13; Luke 13:23–25). Those are the ones who stay the course (John 15:4–10; Acts 14:22, 1 John 2:18–24) and refuse to compromise the Word even in the face of great adversity out of reverence for the living God (Matt. 10:32–33).

Hebrews, like all of God's Word, transcends time. It is the timeless Word of God and is as relevant today as it was to those living in the first century. True believers are called to hold fast to what is true, even denying the voices of the day. God is forever faithful and beseeches us to know Him above all else, living in obedience to His Word and not to the world (Deut. 6:4–9; Mark 12:30; John 14:15). Every human alive is given the opportunity to respond (2 Pet. 3:9), but the response must be on God's terms, not on the individual's terms (Matt. 22:8–14). The message to the Hebrews is a message for those professing Christians of today. Hold fast, live faithfully, and trust in the Lord because His promises are sound.

> So you will find favor and good success in the sight of God and man. Trust in the Lord with all your heart, and do not lean on your own understanding. In all your ways acknowledge him, and he will make straight your paths. (Prov. 3:4–6, ESV)

> I know, O Lord, that the way of man is not in himself, that it is not in man who walks to direct his steps. (Jer. 10:23, ESV)

> Keep your life free from love of money, and be content with what you have, for he has said, "I will never leave you nor forsake you." So we can confidently say, "The Lord is my helper; I will not fear; what can man do to me?" (Heb. 13:5, ESV)

Review:

Key Theological Themes

1. Trust in the promises of God.
2. Do not compromise the Word of God.
3. Watch for the dangers of apostasy.
4. Be prepared for adversity.

Study Questions

Assessing Lower Textual Criticism

1. What is the oldest surviving document that contains the message to the Hebrews? What type of internal evidence helps to date this document?

2. What external evidence is there that has aided scholars in the dating of the original writing?
   List at least two examples:

   a.

   b.

3. What internal evidence has aided scholars in the dating of Hebrews?
   List at least two examples:

   a.

   b.

4. Write down the names of three individuals whom scholars believe could be the author of Hebrews. List why they believe these are viable potential authors.

   a.

   b.

c.

5. Is the evidence for the potential author considered internal or external?

For Theological Reflection

1. Where have you experienced apostasy? What other scripture warns about apostasy?

2. Is it possible to be an apostate and still believe that you are a Christian? Explain your answer, making sure to back it up with scripture references and not personal opinion.

3. Give three examples of modern-day persecution:

   a.

   b.

   c.

4. Do you know of someone who professes to be a Christian but compromises the Word of God by accepting humankind's word over God's?

   Explain how such a person justifies accepting humankind's word over the Bible:

Group Discussion

1. Do you believe that people living in First World countries are more in danger or less in danger of apostasy than those living in areas considered to be Second and Third World? Explain your response. If you are a missionary or participate in missionary trips, share your personal experience in relation to your response.

2. How are the churches in the West in danger of apostasy?

    a. Do you know of any churches that are currently operating as apostate churches?

    b. Explain why you believe this, making sure to back up what you are saying with scripture.

3. Discuss how you can make a difference in your community to help Christians stay on track.

Key Terms

Alexandrian Judaism: A philosophical form or way-of-life pattern that developed in the Diaspora of the third century BC with the Jewish people who were driven to the area of Alexandria, Egypt.[649] As a result of the effects of Hellenism and the distance from their Palestinian roots, there was a tendency to adopt the Greek language and some of the customs of the local people.[650]

apostasy: The act of denying the Word of God and no longer following the God described in the Bible.

chrestus: A Greek term given to "good" or "useful" Roman slaves.[651] Clearly the Roman historian Suetonius (Claudius 25.4 [AD 120]) was not familiar with either the Jewish beliefs or the Christian movement, as he refers to Jesus as Chresto. This term, along with Suetonius's documentation, inferred that this individual was an instigator with a police record.[652] The term was later used to further insult Christians as it was used as a slur against their chosen loyalty.[653]

Chester Beatty Papyri (P46): A collection of many of the earliest New Testament manuscripts in possession today written in uncial form. The papyri is aptly named after the twentieth-century private collector of ancient manuscripts Chester Beatty. This collection of biblical manuscripts date to AD 200–250 and contains the four canonical Gospels, Acts, the earliest copies of Paul's letters, all of Hebrews, and portions of the earliest surviving document of Revelation.

homily: A teaching message to an audience. It is another term used for sermon.

---

[649] Paul Wendland, "Alexandrian Philosophy," in Jewish Encyclopedia.com, 2002–2011, accessed July 16, 2018, http://www.jewishencyclopedia.com/articles/1174-alexandrian-philosophy.

[650] Ibid.

[651] Lane, *Word Biblical Commentary*, vol. 47A, *Hebrews 1–8*, lxv.

[652] Ibid.

[653] Ibid.

Promised One: The Hebrew scriptures frequently speak of a future Savior who would redeem Israel and raise worldwide awareness of the one true God. This Savior will make the nation of Israel the center of the world. This Messiah is known as "the Promised One."

Torah: The Torah is the Jewish law. It is the first five books of the Old Testament.

Yahweh: The proper term used for the Lord God of Israel in the Hebrew language. Many Hebrew scholars also recognize the various forms of the Hebrew word that equate to "the Giver of Life," and many other equally revealing terms for an ultimate Being.

God's Attributes

faithful – God continued to reach out to the chosen people of Israel with knowledgeable spokespeople in an effort to redeem the chosen race (Hebrews). He never stops being faithful to His promises as His Word continues to promise redemption for those who repent and return to Him.

sovereignty – In God's perfect plan, He made certain that throughout the generations there would be both internal and external evidence for His written message to survive.

Literature Cited or Recommended

Brown, Michael L. *Answering Jewish Objections to Jesus: General and Historical Objections.* Grand Rapids, MI: Baker Books, 2000.

Bruce, F. F. *The New Testament Documents: Are They Reliable?* 6th ed. Grand Rapids, MI: William B. Eerdmans, 1981.

Johnson, Luke Timothy. *The Writings of the New Testament.* 3rd ed. Minneapolis: Fortress Press, 2010.

Lane, William L. *Word Biblical Commentary.* Vol. 47$_A$, *Hebrews 1–8*, edited by David A. Hubbard, Glenn W. Barker, and New Testament editor Ralph P. Martin. Waco, TX: Word Books, 1991.

Wendland, Paul. "Alexandrian Philosophy." Jewish Encyclopedia.com. 2002–2011. Accessed July 16, 2018. http://www.jewishencyclopedia.com/articles/1174-alexandrian philosophy.

INDEX

Episkopos 94
epistemology 3, 15, 107, 113
Erastus 170
Eros 151, 157
eschatological 7, 15, 30, 73, 74, 82, 90, 98, 99, 100
eschatology 153, 157
essence 22, 32, 44, 46, 51, 53, 56, 68, 76, 86, 88, 94, 179, 197, 198, 210, 211, 214
Euodia 194
Eusebius 131, 132, 144, 175, 194, 200, 203, 216
extant manuscripts 38, 45, 46, 202, 203, 204, 205, 206, 207, 208, 209, 210, 211, 213, 225, 227, 228
external evidence 86, 88, 123, 142, 202, 205, 211, 212, 213, 234, 235, 241, 244

F

fallible 115, 121
Flavius Josephus 126
Flavius Sabinus Vespasianus 39
form criticism 64, 66, 67, 70, 71, 230
fornication 150, 157

G

Gabbatha 171
Gallio 170
Gemara 124, 140, 141
Gentile 11, 12, 15, 21, 22, 25, 30, 32, 51, 56, 57, 58, 66, 72, 73, 74, 75, 76, 77, 78, 79, 80, 81, 82, 89, 92, 95, 98, 117, 127, 128, 130, 131, 136, 139, 141, 143, 145, 149, 150, 152, 157, 177, 178, 185, 186, 187, 189, 191, 192, 193, 194, 195, 196, 206
Gnostic 66, 117, 121, 132, 133, 135, 136, 137, 140, 144, 154, 157, 228
God-fearers 141, 145, 157
Gospel 3, 8, 11, 12, 15, 19, 20, 21, 23, 26, 27, 28, 29, 31, 32, 34, 35, 38, 39, 40, 41, 42, 43, 44, 45, 46, 47, 52, 58, 61, 63, 64, 65, 66, 67, 72, 80, 85, 87, 90, 92, 94, 95, 97, 100, 113, 114, 118, 119, 120, 129, 130, 131, 132, 133, 134, 135, 136, 137, 139, 141, 145, 147, 153, 155, 161, 163, 165, 167, 168, 169, 170, 171, 174, 183, 185, 186, 190, 191, 192, 196, 203, 204, 207, 208, 227, 228, 243

H

halakha 188, 190, 198

Herod 22, 39, 90, 91, 127, 167, 168, 169, 170, 174, 175, 191, 200
Herodotus 40, 209, 230
historiography 105, 110, 112
Homer 38, 208, 209
homily 238, 244

I

Ignatius of Antioch 86, 94, 130
Imago Dei 11, 15
immutable 6, 15, 55, 118, 121, 240
imperial cult 53, 61, 77, 83, 149, 157, 159, 195
Infancy Gospels 66, 134, 135, 141
intelligent design 10, 15
internal evidence 88, 90, 123, 130, 139, 142, 202, 205, 211, 212, 213, 236, 238, 241
Irenaeus 131, 132, 135, 144, 175, 204, 215

J

Jewish Talmud 124, 139, 140, 141
John Rylands Fragment 207, 226, 233
Jon Hus 107
J. P. Moreland 18
Julius Agricola 128
Julius Müller 40

K

Karl Ludwig 64
kerygma 32, 35

L

last day 4, 15, 73, 80, 82, 98, 124, 141, 153, 157, 158, 179
law of Moses 52, 57, 125, 141
Loveday Alexander 87
lower textual criticism 201, 202, 212, 213, 214, 221, 225, 232, 234, 241
Lycus valley 176
Lydia 194
Lysanias 90, 170

M

Mahabharata 209
majuscule 227, 233
manuscript 18, 19, 21, 23, 25, 26, 38, 39, 41, 43, 44, 45, 46, 50, 85, 89, 107, 110, 111, 123, 128, 130, 131, 132, 133, 134, 137, 140, 161, 166, 172, 202, 203, 204, 205, 206, 207, 208, 209,

U

unchurched 11, 63, 72
uncial 227, 228, 233, 236, 243

V

vellum 38, 208, 213, 226, 232, 233
Vespasian 126, 143, 168
vestal virgin 187, 188, 195, 197, 198
volitional 9, 10, 15, 172

W

Warren Cup 196
the Way xi, xiv, 1, 7, 9, 12, 23, 27, 29, 43, 44, 47,
        50, 56, 64, 65, 67, 72, 75, 78, 79, 83, 86, 87,
        92, 97, 100, 102, 103, 106, 109, 110, 112, 114,
        115, 116, 118, 120, 121, 125, 128, 136, 141,
        143, 145, 146, 148, 150, 153, 157, 161, 162,
        171, 178, 179, 182, 186, 187, 189, 196, 198,
        199, 203, 223, 228, 239, 240
William F. Albright 41, 169

Y

Yahweh 69, 78, 186, 198, 238, 244
Yeshu 124, 125, 127, 139, 141